Practical Guide to Computer Forensics

D1281848

Disclaimer

In the process of writing this book we discovered that several companies do not allow their employees to publish articles or books on computer forensics. The reason and fear is that these written words will come back to haunt them in court or other legal proceedings. Someone will bring out a published piece of work, cite the procedures the author said should be used, and then ask the author, who happens to be in court testifying as an expert in computer forensics, why they did not follow these procedures. Computer forensic examiners will use different procedures for cases for a very simple reason.

The reason is no two forensic examinations are the same. The procedures a computer forensic specialist will use in a review will vary based on the type of hardware they are dealing with, the software installed and its configuration, the forensic tools being used, time or legal constraints, the objectives of the review, and many other variables that determine the course of action the specialist will take. With this in mind please realize that this book is meant to provide the reader a basic understanding of computer forensics and to be used as a general guideline for areas that deal with computer forensics. Different labs and specialists will have different procedures, which is fine as there is more than one way to do just about everything. We, the authors of this book, will use different procedures during the course of our forensic reviews. This is caused in part by the evolution of computer hardware and software, its use and configuration, and the tools used by computer forensic specialists. These deviations can also be influenced by company policy, advice from legal counsel, and changes in federal and state laws.

To order additional copies, please contact us.
BookSurge, LLC
www.booksurge.com
1-866-308-6235
orders@booksurge.com

Practical Guide to Computer Forensics

For Accountants, Forensic Examiners. and Legal Professionals

David Benton & Frank Grindstaff

Publisher
2006

Practical Guide to Computer Forensics

Table of Contents

Acknowledgements

We would like to thank the following people for their assistance putting this information together.

Andy Rosen

Bob Sheldon

Bill Spernow

Dan Mares

Eric Thompson

Fred Cotton

I would like to thank my Mom and Dad (Bud and Audrey), who have always been there for me. You have held me when I cried, laughed with me when I laughed and have always been a source of encouragement and inspiration. My prayer has always been to have the steadfastness of my mother and the wisdom of my father. Also I want to thank my adorable children Joshua and Jessica and Frank's son Trey for endured hours of photography while I was shooting the pictures for the front cover.

—David Benton

I would like to thank my wife Melanie and children, Trey and Kaylin, for their support during the hours I spent working on this book. Also, I would like to thank my wife for taking the time to proof read parts of this book. If there is a grammatical or other error in the book you can assume that it is a part she did not proof read for us.

—Frank Grindstaff

David Benton, CFCE, CISSP, EnCE

David is on the computer forensics team of a Fortune 500 company. Prior to joining the private sector David was the Chief Forensic Computer Specialist for the Georgia Bureau of Investigation (GBI), and a supervisor with their Internet Crimes Against Children Taskforce. While at the GBI, he worked on such high profile cases as the Hope Scholarship case, the Dewin Brown Homicide case and the hacking cases of a major university. He has also testified as an expert witness in numerous jurisdictions throughout Georgia.

Prior to his involvement in the computer forensics field, David was a Counterintelligence Special Agent with the US Army. His primary focus was the collection of Human Intelligence (HUMINT). In 1996 his unit received the Meritorious Unit Citation from the Director of the Central Intelligence Agency for their work in support of Operation Uphold Democracy in Haiti.

David is a member of the advisory board for the Cybercrime Institute of Kennesaw State University and has been elected an officer in various positions for the Atlanta Chapter of the High Technology Crime Investigation Association (HTCIA). He is also the founder and primary administrator of the largest vendor neutral computer forensics portal called http://www.forensicexams.org. He is cofounder and Vice President of the Cybercrime Summit Group, which is a non-profit organization responsible for running the Cybercrime Summit. The Cybercrime Summit is an international computer forensics/security conference held annually in Atlanta, Georgia.

J. Frank Grindstaff, Jr., CPA, CISA, CIA, CCE, EnCE

Frank is on the computer forensics team of a Fortune 500 company. Prior to this position, Frank has worked 17 years mostly in information systems auditing, but has significant experience in computer programming, computer security, and financial auditing. This breath of experience has helped Frank to understand how computer forensics can be a valuable part of a company's internal resources and how it can help in investigations.

Frank is a past president of the Atlanta Chapter of Information Systems Audit & Control Association (ISACA) and a past treasurer of the International Information Systems Forensics Association (IISFA). He is also one of the administrators of the largest vendor neutral computer forensics portal called http://www.forensicexams.org.

Frank completed his undergraduate degree in Computer Science at the University of South Carolina and completed his MBA at Georgia State University. Frank is active in several professional organizations including the High Tech Crime Investigation Association (HTCIA), ISACA, and the Georgia Society of CPA's. He and his family currently reside in Atlanta, GA.

"Computer forensics plays an ever increasing role in my investigations. Our forensic examiners arm me with the information I need to get the most out of an interview."
Pete Maddox
Loss Prevention Manager for a Fortune 500 company

Forward

The American public has developed an almost feverish fascination with medical forensics. Think of how easily such phrases as *DNA sample* and *reticulated hemorrhage* roll off the tongue nowadays. You may be surprised to learn that equally fascinating investigative scientific breakthroughs are also taking place in the vast and complicated world of computer technology. Computer scientists Frank Grindstaff and David Benton have addressed these advances and much more in *Practical Guide to Computer Forensics.*

Every individual and company using electronic data, including data of the most confidential nature, is susceptible to thieves and hackers. Worse, the altering of data is no longer confined to college students breaking into a system to change grades. Today, a worldwide level of illegal activity exists that is capable of shutting down a nation's financial markets and destroying major corporations. In order to counter the plethora of disasters resulting from the illegal electronic transfer of data, the role of the computer forensic specialist has attained new prominence. These specialists are trained to unearth the most sophisticated electronic-based illegal activities and follow the trail to the perpetrators.

From the opening chapters dealing with the advent of computer forensics to the comprehensive descriptions of how these technological processes are used by forensic accountants, auditors, attorneys, etc., the message here is starkly clear: Tough procedures must be put into place and legal consequences must be honored.

Why? Because data that can be accessed can be modified, and those modifications can, and often do, result in the grave of consequences.

Grindstaff and Benton are eminently qualified to disclose pertinent information about this growing field. Their section titled *Annotated Case Law on Electronic Discovery* adds even more weight to what is already a very important book.

Ellen Tanner Marsh

January 2006

Chapter 1
History of Computer Forensics

Computer forensics is still relatively new to experienced investigators and seasoned legal professionals alike. While it is becoming a more common investigative practice among these professionals, it is being forced upon the veterans of many other various disciplines. In the past retrieving items from computers was considered too expensive and difficult to validate, especially in court. This is because electronic evidence is very volatile. It can be easily changed and often these changes leave little or no audit trail. So if you found the "smoking gun" for your investigation, how could you prove that you did not create it? Even if you wanted to use computer forensics or data recovery in your investigation, who would you call? It seems as if every day I meet someone who claims to be doing computer forensics. When I ask them what classes they have attended, they proudly list two or three and pronounce "I'm an expert." The other end of the spectrum is a traditional computer security professional, who has hung his/her shingle out as a forensic examiner. They mistakenly believe their computer security training makes them a forensic examiner. While there is a small amount of overlapping knowledge when it comes to log files and a computer's interaction on a network, computer forensics is very different from computer security. A network security person does not need to be able to explain what the Master File Table is or what it is used for. However, it is critical for a forensics examination on a NTF formatted hard drive.

Another critical element is evidence handling; the lack of experience in evidence handling can prove to be fatal. In many cases it seems to be treated as a glib after thought. To prove my point, just ask one of these self proclaimed forensics experts for a copy of their evidence sheet. When you see the blank look on their face, you know that you are dealing with a forensic hobbyist. A forensic hobbyist is akin to a script kiddy in the computer security community. This might come as quite a shock to many people; however, it is nevertheless true. They might be able to talk the talk; however they can't walk the walk. This is why there has been a trend for experienced law enforcement officers retiring or otherwise leaving their respective agencies to fill the upper ranks of the private sector computer forensics community.

Computer Forensics has finally emerged as a completely separate discipline in and of itself. It has developed its own language and terminology. Classes on computer forensics are taught around the world. In fact Guidance Software, the industry leader, boasts over 14,000 clients worldwide. In order to fully understand where its roots lie, it is helpful to take a walk down memory lane and review the history of the personal computer.

Intel released the first commercial microprocessor on November 15, 1971. In 1975 Bill Gates and Paul Allen founded as small company called Microsoft. The second generation of microcomputer was sold under the title of a home/personal computer. In 1979 while working at Apple computer Jeff Raskin started a project called Macintosh. During this time the fight over who would dominate the personal computing market was born. IBM was backing the Intel PC, and Apple was pushing Macintosh. As these personal computers began to play a larger role in daily life, the California Department of Justice recognized that criminals could capitalize on computer technology. In response it created a computer security training program.

Conception of Computer Forensics (1980's)

By 1981 Microsoft released the Disk Operating System (DOS) for the personal computer. DOS was a command line or shell interface for an individual user to control their computer. DOS was a vast departure from the Terminal Emulation programs of that era. The user was no longer constrained by the administrators of the mainframe computers. When a user typed in "c:>delete *.*" by mistake or on purpose, it deleted everything on their hard drive. This also meant that any user could wipe out critical business data. Understanding the possible damage a user could do, Peter Norton released a program called "The Norton Utilities." One of its first programs was an unerase utility. Many users considered this a miracle tool. Along with unerase, other programs soon followed to help increase a computer system's performance.

In 1983, Apple released it's first computer with a Graphical User Interface (GUI) called Lisa. GUI meant it was a departure from the good old days of typing commands at a command prompt and started the age of point-and-click. The purpose of the operating system was to provide an easy to use environment for a user. This same year Microsoft released its first Windows based Operating System (OS), which could be purchased for approximately $100. Windows is considered a Graphical User Interface (GUI). During its earlier days the focus of the Windows operating system was end user functionality. This was just the beginning of the age of the personal computer.

Keep in mind that up until this time computer records existed on main frame computers. The personal computer began a shift in office records management. Many records that were kept on mainframes or in paper form could now be stored electronically on the personal computer. When a police officer believed that someone was conducting fraud they would get a search warrant and go into the business and look at their records. In most cases they would try to identify the pertinent ones and have their records copied. Many times the originals were retained and the duplicate records were placed back into the business so it could continue to operate. However as time went on these financial investigators and auditors began to encounter personal computers. This posed a problem; they needed the records stored on the computers to prove their case. They were the very first profession to really need computer forensics.

As an organization one of the first to seek training in this area was the Association of Certified Fraud Examiners. During their fraud audits more and more of the records were kept on computer media. In order for this information to be accepted in the court, a methodology needed to be developed. Although most people didn't realize it, a new profession was being conceived called computer forensics.

In the mid 1980's, it is rumored that Don Ingram of the Alamana County District Attorney's Office wrote and obtained the first search warrant for computer data. This case involved two competing mainframe computer companies. It was alleged that one computer company had taken information and data from the other. Mr. Ingram obtained a search warrant for the digital evidence. During its execution, the owner of the computer company was very uncooperative until one of the deputies took a crow bar and placed it on top of one of the computer mainframe computers and asked Mr. Ingram, if the data that he needed to search for was located inside. The computer owner quickly realized that it was in his best interest to assist the police with their "search," and the incrementing information was located.

In 1984 computer forensics was conceived by two separate driving forces. As businesses began to be impacted by crimes it became clear there was a gap in knowledge between the law enforcement community and private sector. In order to combat this, Leo Himmelsbach, from the

Santa Clara District Attorney's office met with the Industrial Security Mangers Group. Himmelsbach obtained a grant from the Office of Criminal Justice Planning Project for $238,216.00. On August 31, 1984 Bill 1078 was passed by the California Legislature. It provided for the creation of the District Attorney's Technology Theft Association (DATTA). This same year another small consulting company was created which would end up playing a huge role in computer forensics. It is called ASR Data, which stands for Andrew S Rosen Data. Andy began this company; it focused on custom computer software.

In the late 1980's a group of professionals including Fred Cotton and Bill Spernow from the SEARCH Group; Chuck Rehling, Michael Anderson, Andrew Fried of IRS/CID at the Federal Law Enforcement Training Center; Howard Schmidt with the Chandler Arizona Police Department; and Gail Thackery from the Maricopa County District Attorney's Office began teaching "high tech" classes in the state of California and at FLETC in Glynco, GA. At this time there was little or no other training available, as a result these dedicated professionals had to improvise or develop most of the classes they taught. Generally these trainers were law enforcement officers who happened to enjoy working with computers. Some of the tools they relied on were home grown, made by the examiner as they did their investigations. At that time many computers only had a 5 ¼ inch floppy drive, not a hard drive as they were too expensive. If they were really cutting edge they would have a 3 ½ inch floppy disk drive. Those would cause the investigator to have dozens or possibility hundreds of floppy disks to review. Each floppy would take some time to process depending on how much information was contained on it; and some exams could take months to complete. At this time the forensic examiner used these tools to work on the original media, typing the needed commands in on the command line (that is the 'C:>' prompt). The exam of a 10—20 megabyte hard drive could take weeks of tedious work. In fact some people proclaimed that one megabyte of data could require up to eight hours of analysis time.

Investigators would use Norton's file recovery tools and other command line tools to recover intact deleted files on the computer storage media. After this they would get to examine the media manually with a Sector Editor such as Norton's Disk Editor. Using Disk Editor investigators could now view the data very close to the form it was stored on the physical media. This view is often referred to as "Hex" or more accurately hexadecimal. This view is still present in almost every major computer forensics product. It is also taught in most introductory computer forensic courses. By using the Hex view a computer forensic professional can locate partial files in the unallocated areas of the floppy or hard disk and partial files in the file slack area on the disk.

In these early years this process required long hours at a computer and lots of caffeine as the examiner reviewed each chunk of data, and often recovered the deleted files one at a time manually. Considering the difficulty in conducting an exam, the time it consumed, the lack of any previous case law, the expense, and the small number of people actually experienced to do this type of work, it is no wonder that computer forensics was not even a consideration in an investigation, much less in a legal proceeding.

In 1986 the first chapter of the High Technology Crime Investigation Association (HTCIA) was formed in Southern California with 12 members. This was the first formal nationally focused professional organization for computer investigators or high tech investigators. Building on the DATTA concept it realized that by creating synergy between law enforcement and the private sector much more could be accomplished. It allowed and fostered information sharing by having membership open to law enforcement and information security professionals, agreeing to adhere to a set of by-laws. Its structure allowed for the formation of local chapters with a national umbrella organization. As you read its current by-laws the one item that will stand out is the prohibition of doing criminal defense work. This is due in large part to the group's law enforcement roots. Oddly enough, unlike many professional organizations the HTCIA has not developed a certification, though it is usually the subject of a lively discussion and debate at its annual conference. These conferences are hosted by various local chapters around the United States. Many times these conferences have the most cutting edge presentations and professionals showing off their wears. The HTCIA's growth was explosive. By 1988 the HTCIA membership had expanded to include members from over 30 different Law Enforcement agencies. The HTCIA also filed for nonprofit corporation status this year.

In 1988 a young college student named Eric Thompson was working his way through BYU in Utah. Many Brigham Young University (BYU) students found part time work at the corporate headquarters of Word Perfect, which dominated the word processing marketplace at the time. "People stored their work on low density floppy discs, which were easily corrupted…, the code for disk corruption was error 32", Eric Thompson recounts. "I began charging $30—$50 to recover Word Perfect documents from corrupt floppy disks." Someone suggested that he could make more money recovering the password protected documents. After countless hours of linguistics analyses, he first broke the password protection on Word Perfect® with Lotus 1-2-3® soon to follow. That year he founded Access Data®.

In the personal computer field this year (1988) Apple filed a law suit against Microsoft and Hewlett Packard claiming copyright infringement. In Microsoft Windows version 1 it actually licensed some GUI elements from Apple. When Windows version 2 contained even more Mac like features, Apple headed to court.

In 1989 Bill Spernow joined Fred Cotton at the National Consortium for Justice Information and Statistics also known as SEARCH. They created a hands on course called "Introduction to Microcomputers."

The Birth of Computer Forensics (1990's)

If computer forensics was conceived in the mid 1980's, it was born in the 1990's. The 1990's marked an era of explosive growth in the computer field and an era of evolution for the computer forensics community. In the early 1990's, SEARCH started launching a series of training. These classes came to be called "The Investigation of Computer Crime" and "Search and Seizure of Microprocessors". These were taught all over the state of California. Also the first HTCIA regional seminars were held by the Santa Clara and Los Angeles HTCIA chapters. These ranged from 1—3 days in length.

In 1992 Microsoft released Windows 3.1® and Windows for Workgroups®. This year was when Microsoft began its march to dominancy in the computer market. It sold over two million copies of its operating systems. The Windows for Workgroups was specifically geared toward businesses while Windows 3.1 targeted the home user. While the computer forensics profession was still dominated by Law Enforcement Officers from Federal, State and Local agencies, the private sector began to play an ever increasing role in the community.

This fruits of this synergy between the public and private sector are evidenced in the first HTCIA national conference held in San Jose, California in 1992. This same year Andy Rosen began working for the Peter Norton Group in Santa Monica, California. His role was software development, technical support, design and low level disk editing. One day he received a support call from a criminal investigator in Canada. The investigator was trying to view deleted data. Andy didn't understand why someone would want to view a deleted file structure and leave the problem uncorrected. After realizing this was doable, he quickly wrote a tool and sent it to the customer. As a result, Andy was later invited to teach a class at the Royal Canada Mounted Police College (RCMP), in Ottawa, Canada. In 1993 Peter Norton's company relocated to Eugene Oregon, Andy declined the offer to move.

The software that he pioneered lead to a product called Expert Witness. Prior to this time conducting a computer forensic examination involved using numerous software command line tools to identify and extract the data. Expert Witness was the first tool to provide acquisition, analysis, and was fully document/supported as a "non-invasive forensic data acquisition and analysis protocol."1 Expert Witness also had many other significant improvements over Norton Utilities, including imaging capability. This allowed examiners to make a bit stream image file of the computer storage media. This image file could be verified with a unique combination of CRC and MD5 hashes. Gone were the days of working on the original evidence. Expert Witness also greatly reduced the amount of time needed to conduct a review of storage media such as hard and floppy disks. This revolutionary software was designed to probe the computer configuration files and creates a dynamic representation of the file system.

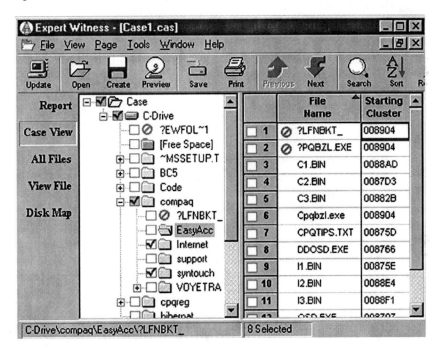

Figure 1.1—Expert Witness

Even with the increase in productivity Expert Witness brought to the industry, government and law enforcement were still the primary users of computer forensic services. Some individuals were less enthusiastic about this partnership between the public and private sector. They regarded the sharing of forensic practices and procedures outside of the rank and file law enforcement as "giving away the keys to the kingdom." This mindset coupled with the fact that law enforcement tends to be a very close knit community it seemed only natural that some of them would bond together to form another professional organization. It was based out of Portland, Oregon and later came to be one of the most widely recognized groups in the computer forensics profession. Today the group is called the International Association of Computer Investigative Specialists (IACIS). IACIS was the first organization to create a certification that was to be called the DPC. This was later changed to the Certified Forensic Computer Examiner (CFCE). Because of it's complexity and rigors its remains one of the most aggressive in the industry with only a fraction of the people who embark on the certification process actually achieving it's prestigious status.

In the early 1990's as computer forensic training and professional organizations began to spring up around the country, the software market was soon to follow. During this time SafeBack was created for the U.S. Treasury Department by Chuck Guzis and Sydex. It was one of the first forensics imaging programs.

In 1994 two earth shaking events occurred, one quite literally. This was the year the US Supreme Court turned down the petition by Apple to hear its case. This finally ended the Apple lawsuit. Also, the Northridge earthquake occurred in CA, which resulted in Andy moving to Texas.

During this time the outcry for computer forensics training was becoming greater and greater. The National White Collar Crime Center (NW3C) was delivering training courses on forensic auditing. The same auditors also required computer forensics in order to get their critical financial records off of computers and into a court. Because of this it seemed only natural for the NW3C to fill this need. So in the mid 1990s NW3C placed a focus on computer forensics training. Director Dick Johnson hired Bill Spernow as the Assistant Director of Computer Crime along with Ben Lewis, Chris Sanft, Chris Stippich and Ray-Marie Schmidt as instructors. The most interesting part about this group of dedicated professionals, Bill recounts, "they were all teleworkers—100% of them." It is also interesting to note that Ray-Marie Schmidt is the wife of Howard Schmidt briefly mentioned earlier. NW3C received a grant for 1.75 million dollars to provide training and assistance to state and local law enforcement.

During these years computer forensics began to immerge from an obscure cottage industry to a separate discipline. In 1996 various computer forensics professionals came together to join Michael Anderson at New Technology Inc. Eric Thompson was part of this group initially; however, he left after a personality clash with Michael Anderson. Interesting enough Michael is a former Internal Revenue Service high tech investigator. This same year the Cleveland Office of the Federal Bureau of Investigation (FBI) also recognized the need for a partnership between the public and private sector. Their hard work and constant outreach evolved into an organization which came to be called Infragard. This was a local effort to form a bridge between the information technology industry, educational institutions and the FBI's cyber investigations.

This same year another small software company was founded in Santa Monica, CA which would later dominated the computer forensic community—Guidance Software. In southern California Shawn McCreight, of Guidance Software, started working on a software package to allow people to search for local restaurants. The software package was called cyberDine. He called it "Simple software in a complex world." It evolved into a package called IntelliDine™, which allows the user to search hundreds of restaurants in the Los Angelise area.

Figure 1.2—Early Guidance Software Website

Even though it was growing every year still many people in information systems security and auditing had never even heard of computer forensics. Just as Bill Gates and Paul Allen had dramatically changed the computer landscape with the graphical user interface, two others would dramatically change the computer forensics community. They are Andy Rosen and Shawn McCreight. By joining forces the brilliant programmers were destined to change the face of computer forensics forever. Andy Rosen realized that he needed some help migrating his computer forensics program over to windows platform. He turned to his friend Shawn McCreight to develop a Windows version called Expert Witness for Windows. With Andy's Mac knowledge and Shawn's Windows knowledge it seemed only natural for them to work together. They both set about building a product, which would expand the scope and mindset of the computer forensics world. Little did they know the seeds were being sown for an epic show down.

The following year in October 1997 HTCIA's national conference was held at the Embassy Suites Hotel, Lake Tahoe, California. Andy and Shawn presented this GUI software to a very skeptical audience. This was perhaps one of the first times that anyone had ever mentioned doing computer forensics in a graphical environment. It was a completely revolutionary idea. Up until this point computer forensics was driven by the command line. Bob Sheldon, now Vice President of Guidance Software recalls, "I remember listening to this presentation about doing forensics in a GUI environment, and thinking this makes a lot of sense." This same year Encase forensic software (originally called Expert Witness) hits this very small market. It sold for $425 with a volume discount. It arrived with very little fan fair. Many computer forensics soothsayers completely discounted the software as being a short cut for doing "real" forensics. Bob Sheldon approached Shawn after the HTCIA presentation and said he wanted to be one of the first beta testers of this new software. Bob remembers "we were up past midnight in the lounge at the hotel of the talking about this software." He laughs that what was really surprising is that they lived within miles of each other. Bob had assumed that Shawn lived in Texas because Andy was from there. To their surprise they realized that they both drove by the same grocery store every day. The distance made the beta testing a lot easier. "In those early days, Shawn would come by my work. He would look over my shoulder and ask what are you doing? Why are you doing that? What do you need to do next?"

By 1998 the use of computers to commit crimes as well as a repository of records had really hit its stride. In 1998 under the direction of the Clinton Administration's PDD 63, the National Infrastructure Protection Center (NIPC) was created and housed by the Federal Bureau of Investigation. This organization of highly dedicated professionals was divided into three organizational units.

- Analysis and Warning Section (AWS)
- Computer Investigations and Operations Section (CIOS)
- Training, Outreach and Strategy Section (TOSS)

The Computer Analysis Response Team (CART) program provides computer forensic support to the various NIPC units throughout the agency. CART conducted over 1,260 computer forensic examinations and by 1999 the CART case load exceeded 1,900 cases. These forensic examinations resulted in over 17 terabytes of data examined. As the case load was expanded in the federal law enforcement arena, the same was occurring at the state and local level. The industry began to see highly qualified individuals leaving law enforcement ranks and joining the private sector. Also this same year Spernow left NW3C to join the private sector, and Bill Crane was hired to fill his position. It should also be noted that later Bill completed his CFCE certification. He was also elected to the Board of Directors of IACIS.

> The demand for accessing, examining, and analyzing computers and computer storage media for evidentiary purposes is becoming increasingly critical to our ability to investigate terrorism, child pornography, computer-facilitated crimes, and other cases. In the past, the Subcommittee has supported FBI efforts to establish a data forensics capability through our Computer Analysis Response Teams. There is a need to further expand this capability to address a growing workload. Indeed, our limited capability has created a backlog that impacts on both investigations and prosecutions.
> Around the turn of the century the computer forensics community began to radically transform. The number of computers requiring a forensic examination was beginning to explode. As the FBI was requesting 20 additional positions and $13,835,000 for our cryptanalysis and network data interception programs and adding 79 positions and $9,861,000 to expand the Computer Analysis Response Team capabilities."[2]

In 1999 all of the forensic examiners in the FBI's lab in Washington and most of its field examiners were provided a new tool to conduct their forensic examination called ACES. It combined hardware and software to automate routine tasks performed by their forensic examiners. By the end of 2000 most CART examiners had received ACES.

Just like the Apple and Microsoft disagreement, Andy of ASR Data and Shawn of Guidance Software had a parting of ways. This was eventually settled by arbitration. During the three day arbitration hearing, both sides presented their arguments. On July 20, 1999 the arbitrator issued his ruling that Guidance Software was to pay an undisclosed sum of money to Andy Rosen. This ruling also put other restrictions in place on both parties. Guidance software continued marketing the Encase product, and it has become the most widely used single piece of computer forensic software in the market place. Andy created an excellent computer forensics tool called SMART. The best part of the ruling is it gave both parties a chance at a new beginning. By going their separate ways both companies have created software which has helped the computer forensics community as a whole.

Computer Forensics goes main stream (2000 and beyond)

The dawning of the new century brought the dominance of the

private sector. The sleeping giant was awakened as criminal cases began to spin into tort cases. Computer forensics and ediscovery became the buzz words of the modern courtroom. As fortune 500 companies began to answer subpoenas for documents, corporate counsels saw the need for a computer forensics capacity. The profession of the computer forensics examiner has gone main stream. Fueled by the outsourcing trend the Big Four of the Accounting and Auditing world began adding computer forensics teams to answer the call from their clients. The best example of the importance of computer forensics and ediscovery received national attention when in 2001 Andy Rosen was contracted to image over 210 terabytes of data as part of the Enron scandal.

In the product arena the software development companies were going full blast. Access Data entered the computer forensic software market with The Forensic Toolkit. It was a significant departure from the Expert Witness / Encase versions by adding the power of databasing to the computer forensics. Now keyword searching became almost instantaneous and simple. The year 2001 saw the release of Encase version 3 with version 4 following in early 2003 and version 4 in early 2005.

While some soothsayers trumpet that computer forensics is a firecracker about to pop and fall to the ground, most skilled professionals understand that computer forensics will continue to demand an even greater role in corporate America. In the early 2000s I heard people preaching the death of computer forensics because Windows was adding encryption to their operating system. While encryption does complicate the computer forensics examiner's job, it is not the death nail. With Microsoft's Longhorn on the horizon, everyone is waiting to climb the new walls of encryption. Just as Mount Everest was conquered by discipline and skill, I feel confident that anything man engineers can be reverse engineered and conquered.

Chapter 2
Electronic Evidence

Electronic Evidence is changing the scope and face of many regulatory and judicial investigations. People may wonder why they need computer forensics in an investigation if they are already using an electronic evidence specialist. Why should they pay twice for what they perceive as being the same service? In an investigation if there is a large amount of items like documents and emails from a large number of computers, an electronic evidence firm can effectively and efficiently gather the files and organize them. If the documents are not in electronic format they can be scanned and included in the process. Once these items are in electronic format they can be filtered, searched, and reviewed with relative ease. In a small investigation where there is only one or two personal computers involved, you use a computer forensics specialist for this. While there is some truth to this there is also a lot wrong with it.

In a large investigation it is common to use a firm specializing in electronic evidence to handle the electronic discovery needs in the investigation. The electronic discovery could cover ten's to thousand's of hard drives depending on the scope of the investigation. If this is the only type of electronic discovery being utilized, your investigation could be missing a lot. While it may be impractical and cost prohibited to forensically review all of the hard drives at a company, it may also be seen as negligence to not forensically review a few selective hard drives in an investigation/discovery process.

When do you need a computer forensics specialist and when do you need Electronic Discovery services? First it is perhaps helpful to define computer forensics and EDiscovery. Computer Forensics is the application of the scientific method to digital evidence during an investigation in order to establish fact, which may be used in judicial proceeding. EDiscovery is the providing of electronic document(s) pursuant to a request or order from a regulatory or judicial authority.

A forensic review of selective computers can help an e-discovery team work more efficiently by helping them narrow their scope in its time frame, number of locations, number of computers (email servers, network servers) and number of people. Another item to consider is do you want to review deleted items? If so, a forensic review is a must for that computer. Below is a table comparing electronic discovery and computer forensics on some of the key points.

Computer Forensics	Electronic Discovery
• Investigate & detailed analysis	• Gathering, searching, filtering, and producing large amounts information for review
• Typically targets selected hard drives	• Can cover thousands of hard drives
• Searches everything on the hard drive, "deleted" information and active data	• Active and archived data, normally does not include deleted, discarded, or hidden data
• Determine who, what, & when	• Data is accessed, but not analyzed
• Re-creation of time critical events	• Can include backup tapes, email servers, network servers
• Reporting & expert testimony	• May or may not include Meta-data
• Breaking of passwords/encryption	• Reviewed by numerous people in multiple locations
• May include backup tapes, email servers, network servers	• Searches can take minutes or hours
• Includes Meta-data	
• Normally reviewed by one person at a time, in one location	
• Searches takes can take hours or days	

Figure 2.1—Compare Computer Forensics to Electronic Discovery Table

You may notice that searches in computer forensics can take days, compared to minutes for electronic discovery. This seems odd until you look at the way searches are done using computer forensic software. Consider that a typical personal computer has an 80 GB hard drive can have 18,181,820 pages of data on it. Electronic discovery may only look at a small fraction of this data, and the search is a text search (byte by byte). In computer forensics every bit of the hard drive is searched bit by bit, (note: eight bits equals one byte). In general, the bit by bit search algorithm is much slower than the text search. This speed difference and the searching by bits instead of bytes requires much more time.

At one time computer forensics was very expensive and was viewed as unaffordable for the average case. This meant that if any electronic evidence was reviewed it was done through electronic discovery, not computer forensics. Now, with innovations in computer forensic software a forensic examination of a hard drive is reasonably affordable. This has caused more and more cases to include electronic evidence that just a few years ago would have ignored it. This has caused some interesting developments as there was very little case law to guide attorneys and judges in these matters. The past few years has seen more and more rulings on items found using computer forensics and more conferences and work groups formed to publish guidelines on electronic discovery and computer forensics. One such organization is The Sedona Conference®, which is a non-profit, non-partisan law and policy think-tank (more information is available at their website—http://www.thesedonaconference.org).

One of the Work Groups, WG1: Electronic Document Retention and Production, purpose is to develop principles and best practice guidelines concerning electronic evidence retention and production. These guidelines were developed as a joint collaboration between attorneys in the public and private sector, judges, and other experts. Below are the 14 proposed guidelines:2

1. Electronic data and documents are potentially discoverable under Fed. R. Civ. P. 34 or its state law equivalents. Organizations must properly preserve electronic data and documents that can reasonably be anticipated to be relevant to litigation.

2. When balancing the cost, burden and need for electronic data and documents, courts and parties should apply the balancing standard embodied in Fed. R. Civ. P. 26(b)(2) and its state-law equivalents, which require considering the technological feasibility and realistic costs of preserving, retrieving, producing and reviewing electronic data, as well as the nature of the litigation and the amount in controversy.

3. Parties should confer early in discovery regarding the preservation and production of electronic data and documents when these matters are at issue in the litigation, and seek to agree on the scope of each party's rights and responsibilities.

4. Discovery requests should make as clear as possible what electronic documents and data are being asked for, while responses and objections to discovery should disclose the scope and limits of what is being produced.

5. The obligation to preserve electronic data and documents requires reasonable and good-faith efforts to retain information that may be relevant to pending or threatened litigation. However, it is unreasonable to expect parties to take every conceivable step to preserve all potentially relevant data.

6. Responding parties are best situated to evaluate the procedures, methodologies and technologies appropriate for preserving and producing their own electronic data and documents.

7. The requesting party has the burden on a motion to compel to show that the responding party's steps to preserve and produce relevant electronic data and documents were inadequate.

8. The primary source of electronic data and documents for production should be active data and information purposely stored in a manner that anticipates future business use and permits efficient searching and retrieval. Resort to disaster recovery backup tapes and other sources of data and documents requires the requesting party to demonstrate need and relevance that outweigh the cost, burden and disruption of retrieving and processing the data from such sources.

9. Absent a showing of special need and relevance, a responding party should not be required to preserve, review or produce deleted, shadowed, fragmented or residual data or documents.

10. A responding party should follow reasonable procedures to protect privileges and objections to production of electronic data and documents.

11. A responding party may satisfy its good-faith obligation to preserve and produce potentially responsive electronic data and documents by using electronic tools and processes, such as data sampling, searching or the use of selection criteria, to identify data most likely to contain responsive information.

12. Unless it is material to resolving the dispute, there is no obligation to preserve and produce metadata absent agreement of the parties or order of the court.

13. Absent a specific objection, agreement of the parties or order of the court, the reasonable costs of retrieving and reviewing electronic information for production should be borne by the responding party, unless the information sought is not reasonably available to the responding party in the ordinary course of business. If the data or formatting of the information sought is not reasonably available to the responding party

in the ordinary course of business, then, absent special circumstances, the costs of retrieving and reviewing such electronic information should be shifted to the requesting party.

14. Sanctions, including spoliation findings, should only be considered by the court if, upon a showing of a clear duty to preserve, the court finds that there was an intentional or reckless failure to preserve and produce relevant electronic data and that there is a reasonable probability that the loss of the evidence has materially prejudiced the adverse party.

Over the last year or so there has been more merging of electronic evidence tools with computer forensic tools. Where electronic evidence tools would search the storage media on a computer or network, it generally would only look at undeleted or active files. If you thought the file you needed had been deleted, then you called in the computer forensic person. They would get the deleted files, file fragments, and other artifacts left on the computer storage media. As electronic evidence becomes more prevalent in court, vendors are beginning to develop more sophisticated tools. One such tool that is becoming a combined tool is from Guidance Software. Guidance Software has recently come out with EnCase Enterprise, the next evolution of their computer forensic software, EnCase.

EnCase Enterprise extents the functionality of EnCase Forensics so it can access and image computer storage media (Hard drives, Blackberry's, etc.) over a network. Encase Enterprise also allows the user to search and collect files from any or all of the computer storage media on the network without having to image each one. This type of tool will become increasingly important as companies must now be sure they comply with the new Federal laws such as Sarbanes-Oxley.

Chapter 3
The Forensic Process

In computer forensics the importance of having a through and transparent process can not be over stressed. This process is generally outlined as a set of procedures and will vary some from office to office and examiner to examiner. Also these processes will be separated into two completely different categories based on intent. By this I mean the request is being conducted for law enforcement or civilian purposes. While computer forensics is rooted in law enforcement, this has been completely surpassed by the civil courts and the requirements placed on companies by these courts. The process of a forensic examination is similar in some ways to a regular financial audit. Some of the qualities they share include:

- Repeatability
- Objective
- Logical
- Predictable
- Conservative its approach
- Governed by Legal parameters

The premise of the forensic examination is to seek the truth. As examiners it is important to realize that we are not the decision makers, but only the objective presenter of fact. The premise of this chapter assumes the necessity of a computer forensics examination has already been established. This can become a process of a mire of individuals and decisions.

One of the first steps in this endeavor is to meet with the client and obtain all of the initial information. This will help avoid confusion and hopefully head off any misunderstandings. In this meeting you should obtain a clear understanding of the following:

- Scope of the Engagement
- Outline the Steps
- Identify Points of Contact
- Obtain all relevant policy and procedures
- Establish time tables
- Outline the deliverables.

In this initial meeting you should also discuss the type of investigation you are dealing with Internal, Civil, or Criminal. Any legal issues and/or compliance issues should be discussed that may be unique to the industry. Copies of the company policies and guidelines that relate to the scope should be provided to the examiner. Special emphasis should be placed on the company's policy and procedures for the backup of the computers and the retention of these backups. Additionally this is the time to outline how to obtain user identifiers and associated passwords to the computer system and/or files. Once this initial meeting has been completed the work begins. In order to understand the process it is perhaps easiest to think of it in terms of a series of sequential steps. These steps are generally conducted in a defined order and contain various processes and sub processes. While cases can vary widely they generally always fall into this overall process.

Identification/Scope

This initial stage might seem like an easy first step. I have heard forensic examiners describe it as either simple or straight forward or leave them asking "where is the bar because I need a stiff drink." In the early days of computer forensics identification, it was a fairly simple process, and in some cases it still may be. However this landscape is rapidly changing. Five or ten years ago when you walked into a business and started looking for the electronic records—one of the employees would say—here is the computer. In the modern office environment, it is quite different. While many offices have their records on site, it is more and more common for these same records to be kept in a wide variety of formats and on increasingly diverse devices at many locations.

For example let's say that your firm has a contract with the state police to provide forensic accounting services in highly complex cases, which exceed the ability of the state police to perform. Today you have been asked to help the police with a local search warrant because of your knowledge of computers and accounting. The police suspect that a local doctor has been over billing Medicare. This is commonly called upcoding. You are tasked to work with the police to help them recover the electronic records then conduct an audit of them to prove or disprove this allegation. The police raid team assembles and you check to make sure that you have all of your equipment. Your goal is just to locate the computer and take them back to your office for processing. Since this is your first search warrant, you are really unsure exactly what to expect. The police assemble in the parking lot at the local Dunklin Donuts. Actually in real life it is very common for the police to assemble in parking lot within 5 or 6 blocks on the target site, especially if there are multiple agencies involved.

The head agent conducts a very through raid plan briefing. This raid plan looks and sounds at its heart very similar to the early meeting outside with some notable additions such as body armor and firearms checks. She explains that she has been conducting this investigation for months based off of a tip from the State Medicate Fraud Unit. She has obtained sufficient information for a judge to issue a search warrant for the medical records to include the electronic records. Since this is a doctor's office, she does not expect there to be any resistance, however just in case a six person entry team will be going into the office building first. These officers are not taking any chances. All of them are wearing body armor and each has checked their weapons at least twice to make sure that everything is working correctly. The head agent explains that once the scene has been secured, the rest of the raid team will be allowed onsite to conduct the search. After the briefing and a communications check has been completed, everyone finds a seat in one of the several unmarked Ford Crown Victoria or the small mini van for the short ride over to the doctor's office.

As the initial cars arrive in the parking lots, several patients are getting out of their cars and give the convoy a curious look. The first two Crown Vics stop directly in front of the office doors. The entry team exits the two vehicles and very quickly enters the doctor's office. Since this is not suspected to be a hostile environment, their pistols are not drawn; however their hands are on their weapons just in case someone decides to do something stupid. When you ask the officer, who is driving the vehicle, why they still need to secure the scene this way, he explains to you that while the doctor will probably not be armed. You can never tell—when someone, who sells drugs might be in the lobby to see the doctor and thinks that the police are coming to get him instead of the doctor. This can be very common if the search warrant is conducted on a business such as a 24 hours pharmacy, where it is possible to have a large number of customers in the building at an odd hour. You can never been too careful, because these officers have families that they want to see at the end of their shift.

You hear the "all clear" raid call, which is the clue that the scene has been secured and is ready for processing. As you enter the facility you notice there are several office staff and patients, which are still seating in the waiting area chairs. There is a uniformed police officer, who is taking their information. Since they are not suspects, once they have been properly identified they will be released with an apology for the inconvenience. An agent is almost finished with videoing the various rooms. This is done in order to establish an accurate record of the areas' condition prior to the records search beginning. Each room has been labeled, and an agent is setting up a laptop computer and printer in the waiting area. These individuals will be responsible for recording all items, which are removed from the facility.

Your first task is to locate the electronic evidence. You ask the remaining staffs, who handle the computers. An interview of the "computer guy" reveals that the doctor's office has two other locations. Each of these locations links via a Windows 2003 server. You have caught a break in that the actual server is residing in this building. He also explains that the other doctors at the other sites are using the Windows server for actual patience files. If the server is taken offline—it will severely impact the other locations and the ability of the doctors to update medial information. You suspect this is not entirely true, since these computers are only linked via a DSL internet access with dial up backup. All of the billing is handled by a proprietary computer program. Also you discover the actual electronic billing is outsourced to a third party company in the neighboring state. The computer individual tells you there is a server in the computer closet. Also, there are five computers in this office that are linked together. You locate the server closet and notice that the screen is locked. The "computer guy" is very corporative; however he is very concerned about the impact on the connectivity of the computer systems. More importantly he is trying to determine if he needs to be looking for another job, just incase his doctor goes to jail.

You begin a room by room search of the office faculties. You notice that in addition to the five desktop computers, there are three running laptop computers scattered throughout the facility. In the server closet you locate 4 old computers and an old IBM rack mount server. The "computer guy" explains that this past year all of the computers were upgraded to dell systems. In additional to all of the other computer devices there are numerous floppy diskettes, compact discs, installation manuals, three USB thumb drives and as well as a RIM blackberry device on Doctor X's desk.

This scenario is a far cry from the early days of computer forensics when it comes to the first and most simple step, which is the identification of electronic evidence. The data either resided on a large main frame computer or on the hard drive of a central or shared desktop computer. As technology has increased, microprocessors have become much smaller, and computers are more pervasive. This once simple task of identification has become much more complicated. Also the myriad of computer devices and assorted types commonly used increases the likelihood that the electronic evidence can simply be overlooked. While this wide variety of devices presents a challenge for the forensic examiners, it is also a blessing. These new devices can hold a treasure trove of electronic evidence. Additionally as computer systems become more complicated, the likely hood of residual traces of evidence increased. Even as the threshold of computer security becomes lower and lower thereby becoming more and more common—this can also hold vital clues for the examiner. Here is just the beginning of the different types of devices used in almost every office.

Media Type	Read Device	Capacity (est.)	Comment
3.5" Floppy Disk	Floppy Disk Drive	1.44 MB	Less common on newer computers
CD's	CD Drive	600MB to 800MB	Very common, on most computers
Hard Drive	IDE or SCSI connection	540MB to 500GB+	Very common on PC's and Servers
DVD's	DVD Drive	1GB to 15GB	Very common
Zip Disk	Zip Drive	100MB to 1GB	Common on PC's
Backup Tapes	Tape Drive	20MB to 300GB+	Common on servers, very proprietary
Flash Card	PCMCIA slot	Up to 2GB	Compact and common
Thumb drive	USB connection	Up to 2 GB	Very common
Smart Media	Card Reader	8MB to 128MB	Common and small

Figure 3.1—Media Type Table

Preservation—Imaging

Before the examiner can begin the next stage of this process there is preparatory work that must be done. In the initial discussions the forensic examiner will inquire about the size and number of the computer media that will be reviewed. This is important because the examiner must prepare "sterile" hard drives to store the images on. The examiner can sterilize the hard drive by writing "00" over the entire hard drive, this process is also known as wiping. Then the examiner conducts a search of the hard drive to insure that the hard drive has been completely wiped. After this the drives are bagged up so the examiner knows they are sterile and ready for use. Some examiners keep a log of the date and time that each hard drive was wiped. This has both pros and cons, which are really beyond the scope of this book. Also, just because a hard drive is new; does not mean that it is forensically clean. Even new hard drives have been found with data already on them. By wiping the hard drive before an image is sent to it you can testify to the validity of the image. This helps to quash the opposition's argument that the evidence is contaminated or tainted from residual data left on the disk. If the forensic examiner has properly document the steps he used, this can be dismissed in a routine manner.

As computer forensics has matured as a disciple, so have the tools and methodology. After the evidence has been identified the next task is to insure that it can be presented into court in a state in which no undocumented changes have occurred. This is accomplished as a two step process. Just like in medicine the first rule is to "Do no harm." This rule is the mantra of computer forensics. The question is how we insure that the media remains in its original state. This is why at the heart of any computer forensics examination is the forensic imaging process. There are generally considered to be two completely different types of forensic images. These include a bit-stream image (sometimes called a mirror image) and a file image.

Bit-stream imaging was the first true forensic imaging process. This process involved using specialized software to create the bit-stream image. This process has also been called a clone image or a hard drive twin. It involves the connecting of two very similar hardware devices to a computer or a device and copying all of the information from one hard drive onto another hard drive of very similar size and design. In the beginning this was accomplished with the use of special software, however several companies produced software for this sole purpose. The oldest true forensic imaging software package was called Safeback. It was the most common for a number of years. Later hardware imaging devices were created which could image the hard drive significantly faster.

The purpose of the bit-stream image (or image) was to provide a working copy of the evidence, which an investigator could examine, while still insuring that the original media was essentially changeless. The original media could then be presented as "best evidence" in a court of law. In many cases the image was placed back into the original computer, which could be booted. This allowed the investigator to look at the evidence in the same manner as the suspect could. In fact many investigators thought of this process as stepping back into time because they could essentially see the evidence the same way that the suspect did. However this method presented the examiner with some challenges. The examiner was limited to the same tools that the suspect was using in order to conduct the forensic examination. Also there was no place to store items, which were discovered. In order for them to be presented—they needed to be printed. Now what is the likelihood that the computer forensic examiner would have the same exact printed file as the suspect? Some departments actually required that their officers seize every single computer connected item at the suspect's location— just for this reason. However as the number of devices and cases grew this became completely impractical. The next evolution in this process was the connecting of the image to the computer of the forensic examiner. While this method did not allow the investigator to view the information exactly as the suspect, it did allow the use of specialized tools. These were installed on the forensic examiner's computer to be used on the images. This provided an area to store data for the forensic examiner's report. Also this eliminated some of the more annoying problems, such as installing printers and obtaining internet connectivity. Some of the more through forensic examiners would actually conduct both two steps. First they would connect the image to their forensic computer and run a series of programs to recover deleted information and other items. Then they would place the image back into the original system and take a look at the computer. This was probably the most productive method; however it was still a matter of personal preference for the forensic examiner. It also required a lot more time. The main problem with this sort of forensic examination is it lacked a common interface for forensic examination and it required an extensive amount of time for the examination to be conducted.

As more computer software companies entered the computer forensics software market, it was quickly apparent that a common interface for forensic examinations would be able to increase productivity. This problem was solved with the file image. As the name implies a file image is a forensic image of media, which is encapsulated into another file. These files can then reside on any media of the examiner's choice. While the image would require an entire hard drive for each case, the new file image would allow two or three forensic images to reside on the same hardware. The usefulness of this sort of forensic image was greatly increased as the manufacturers of these programs began to incorporate compression into their programs. There are two programs, which have dominated the market place in this respect. They are Encase by Guidance Software and DD, which is part of Linux. In fact some Windows based forensic products have actually based their tool on the open source version of DD. An Encase forensic image is easy to recognize by the use of the extension e01 as the beginning of the forensic image.

By placing the forensic image inside of a standardize format, this allowed the forensic image to be treated like any other file. It also aided to process of backing up forensic images. In order to insure the maximum flexible and validity in the process, many labs implemented the "2 by 2" rule. This rule requires that you get the same result using two different methods. Basically this meant that for every forensic image there would be two difference forensic images created. This was accomplished by using two different tools onto two completely different types of media. For example the imaging of a hard drive would involve creating a forensic image with the Safe back software package onto a 4 millimeter digital audio tape (DAT), and the creation of a file image using Encase onto another hard drive. This provided the maximum survivability of the forensic image. Consider if one forensic image was corrupted by a virus or thrown out of court, there is always another image to reply upon. This makes allowances for cases where a licensing issue would prevent a forensic examiner from using one type of software—then the other file image could be used. Also, it allowed for hardware failures such as the hard drive with the Encase file image being dropped and damaged in the lab. Now the forensic examiner had a safe tape image to rely on. Many forensic examiners, who were trying to cut corners, found themselves answering some very difficult questions in courtrooms all across the country about their procedures. These examiners might argue there was always the original media that another forensic image could be created from. This was true is most cases, however in many civil cases it was necessary for the original hard drive to be returned to the owner. Once returned it was generally re-installed into the computer and used, making it almost useless for re-imaging.

Now we have discussed the process of creating a forensic image, however does creating a forensic image insure that your original media has not been change—absolutely not? This is done by skillfully using write protection software and/or hardware.

Under the "do no harm rule" when imaging a hard drive or any piece of computer storage media it is very important to never, never, ever alter the contents of the computer storage media. This can be done with write protection. It does not matter if the operating system the examiner is using to image the computer media is DOS, Windows, Linux, or some other, the main concern is evidence preservation. Several popular tools to image computer storage media are:

- EnCase for DOS,
- EnCase for Windows with a hardware write blocker,
- FTK in Windows with a hardware write blocker,
- SMART for Linux,
- DD—a Unix/Linux command, and
- A hardware imaging device.

Once you get to the actual computer the fun begins. If the computer is turned off then do NOT turn it on. Booting up a computer (turning it on) can cause changes across hundreds of files on the hard drive. These include the accessed and last written date/time stamps. The actual number varies with the version of the operating system, the application on the computer, and how they are all configured. This simple act could leave the door wide open for a skillful litigator to argue that the evidence found on the hard drive is tainted and should therefore not be allowed into evidence.

If the computer is on there is a possibility that a destructive program is running. These could include a wiping program or a routine disk defragmentation program. So the rule of thumb is it the computer is running then pulls the power plug from the back of the computer. One reason for pulling the plug from the back of the computer is the computer may be hooked into an uninterruptible power supply. Some of the more complex UPS systems can cause the execution of a series of bat programs, which are designed to shut the system down properly. It would be quit simple to include a series of commands to destroy certain residual traces of evidence should this occur. If you pull it from the back of the computer these problems are no longer issues. If destructive programs are not a concern then there are a few steps that can be done prior to powering down the computer.

The examiner then disconnects any network communication lines from the computer and tags them. The examiner should then note the date and time of the computer's clock (if it is turned on) and compare it to accurate clock (such as one in sync with the atomic clock) and document every program that is running on the computer. A photograph of the computer's screen is a good way to help document that the computer was turned on and what programs were running on it at that time the examination began. This photograph is not a substitute for hand written notes though. The examiner may also run a program from a floppy disk or CD that downloads the contents of Random Access Memory (RAM) onto it. This process does destroy a little bit of what was in RAM at the time, but if the computer is powered down or has the plug pull the data in RAM is lost. Depending on the computer system the examiner will pull the plug from the back of the computer or power down the computer gracefully.

After the computer is off, a forensic boot disk is placed into the floppy drive and tape placed over the drives. This prepares the computer so it can be transported to a lab for imaging and helps to ensure that no one accidentally boots up the computer. If the computer is to be imaged onsite, then skip this part. Now that the computer is powered down, take note of any networking equipment that is in the area such as hubs, routers, wireless routers, etc. This could indicate there is an additional computer that needs to be imaged.

The examiner then begins to take detailed notes of the computer's surroundings. Document any books, printouts, papers, post-it notes that could be relevant to the exam of the hard drive or other computer storage media. Basically this is an inventory audit of the computer's room or space. In documenting the surroundings the examiner may find additional computer storage media such as floppy disks, CD's, DVD's, Tapes, external hard drives, thumb drives, etc. After these have been inventoried and photographed they should, if possible, be boxed up.

Once everything has been inventoried, photographed, tagged, and documented the examiner starts on the computer. The examiner will normally open the computer up and physically remove the hard drive from the computer (taking pictures of it all). The hard drive and the computer it came from are documented, including serial numbers, models, and possibly photographs.

Company Name – Forensic Exam Worksheet

Case Number:		Client Name:	
Date:	Examiner:	Client Case Name:	
Location of Exam:	☐ Co. Lab	☐ Other (Complete Address)	

COMPUTER DESCRIPTION

Evidence #:	Make:	Model:	Serial #:

Case Type: ☐ Tower ☐ Desktop ☐ Laptop ☐ Rack/Server ☐ RAID ☐ PDA ☐Other	CPU:	RAM ☐ KB ☐ MB

Date Seized:	Status When Seized: ☐ On ☐ Asleep ☐ Off ☐ Suspended ☐ Unknown ☐ Other
Seized By:	System Shutdown Method: ☐ Hard ☐ Normal ☐ Unknown	Date/Time of Shutdown:
BIOS Date:	BIOS Time:	WAN Type: ☐ T1 ☐ Dial-Up ☐ DSL ☐ Cable ☐ Other
Current Local Date:	Current Local Time:	LAN Present: ☐ Yes ☐ No Type:

DRIVE INFORMATION

3.5 Floppy ☐ Internal ☐ External	CD/RW ☐ Internal ☐ External
Zip Drive ☐ Internal ☐ External	DVD ☐ Internal ☐ External
CD ☐ Internal ☐ External	DVD/RAM ☐ Internal ☐ External
CD/R ☐ Internal ☐ External	Other: _____ ☐ Internal ☐ External

HDD #1:	Make:	Model:	Serial #	Connection:	Jumper: :::::
HDD #2:	Make:	Model:	Serial #	Connection:	Jumper: :::::
HDD #3:	Make:	Model:	Serial #	Connection:	Jumper: :::::
HDD #4:	Make:	Model:	Serial #	Connection:	Jumper: :::::

MISCELLANEOUS HARDWARE

SCSI Card:	NIC CARD:
Modem:	Other:

ACQUISITION

☐ Encase ☐ Ghost ☐ SafeBack ☐ FTK Imager ☐ Field Hardware ☐ Other: _____
☐ FastBloc ☐ DriveLock ☐ Other Write Protection: _____
Notes:

Figure 3.2—Sample Acquisition Form

Images can also be made over a network using tools like EnCase Enterprise or ProDiscover. These two tools are gaining in popularity in the corporate environment as they allow an examiner to image any hard drive on the company's network without traveling. For a large national or international company this can represent a sizeable financial savings.

If it was not done in the imaging process, the images of the computer storage media must be validated. Just as in an audit the auditor should validate that the client gave them all of the requested data (and the correct data), the forensic examiner must validate the images they make. Failure to validate the images could cause any finding to be thrown out in legal proceedings. The examiner validates the two images they made with a hash number and then validates any copies of the image with a hash. If the hash numbers agree, then the image is valid. If they do not agree, then you have a problem. Think of a hash number as the DNA or fingerprint of the computer storage media. Once a hard drive has been hashed if a single bit is changed from a '1' to a '0' some where on the image of the computer storage media, the resulting hash number will be different. In the computer forensic community two of the more popular hashing algorithms are the MD5 and SHA-1 (these are 1 way hashes). The imaging process and the hash values must be documented by the examiner.

The importance of documentation in a forensic review can never be stressed enough. Once the images are made and validated, the examiner must document everything or person that touches the images physically and/or virtually. To help ensure this, the forensic images are kept in evidence lockers or rooms where access is restricted to a select few that have to have access to do their job. Every time someone touches, moves, or works on an image it needs to be documented on some type of log sheet. In a financial audit, you would generally control who has access to the work papers and track who has them. This is why most audit departments have rooms to store audit work papers that are kept locked, and access to this room is very restrictive. Forensic examiners similarly keep images and the work papers of their reviews in an evidence locker or safe. This restrictive access is important because the examiner must be able to prove the chain of custody of the images. If the chain is broken, anything found on the images could be disallowed in court.

If you are curious how strict the rules are in handling the images of computer storage media, evidence, the Federal Rules of Evidence and Federal Rules of Civil Procedure is a good place to start. This set of rules provides a working framework to address these issues. Following sound computer forensics procedures decrease the chance of items being disallowed in court.

In the imaging process there are several mistakes that the examiner could make. One is kind of ironic actually; an examiner may ignore a potential source of evidence because it is hard to deal with. This is the same reason auditors use to ignore computers in their audit and would audit around the box. Auditing the computer itself was deemed to be too hard to deal with, so extra financial audit steps would be done to 'compensate' for this. Another is using a system administrator, information system auditor, or some other computer type person that has not been adequately trained in computer forensics. This inexperience could lead to some of the common and preventable mistakes, including:

- Not making a bit-stream image
- Booting the computer
- Just Poking around first, to
- Not making forensically sound images as soon as possible

Examination/Analysis

Assuming that you now have valid images to work with, the examiner can start the analysis work. This work should be done in an environment that is completely under the control of the examiner. No actions or examination steps can take place without the examiner doing it. This means that the examination is done in a room where the access is restricted to only those that absolutely must have it. One of the first steps is to make a copy of the image and to validate it to the image. Then the examiner will perform the steps needed to accomplish the objectives established in the meetings with the client. The examiner should be able to perform any of these tests with more that one tool. So if the examiner uses the EnCase software to conduct the examination, then someone should be able to get the same findings using another tool such as SMART. The steps in the examination can include:

- Keyword Searches, this is where the forensic software searches the hard drive bit by bit for the search terms the examiner entered.
- The system area of the volume should be examined for possible irregularities or unusual items.
- Review of the Internet History items and artifacts.
- Review the email folders (mailboxes) and settings, including the Address Book.
- Metadata of files, if relevant.
- User settings, such as the registry or user profile files.
- Inventory the software on the image and review these programs for unusual programs or programs that may relate to the investigation.
- Timelines created of activity, based on the time stamps from the computer's internal clock (not always accurate).
- Search for specific file types base on the file headers.
- Password breaking.

The review of the image(s) must always be done in accordance with Federal and State laws. In a forensic review this takes on new meaning when compared to a financial audit. While both observe the legal requirements of Federal and State laws, such as HIPAA or SOX (Sarbanes-Oxley), in a forensic exam there are other laws to be aware of. If there is child porn, then the appropriate law enforcement is notified (18 USC 2251 and 2252). This is not an option for the examiner. So if you think there may be child pornography on a piece of computer storage media and you so not want anyone to know about it, then do not hire a computer forensic specialist to examine it. If a party beyond your control, opposing legal counsel or corporate examiners, image your computer to examine it and there is child porn on it you may want to consider moving to a country that does not have an extradition treaty with the United States.

Forensic examiners may also run into items that you would not normally find in a financial audit. This can include email it instant messages that are threatening some one or harassing someone. The examiner may uncover items that indicate suicidal thoughts or violation of corporate guidelines. While these may not be in the scope of the review, the examiner should notify the appropriate people at the company or his client.

When the examiner is done with the examination and analysis of the images that were made it is time to write the report. The format of the report may vary from examiner to examiner, but is usually very similar to an audit report. Most will have a summary section, a purpose and scope section, a conclusion and opinion, and a summary of findings. Unlike an audit report, the forensic report will normally get a legal proof reading if it is likely to end up in court or other legal proceedings. The forensic report will also normally have CD with the items the examiner found on the images, organized according to the examination's objectives.

This report should be well organized and written so someone with little or no understanding of computer forensics can understand it. To someone with an understanding of computers the report may appear too elementary or basic, but remember that the report's audience is non-computer people and possible a jury if the report ends up in court. A wise prosecutor once told me that an examiner should write all of their reports as if it needed to be explained in a sixth grade science class. The examiner may also need to prepare a presentation, like a PowerPoint presentation, to go along with the report to help explain it to the Board of Directors or a Judge in court. It is important that the forensic examiner can tie the report and presentation together in non-technical terms. If requested the examiner needs to be ready to re-perform any or all of the steps in the forensic examination if requested and achieve the same findings. If the examiner is unable to do this then the findings could the thrown out and the examiner's credibility will be damaged. If the examiner's report ends up in court, then the examiner may need to qualify as a direct witness or expert witness.

In any audit the work papers should be sufficient to support any findings or lack there of. It is also interesting to note there are two schools of thought. While some people argue that work papers are essential to a case presentation, others argue these documents are subject to privilege and should not be disclosed. The former argues that when a person reviews the work papers they should be able to understand what is being audited, why it was being audited, what each test's objective was, what procedures were done, and what the conclusion is. Basically someone should be able to repeat the entire audit test and arrive at the same conclusion based on the documentation alone. It is the same with computer forensics. A difference with computer forensics is that often the person reviewing your work is the opposing legal counsel and their computer forensic specialist. This makes good documentation even more important in a forensic examination. In this chapter we look at the process of a forensic review of a computer, where you will probably notice similarities to a financial or information system audit.

Presentation

The final step is providing the information. This is generally done in a formal written report. Some examiners provide an extremely detailed written document, which others just present their findings with only an explanation of their finds. Remember the ultimate goal is to give the decision makers a clear understanding of the facts as you uncovered them. This information must be presented in a meaningfully way. The audience could range from a judge, a jury, a corporate board or a manager. Just like the old television show—"Just the facts sir—only the facts."

If your endeavors have provided some critical information then it may be necessary for it to end up in a courtroom. When this is the case it will be presented as testimony, which will be offered into evidence by a witness. There are several different types of witnesses. The first is the direct witness. This is someone, who has first hand knowledge regarding certain information being offered into evidence. The witness can not give any testimony, which is outside of his/her first hand knowledge. The second type is called an expert witness. This is an individual who possess special knowledge, skills and abilities, which is above that of a reasonable individual. It should also be noted that this is defined differently by state and federal courts and the standards also vary wildly between different states. In very general terms being qualified as an expert allows the examiner to offer an opinion regarding the information they reviewed. A question could be along these lines. "Mr. Davis, in your expert opinion is it possible this computer was involved in hacking activities using this exploit?" A direct witness could only provide testimony about items, which he had seen. For instance.

(Question—attorney) "Mr. Davis what did you find?"

(Answer—examiner) "On Tuesday, September 13, 2005, I utilized ABC log viewer to examine the log files from the Dell Spark Two server bearing serial number 8767464. I noted in log file 01011005.txt that there were numerous logon attempts from IP Address 123.48.75.3.

Also you must consider if the examiner is presented as an expert and fails to qualify as an expert witness, then it could open doors for the opposing legal counsel to invalidate the information presented by your expert by someone, who has been qualified as an expert. Some states also allow people, who have been qualified as an expert in a certain area, to be qualified for life as an expert in that area.

Once it appears it is all over, the exam, the report, the presentation, the courtroom testimony, are all finished, it still may not be over. If the examination is involved in legal proceedings, then it may not be over for years. If the defendant does not like the verdict then get ready for the appeal process. If it is in a criminal case, then there could be a civil case after it. Thanks to our wonderful legal system, the findings from an examination could be relevant for years to come. This is the primary reason that your examiner should have a good archival procedure to store images and work after the investigation is over. Also there must be sufficient documentation for the examiner to recount what actually happened. This procedure may need to be altered if the client's policy and procedures are more stringent.

If you find yourself in this position—I would highly suggest that you get a copy of "A Guide to Forensic Testimony: The Art and Practice of Presenting Testimony as an Expert Witness" by Fred C. Smith and Rebecca G. Bace. This is the definitive work on testimony and can help your examiner from falling into some of the common testimony pitfalls.

Chapter 4
Evidentiary Findings

What can you find on a computer that can help an investigation? Generally speaking, a computer can be a Gold mine that computer forensics can recover. Items like deleted files, file fragments, temporary files, swap space, emails, metadata, Internet and Web based activity items, and others can be recovered. Basically an investigation is not complete until the review of the computer storage media has been completed. The reason that forensic examiner can recover so much from computer storage media, like a hard drive in a computer, is because of the way the operating system, various applications, security utilities, and other software function. Unless otherwise noted, illustrations used for the operating system are from the Microsoft Windows operating system. I have chosen to focus on this operating system because it is the most prevalent operating system on the market and the one most users are familiar with. Other operating systems will have similar items a computer forensic specialist could recover, so Microsoft operating systems are not unique in this area.

Operating Systems

The data recovered from a hard drive is intrinsically tied to the operating system that holds it. Since Microsoft Windows is the dominant operating system much of computer forensics is concerned with the various flavors of Windows. As Windows began adding a lot of neat functions these were instigated into the operating system. Functions like printing a file in the 'background' while you do other work i.e. having multiple programs such as Word, Excel, Internet Explorer, etc all open and running at the same time. This functionality is facilitated in part by the creation of items 'behind the scenes' that most end users are never aware of. Temporary files, swap files, spool files, link files, cache files, and *.dat files are some of the items created by the operating system as someone uses the computer. Even the simple 'Delete' command may not function as you think; do you really know what gets deleted? Even more importantly, what does not get deleted? These items can provide a wealth of information to an examiner.

There are numerous fundamental differences in the operating systems. However most of the difference can be attributed to the manner in which the operating systems keep track of files. To better understand how these items can be recovered, we need to look at how the operating system works. When something is written to the hard drive the operating system takes the space needed in clusters from the unallocated space of the computer's hard drive. A cluster contains a fixed number of sectors (1 sector = 512 bytes), the number of sectors can vary, but 8 sectors per cluster is common. If the operating system does not need all of the space in a cluster, then the data previously stored in the unneeded part is left. If the cluster has eight sectors, it could potentially leave 7+ sectors with the 'old' data in it, which is large enough for a one or two page word document.

Think about how much information can be stored in two pages of a word document. In an investigation this could mean finding two pages of a memo or letter that was 'deleted' by the user. It could be that they had two versions of a contract, the original one your client signed and the one they say the client signed (that has been slightly modified). Finding two pages of the original contract could be huge. Even if it does not have the modified part, ask them why there is a deleted version on the hard drive. Items found in slack space can be significant.

Slack space is the area with the old data in it, starting at the end of file marker from the data being written and ending at the end of the cluster being allocated by the operating system to store the data. Another way to look at it is that it is the difference between the file's actual size and the space the operating system uses to store the file. This difference is called Slack Space.

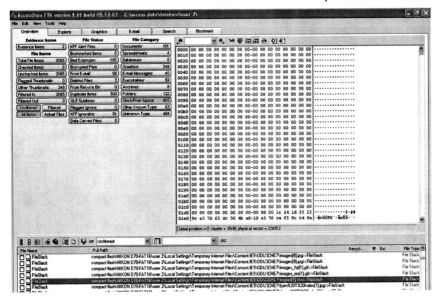

Figure 4.1—Slack Space

This data in the slack space will remain untouched on the hard drive until the file associated with the slack space is 'deleted' and it is overwritten with something else. This can create a situation where the contents in slack space remain on the computer for years. Think about how many files that are installed on the hard drive that are never changed and never deleted, consider program files and their related help files and documentation. This is significant, as I have recovered partial word documents in a file's slack space that was approximately 5 years old.

The unallocated space on a hard drive is the area that the operating system 'thinks' is empty and available for use. In reality the unallocated space is full of all kinds of data that an examiner will find useful. Normally there are a lot of deleted files that can be recovered from the unallocated space, that's right deleted files. This is true even if the hard drive has been reformatted. Actually if the hard drive has been reformatted there may be more deleted files to recover because of how the operating system performs this task. All the reformatting does is 'zero out' (or write over this area with zeros, "0") the file allocation table (FAT), zero out the root directory, but leaves the data area (everything else) untouched.

Deleted Files

Finding deleted files is possible because of how the operating system 'deletes' a file. When a file is deleted the operating system replaces the first letter of the short file name in the directory listing with a Greek sigma or HEX 'E5' and wipes the associated File Allocation Table (FAT) entries. The file is still on the hard drive in its entirety, but is now part of unallocated space and is in danger of being over written. You can think of the delete function like this; you want to delete chapter 5 from a textbook, so you go to the table of contents at the front of the book and mark over all of chapter 5's entries. By doing this you are convinced that the chapter has been deleted. If someone flips through the textbook page by page, they find chapter 5 in its entirety.

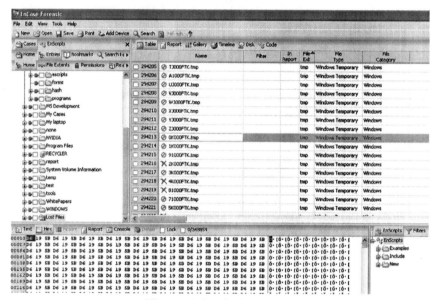

Figure 4.2—Deleted file

Similar to the flipping page by page through a book to find chapter 5, an examiner will scan the unallocated space for deleted files. Instead of looking for the page with 'Chapter 5' on it the examiner is looking for file headers. Almost every type of file on your computer hard drive has a file header. The file header is a set of unique characters at the beginning of a file. This means that every Microsoft Word document created has the same header, "ÐÏ·à¡±·á", as the first X characters of the file. To carve the file out of unallocated space the examiner will basically start from the file header and keep going until the end-of-file (EOF) marker is found. This will normally recover the file, though sometimes the sectors used to store a file are not contiguous. When this is the case the forensic examiner can generally match the sectors together correctly to carve the file out, though sometimes it can be difficult.

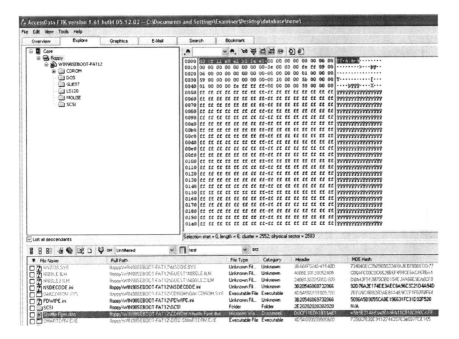

Figure 4.3—File Header

This is attributed to the operating system's method of using and re-using sectors for storage. The beginning of a file might be in sectors 1012 through 1030 and the end of the file in sectors 1040 to 1048. The problem is sectors 1031 to 1039 that for some reason were not used to store the file (probably being used at the time by another file). To get the deleted file carved out correctly these need to be skipped. They could add garbage to the deleted file when it is recovered or if these sectors contain an EOF marker the correct end of the deleted file may not be recovered. These nine sectors may be part of another file (deleted or not) or may be what is called a file fragment.

File Fragments

File fragments are basically just that. A file fragment is part of a deleted file that can no longer be reconnected to the rest of the file it once was a part of. A file fragment is created when a file is deleted and parts of the sectors containing the file are re-used to store a new file. In this scenario the file fragments would be found in the slack space of the new file and in unallocated space for the part of the file that was not re-used.

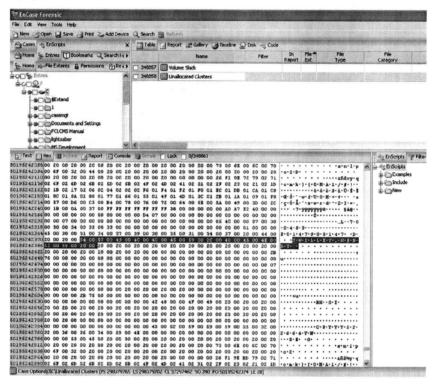

Figure 4.4—File Fragment

Deleted Directory Entries

As mentioned above, when Windows deletes a file it only replaces the first letter of the short file name in the directory listing with a Greek sigma or HEX 'E5'. This means that the rest of the directory listing is left intact until it is over written with a new entry. This directory entry has lots of used information including the file's long file name (if the file's name is more than eight characters), creation time and date, last access date, time of last update, date of last modification, file's starting cluster, and the file's size. If this is present, it allows forensic tools like EnCase or SMART to rebuild the file's directory entry and if the file has not been over written the file is 'undeleted' by the rebuilding of the file's entries into the File Allocation Table (FAT). These date and time stamps are based on the computer's internal clock, so they are not always accurate. It is very simple to resent the date and time on the computer's clock making the date and time stamps easy to manipulate. Knowing this an examiner can generally weed out files with irregular looking time stamps and develop a reasonable time line of what happened on a computer.

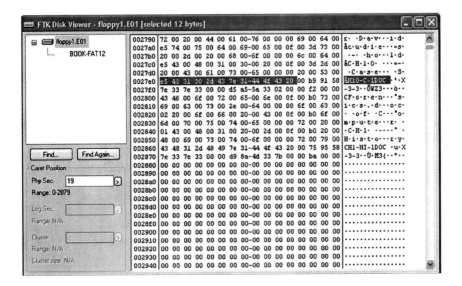

Figure 4.5—Deleted Directory Entry

Date and Time Stamps

Normally, people do not pay much attention to the computer's clock so many of the date and time stamps are relatively accurate to the computer's internal clock. In an investigation these dates and times can be very useful. Investigators also must realize that sometimes these time stamp do not mean what you might think. The 'creation' date and time stamp identify when the file was created. This date and time stamp is changed when the file is moved, copied, or downloaded from a remote location. So if a file was created on July 1, 2003 and then moved in Windows on January 4, 2004 then the creation date and time stamp would be January 4, 2004 not the date it was really created. There are many other functions in Windows that can change date/time stamps so that they are misleading. It is important to be aware of this when analyzing computer storage media.

Recycle Bin

In Windows there is one other place you can find 'deleted' files, the recycle bin. The recycle bin gives the user the convenient option of being able to recover files. When a file is deleted it is normally moved to the recycle bin and can be easily recovered through windows. The user must then empty the recycle bin to delete the file so that it is no longer recoverable through windows. After being emptied out of the recycle bin, the files are still on the hard drive and can be recovered, but are now in danger of being overwritten. Once something is overwritten, it is basically no longer recoverable. Another interesting item in the recycle bin is the INFO2 file that is created. This is a file containing information about files that are deleted through Windows and sent to the recycle bin. This file has information like the files original path and date & time it was sent to the recycle bin. When the recycle bin is emptied this file is deleted as well, but like any deleted file can be recovered.

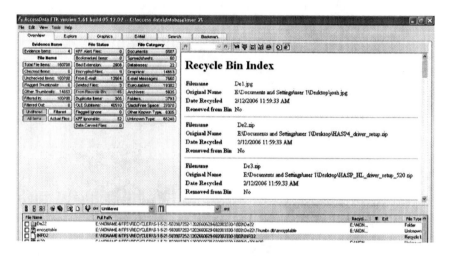

Figure 4.6—INFO2 File

Swap space

Swap space is one of those things the operating system creates and uses without the user's knowledge. When the computer runs out of Random Access Memory (RAM) it swaps items out of RAM and stores them on the computer's hard drive. For a period of time the operating system maintains a link to this file on the hard drive so that it can be quickly recalled if needed. Eventually the computer deletes the link to the file in swap space and the file is 'deleted' as far as the operating system is concerned. Unless otherwise set by the user the size of the swap space is dynamic and will keep growing during a user's time until the operating system runs out of unallocated space to assign to it. When this happens, the operating system begins to recycle sectors used by the swap space. Every time the computer is turned off the swap file is returned to the unallocated space on the hard drive. When the computer is turned on a new swap file is started and is usually in a different location on the hard drive unless the user set the size of the swap file to a fixed size. This creates a huge amount of deleted files on a computer's hard drive that the user may never have known were there. An examiner can also find user identifiers and passwords in this area if the computer was used to access online site's that require this, including bank accounts, brokerage, web based email, etc.

Printer spool files

Have you ever wondered how the print function works at the operating system level? It appears to be straight forward, the operating system takes and sends it to the printer and it is printed. The operating system does it a little differently. When a file is sent to the printer, the operating system makes a copy of the file, called a spool file, and then this file is placed in queue to be printed. When a file is printed the actual file being printed is the spool file copy of the original file. After it is printed, the spool file is deleted by the operating system, which means it is still on the hard drive in the unallocated space. So if spool files are found, they will show what was printed from the computer. This could differ from the file saved on the hard drive that someone claim's they printed.

Think about it, you open a Word document, make changes to the date, dollar amount, etc. and then print it (without saving it). After the file is printed you close the file and select not to save the changes. The only version of the printed file on the computer is the spool file, and even that exists as a deleted file. Spool files also create another possibility, files that are on removable media such as floppy disks or CD's that are printed on a computer may remain on the computer as a deleted spool file. So if a file is on a floppy disk the user can simply print out the file and then destroy and throw away the floppy disk. The spool file could be the only electronic version of the file available.

Link files

Link files (*.LNK) are another item the Windows operating system created to help make the user's life a little easier. Every time a document is opened Windows creates a link file for it. These files contain the path and filename of recently used files and are used to facilitate quick and easy access to these files. If you are using a program like MS-Word, left-click on the 'File' option on the menu bar. Near the bottom you should notice a list of recently access files that can be used to recall the file. The information needed to recall the file is stored in a link file. Link files can show that a file was accessed recently on a computer, even if it has never been stored on the computer. This is important if the file in question was on a floppy or network drive then the link file may be the only evidence on the computer's hard drive relating to the file.

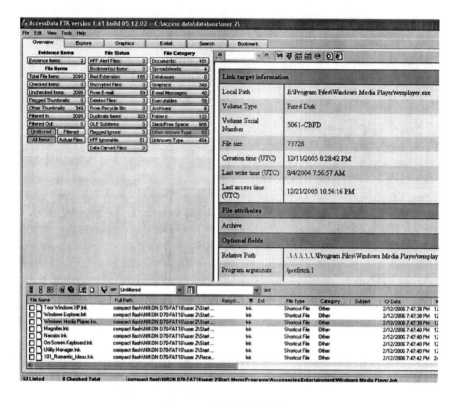

Figure 4.7—Link File

Windows Registry

The registry is the repository for the computer's settings. Hardware, software, services, and users all store information in the registry. Every time you make a change to the computer's environment a value to the registry is added, deleted, and/or modified. The registry information is stored in *.DAT files, such as NTUSER.DAT. While most of the information is of no value in an investigation, there is five or ten percent that is. If a program was ever installed on the computer, there will be evidence in the registry even if the software has been removed. The registry is where you will find the user profile(s), applications started in the boot process, user identifiers and passwords (sometimes), default paths used by applications to access or save files, and other system parameters. Another neat thing that may be in the registry are items generated by web browsers. The registry is where the web browser may store items like the user's profile associated with the browser and user identifiers and passwords for websites visited is desired by the user.

Incorrect Extensions

In the Windows environment the last three or four letters of a file name provide some valuable information. These letters are generally called the file extension. The Windows operating system uses these letters to determine what program to use when the user attempts to open a certain file. How can a file end up with the wrong extension? Many people think that the assignment of file extensions is controlled by the applications that created it. After all when you select the 'Save As' option when saving a Microsoft Word file the application only lets you select a file extension that could be associated with that type of file. The most common of these for a Word file is '.doc'. The extensions used with other file types, such as Excel files (.xls) or a program executable file, (.exe) are not even an option. Another common response is a computer virus or hacker must have done it. While these are both possibilities, the reality is much simpler. To change the file's extension just locate the file with Windows Explorer and right-click on the file. Then choose the 'rename' option and add the desired file extension. There are several other ways to easily change a file's extension, as the Windows operating system is generally very good about providing a user with multiple ways to do the same thing.

Now the questions are why would anyone want to do this and what would it accomplish? Actually it is a good way to hide a file in plain sight. If you are involved in an investigation concerning financial fraud you may look at excel files to see if they posses any data in them that would concern the fraudulent transitions, but you might choose to ignore executable files. So to hide the excel spreadsheet from others the user can just rename the file from 'Fgame.xls' to 'Fgame.exe'. Who would think of looking in this file? Thus relevant evidence is overlooked by the investigator. Even if the investigator doubled on the file the operating system would attempt to execute the program, because of the exe extension. However since this file only contains spreadsheet data, the user would receive an error message.

How can you counter this type of file hiding? In your investigation you can attempt to open every file on the various computer storage media. In modern computer terms this is completely impractical. It accomplished it would be very time consuming, especially when you consider the volume of files on a typical computer hard drive can number in the tens of thousands and even millions. This is why many computer forensics software applications have routines that compare the file's header to the file's extension. This is because a user can easily change the file's extension but it is much more difficult to change a file's header. When the two do not match the person conducting the examination is alerted. These files can be investigated further by the examiner. While there is still a manual review of the files involved, the number of files to review is normally reduced to a fraction of a percent of the total files.

Log files

While an investigation may begin on an individual's PC, in the corporate environment it can quickly grow to include servers, mid-range computers, and even mainframes. The good news is that all of these normally keep logs of user activity; the bad news is that these logs are normally kept for a limited amount of time. This means the identification of computer systems that may be included in the investigation needs to be done quickly and appropriate steps taken to preserve them. One of the first steps in the investigation is to obtain a copy of the company's policy and procedures for computer system backup, computer system logging, and log file retention. This was you know what should be available, and if it is needed have those backup tapes and/or files preserved.

Log files are normally text files that are used by logging applications to store events. What is stored in these log files depends on how they are configured. These log files can be used to reconstruct how a user did something on the computers. It could be as simple as trying to access an inappropriate website from work to access financial data in a database, thus bypassing the application controls to the data. Thanks to Open DataBase Connectivity (ODBC) connections this can be done with tools like Windows Explorer, Microsoft Excel, Microsoft Access, and/or Netscape. I chose these tools because they are common on most corporate personal computers, and if the company's security is not setup correctly on the computer system a user can access remote databases with them.

Log files can also be generated on an individual's personal computer. While using excel to access a remote database to change financial data may not create any logging activity on the personal computer, other activity can. Items like extracting files from a compressed format file (a ZIP file), Internet chat, Internet use, instant messaging and network activity can all create log file. It just depends on how the computer is configured.

Metadata

Today several articles I have read estimate that over 90% of all documents are created electronically. Many times these 'new' documents are not new, but are previously created documents that someone modifies and saves to a new file name. This is quicker and easier than creating the document from scratch, besides who will know. Many applications like Microsoft Word®, Excel®, PowerPoint®, and other create metadata in a file when a file is created or saved. Metadata is simply data about data. What does this data tell you about a file? Many people are surprised in the information that can be found in the metadata of a simple Word file.

This data can include items such as the last 10 authors, hidden text, document last modified, access, created time stamps, editor, owner, publisher of the document, personal information, and more. (Metadata is discussed in more detail later.) In an investigation this information can be very useful. Ever had a contract modified from the original and you were trying to prove who changed it? If the document was a Microsoft Word file there is a good chance you can find metadata that can help you prove who did it. If there was financial fraud at a company, the person(s) involved may use Excel to keep track of the fraudulent activities. If you find the Excel file(s) there is a good chance you can extract metadata that shows who created and modified the file. The reason I say there is a "good chance" or "may be able" is that this is electronic information and it is possible to remove it. Also, if the data fields on the computer are not filled in, like username, company name, etc. then the metadata fields will be empty as well.

There are several tools available from vendors like Microsoft and third parties that can identify, display and remove Metadata. One such tool is available from Payne Consulting Group, Inc. called Metadata Assistant®.

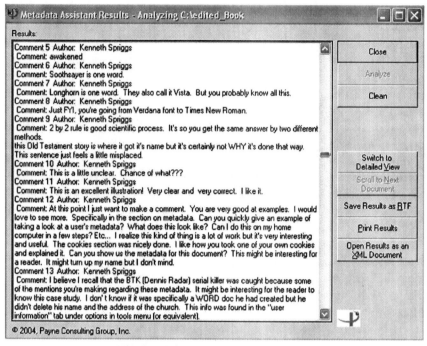

Figure 4.8—Metadata Assistant

Alternate Data Streams

Alternative Data Streams (ADS) were added to the Windows operating systems (NT File System) in the early 1990's to improve its interoperability with Apple's Macintosh file system. The Macintosh file system uses resource forks that basically allow 2 files to appear and act as one file. This may sound neat, but users and most applications will only be able to access the file stored with the default stream. The file connected with the ADS will be 'invisible' to most applications and thus users. Since it became part of the NT file system in the some Windows applications are starting to use ADS's to store metadata about a file.

This makes storing files with an ADS a near perfect hiding place. Someone could use this to send out malicious code, viruses, or to email sensitive data out undetected. A simple way to think about ADS is as an invisible attachment to a file. This attachment is invisible to many security applications like virus scanners, firewalls, scanners, or backup software. The ADS files stay with the file they are attached to until they are intentionally removed, copied to a file system that does not support them, or backed up with software that does not support ADS files. This can be a nice way to get rid of ADS files.

Temporary files

Applications with an auto save or auto backup function creates temporary files that users may not be aware of. This function is in many word processors, spread sheet, database, and similar user applications to provide recovery abilities in case the application or computer crashes. These files are created behind the scenes while the computer is being used and often have a '.tmp' file extension and/or start with a non-alpha character such as the tilde, '~'. These files are stored in a default location or sometimes in a user defined location on the hard drive. Depending on the application and its configuration these temporary files are stored in a folder or they may be deleted and in unallocated space.

Web Browsers

Surfing the Internet has become a daily event for people using computers. Internet Explorer®, Netscape®, Firefox®, and other browsers enable users to point and click their way around computer systems, download files, shop, pay bills, order a pizza, and numerous other activities. Each activity can leave items on the hard drive in many places.

Internet History

If you have ever surfed the Internet with a web browser such as Internet Explorer or Netscape you may have noticed that after clicking on a link and returning to the original page that the link has changed colors. If you click a second time on the link you may notice that the web page loads much faster. Have you ever wondered why? The links change color because the browser keeps a history file of the websites the user has visited. If the webpage has not been visited then the link may be blue, if it has been visited then the link in red. (Note: Users can control if colors are changed and what the colors are, blue and red are only used as an example.) The webpage may load faster because the browser is not going out on the Internet and re-accessing the website to download the webpage, the browser is getting the webpage from the cache files.

Most web browsers keep a number of files that can show a user's activity on the Internet in addition to the INDEX.DAT (history data file) and cache files. These include email addresses, bookmarks, cookies received, preferences, emails sent and received, and news group information. Email, cookies, and cache files are discussed a little later, right now let's focus on the other files. Bookmarks are web-pages that the user has intentionally saved, normally for future reference. In

Netscape there is a 'Bookmarks' menu option on the menu bar of the browser. Once a page has been booked marked it allows the user to return to it in the future by simply clicking on the appropriate option off the 'Bookmarks' drop down menu. Bookmarks have a name that normally describes the location it goes to such as a name 'CNN News' for the website 'www.cnn.com'. What you need to understand is that browsers also allow for users to manage the bookmarks. This allows a user to group bookmarks into folders and even change the name of the bookmark. This means that the name 'CNN News' could send the user to the 'www.pornXXX.com' website. So if you are investigating a person's Internet use, you need to look at the locations bookmarks will send you to, not just the name of the bookmarks.

Preferences are parameters that can be set by the user for the browser, Internet chat, news groups, email, instant messaging, and security. These parameters help determine how the applications function and what kind of history is kept.

Cookies

Many websites a user visits will leave a cookie on the user's hard drive. A cookie is just a small text file with relevant data formatted the way the creating website likes it. This is currently the main way websites store tracking information about people the visit their websites. When you return to the website it looks for the cookie it left last time you visited to retrieve the information in it. These cookies are normally stored in the C:\Documents and Settings\<username>\Cookies directory. This information can be very useful in an investigation as the cookie can hold username and password data, date of last visit, user preferences for the web site, and any other data the web site deems necessary. The six common items found in cookies are name, value (usually an ID string from the website visited), expiration date, path, domain, and secure (a security parameter). Remember, there is no set format for cookies so each one can be different in the data it has and the format of it. Below is a cookie from my personal computer relating to my security software, can you tell which vendor I use? (The cookie's name is "administrator @mcafee[1]".)

lUsrCtxPersist

%3CUserContext%3E%3CAccount+acct%5Fid%3D%222a7d1d3aa f14efd5d777903309b0430e5c40425d510b0117%22+email%5Faddress %3D%22frank%40gsforensics%2Ecom%22+signon%3D%22frank%4 0gsforensics%2Ecom%22+disp%5Fname%3D%22%22+LoggedIn%3D %22d08574791cecadc50172ebf3fad6438e3b010109%22+RememberMe %3D%

mcafee.com/

1536
1372674048
29722287
1614955248
29716337
*

Much of the cookie is cryptic to a human, but to the website it makes perfect sense. If needed in an investigation the company, in this case McAfee®, should be able to provide details as to what everything means. Just looking at this you know it is for the mcafee.com website, my email is frank@gsforensics.com, my email address is also my sign on user name, that I have logged on to this web site, that I was logged on to the computer as "administrator", and I have asked it to remember me. In an investigation this cookie may not provide you with any useful information, but what if it was to a competitors website, an online accounting service used by the company (such as Quicken®), or and inappropriate website such as porn (accessed from work). Cookies from these sites could prove the user accessed the websites and may provide additional information like last access time, username, password, or level of access privileges. Cookies can sometimes be tied to a specific website by reviewing the Internet history file as sometimes website name cookies with names that have nothing to do with the website that created it.

Cache files for Internet Browsers

As mentioned earlier Internet cache files enable web pages to load faster, but have you ever wondered how these cache files work? When you are surfing the Internet the browser keeps recently viewed web pages in folders on the computer's hard drive and are controlled by the browser. The browser maintains a link to these web pages so that they can be quickly recalled. So when you use the back or forward buttons, make a selection from the History Bar of the browser, or just revisit a web site the browser will first check and see if the web page is in cache, if not it will reload the web page from the source.

This accessing of web pages from cache is normally not noticed by users as most web pages are not very dynamic, i.e. the version stored in the browser's cache is the same as the version the browser would download from across the network. This is helpful in investigations in that the user's recent browser activity can be reviewed. This can include web pages to financial companies like banks and investment brokers or site with questionable ethical content.

BLOGS

Blog is the nickname for a weblog. These can be written by a single person, usually the website owner, or by a group. The group can even be open to anyone on the Internet that visited the website and felt like leaving a message. Entries into the blog are stacked one on top of another, which means the most recent entry will be on top. A weblog is a simple log file that can be accessed from the Internet. It is still just a log file, a simple text file. Granted a website can make this a fancy log, adding search capabilities, indexing, weblinks, pictures, and the like, but at the end of the day it is still a log file. Blogs are used for advertising, personal journals, frequently asked questions, or any other test based creation. This can provide a wealth of information in a forensic review of the computer storage media that stores the associated website or it's backup.

Browser Helper Objects

Microsoft developed this functionality for its web browser, Internet Explorer, so programmers could build programs that interact with the browser and startup with the browser as if it was part of it. This is great for functionality, but it also aids programs such as spyware and keyloggers. An example of a browser helper object that is helpful in one from Adobe. This browser helper object enables the browser to open an Adobe *.PDF file in the browser. These programs normally leave artifacts in the registry, but sometimes that is all. Because they operate as part of the browser they can be difficult to detect.

Applications

On top of the operating system there are usually applications that a user will use. These application files are normally compiled executable files that cannot be modified by the user. Many of these applications do allow for configuration modifications. These changes to the application's configuration settings can affect the way the application interacts with users or how it functions internally. Some of the items to look for include:

Configuration Files—these will normally have information that is of no value such as color and font settings, but they can have some very useful information. These file may contain the logging information, is logging turned on, what data elements are captured to the log(s), what events trigger an entry to a log, the location of the log file(s), and the name of the log file(s). These files may specify an automated backup schedule, the parameters for what is backed up, and where the backups are stored.

Log Files—applications can generate several types of log files. These log files can be simple text files, a database, or a proprietary format (mostly found in older applications) and generally have a date and time stamp for each entry. Some of the more common log files are events logs that can be used to record any event within the application as defined by the user. Error logs are used to store application errors including processing errors that can be useful when trying to determine when an event occurs. The installation log can tell you that a certain application was installed and sometimes by who (the computer user identifier). The audit log can be used to audit transactions, user access, files access, field access, or just about anything that happens within the application. This auditing functionality is getting more attention now because of laws like SOX, GBL, and HIPAA.

Data—many applications have data associated with them in databases, but some use other way to store data, such as flat files. These files can hold data for the accounts payables, accounts receivables, or a file of adjusting journal entries. In a financial investigation this can be important. While entries have dates that the users can control when the entry is being made, or even after sometimes, there is sometime a date/time field associated with the record that the user never sees. This is the time stamp the system places on the record when it is created.

If someone changes entries the company's financial data, there should be entries in the various log files. These entries could show which user identifier did what and when they did it. If this information is being captured and is available it can go a long way in reconstructing what happened in application like SAP, Oracle Financials, Lawson, etc. There are also several other types of applications that are common on personal computers that can leave these items as well. These include:

Instant Messaging

One of the most popular programs in this area is AOL Instant Messenger® (IM) and the stand alone version AIM®. There are other instant messaging programs like Yahoo messenger. Instant messaging program are mainly used to 'chat' online with people and for transferring files. These applications can have log files of past conversations over the network, address books containing the instant messaging contact data, file transfer items, configuration files, and other artifacts depending on how they are configured. You may be surprised at what you can find here. People tend to think that while they are hiding behind a computer over a network no one will ever be able to trace their comments back to them. They tend to say things that they would not normally say. This is great for investigations, but bad for those using technology that they do not fully understand.

Email

Emails are becoming more and more apart of our everyday life. In 2003 people sent about 31 billion emails each day and it is expected to double by 2006 (IDC Email usage forecast and analysis, www.sims. berkeley.edu/research/projects/how-much-info-2003). This is a lot of communications going back and forth, most of which will never be printed out to any type of physical format. Depending on the email application being used, email can be on the person computer, on a server, or on a remote storage location across the network. Email can also be found in the unallocated space of the computer's hard drive, these are deleted emails or emails that were open and moved to the swap file for some reason. If the email application is a web based service, such as those available from Yahoo® and Google®, there may be items in the Internet cache files.

In the corporate environment email potentially exist in many locations, the senders machine, the email server used by the sender, the email server used by the recipient, the recipient's computer and backup tapes at both the sender's and receiver's location. Once an email is sent, it can be difficult to get ride of, thought it may take some work to find it. So the sender and recipient of an email may both think they have deleted an email, though it may remain in unallocated space for quite a while on their hard drive. It may also be on one of the corporate backup tapes. Potential evidence can also be obtained from the address books as the email application may save the email address even after the email(s) have been deleted. This could prove contact between the two email addresses.

Once email are found, there is more to them than just the email message, the data in the email header can be useful. Below are two versions of the email header from the same email. The first is 'normal' and the second is 'all', this parameter can be set in the email client on the personal computer. The first one does not tell you much, probably what you are use to seeing on an email. The problem is that these four lines (From:, Date:, and To:) are very easy to spoof or forge, so if you go to court this could be challenged. The second is an expanded view you can see all of the information from the first version of the email header, but there is a lot of additional information. This additional information is harder for someone to forge, though not impossible, especially the 'Received:' information.

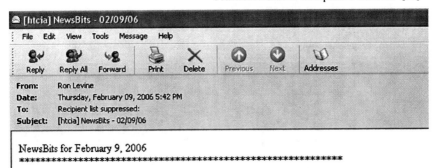

Figure 4.9—Email Header

```
Return-Path: <owner-htcia@htcia1.securesites.net>
Received: from htcia1.securesites.net (htcia1.securesites.net [128.121.62.54])
        by mailhost.cotse.com (8.13.5/8.13.5) with ESMTP id k19NWc4X008054
        for <david@gajedi.org>; Thu, 9 Feb 2006 18:32:44 -0500 (EST)
        (envelope-from owner-htcia@htcia1.securesites.net)
Received: from htcia1.securesites.net (localhost [127.0.0.1])
        by htcia1.securesites.net (8.13.1/8.12.6) with ESMTP id k19N18P3029193;
        Thu, 9 Feb 2006 23:01:08 GMT
        (envelope-from owner-htcia@htcia1.securesites.net)
Received: (from majordom@localhost)
        by htcia1.securesites.net (8.13.1/8.13.1/Submit) id k19N18Zs029192;
        Thu, 9 Feb 2006 23:01:08 GMT
X-Authentication-Warning: htcia1.securesites.net: majordom set sender to owner-htcia@htcia1
Received: from redstripe.fhda.edu (redstripe.fhda.edu [153.18.96.108])
        by htcia1.securesites.net (8.13.1/8.12.6) with ESMTP id k19MhbiT019680
        for <htcia@htcia1.securesites.net>; Thu, 9 Feb 2006 22:43:37 GMT
        (envelope-from rlevine@ix.netcom.com)
Received: from rwdtc.ix.netcom.com ([153.18.226.13])
        by redstripe.fhda.edu (8.9.3/8.9.1) with ESMTP id 0AA29589;
        Thu, 9 Feb 2006 14:43:21 -0800 (PST)
Message-Id: <6.2.5.6.2.20060209142713.025e1330@fhda.edu>
X-Mailer: QUALCOMM Windows Eudora Version 6.2.5.6
Date: Thu, 09 Feb 2006 14:42:39 -0800
To: Recipient list suppressed:;
From: Ron Levine <rlevine@ix.netcom.com>
Subject: [htcia] NewsBits - 02/09/06
Mime-Version: 1.0
Content-Type: text/plain; charset="iso-8859-1"; format=flowed
Content-Transfer-Encoding: 8bit
X-MIME-Autoconverted: from quoted-printable to 8bit by htcia1.securesites.net id k19MhbiT01
Sender: owner-htcia@htcia1.securesites.net
Precedence: bulk
Reply-To: htcia@htcia1.securesites.net
X-Whitelist: Whitelisted (sender *@htcia1.securesites.net)
Status: O
X-UID: 8769
Content-Length: 11117
X-Keywords:

NewsBits for February 9, 2006
*********************************************************

Yahoo Is Accused of Aiding China in Case of Jailed Dissiden
In a development expected to put more
pressure on foreign high-tech companies
operating in China, a free-speech group
<
```

Figure 4.10—Expanded Email Header

Web-base email—such as the services offered by Yahoo or Google can leave all kinds of things behind for examiner to find. You can find deleted emails in the unallocated space, web pages of emails viewed by a user in unallocated space or possible the swap or Internet cache files. This email service may also have address books full of contacts and configuration files. Getting all of this may require help from the web based email service provider. This is another example of an application that lets the user hide behind a computer. Here too, people are generally more open in email than they are in person because they think no one will ever know.

Emails—application such as Outlook®, Outlook Express®, GroupWise®, and Netscape are not web based and are common in the business environment. These applications have address books of contacts, configuration parameters, folders of emails (it is surprising the emails some people keep), and they typically leave deleted emails in the unallocated space of a hard drive. This is also an application that allows people to hide, and consequently say thing they sometimes they should not. Ever wondered if two or more people are involved in a fraudulent scheme at a company, if they ever communicated via email or instant messages? Odds are they do because it is easy, convenient, and they think no one will ever know.

File sharing applications

File sharing hit the headline in the USA with the Napster® trial. Napster allowed people to share the popular music files, MP3, with each other. File sharing applications are peer-to-peer (P2P) networks that allow people to share files, not just MP3 files, with each other efficiently. These programs are also great for moving large amounts of corporate date to another computer, sometimes without being caught by corporate security. These programs such as Kazaa®, Limewire®, Bearshare®, and Morpheus® can provide an examiner with a wealth of information on what the user has done with them. There may be incomplete file downloads, metadata, and database files, registry entries left on the computer that can be of value to an examiner. What you can find depends on the P2P application and how it is configured.

Trojan Viruses

This is when a file is sent to you for some reason, but has another program attached to it. The other attached program is the Trojan. Someone send you a video file, you watch it, and while you watch it a back door program in installed. SubSeven is an example of this type of trojan virus. Many times in an investigation someone will claim that they did not download the files, or mail the confidential files out, it was a virus that did it. Normally this defense is a lot like Phlip's claim that 'The Devil made him do it!'. Well the devil did not make him do it, though he often gets the blame (and may have enjoyed watching). Similarly, a trojan normally did not do it, though in theory they could if programmed correctly. If someone uses this defense, ask them how did they know they had a virus? Which virus did they have? How do they know the virus is the guilty party? A forensic specialist can help determine if the virus actually did anything.

Encryption & Steganography

Two of the more popular methods to hid data or files on a computer are with encryption and/or steganography. These methods of hiding things have been around for thousands of years, so they are not exclusive to computers. Computers are used to enhance these methods though. Various types of encryption have been used for years to store files on a computer. Once encrypted a person needs to know the application used to encrypt the file and the password associated with the file (if one was used). A common tool used for this would include zip files (*.zip). Zip files are a good way to compress files for emailing and the password option adds security. Encrypted files are a good way to keep files private, but are easy to detect and most of the time is only as good as the password associated with it.

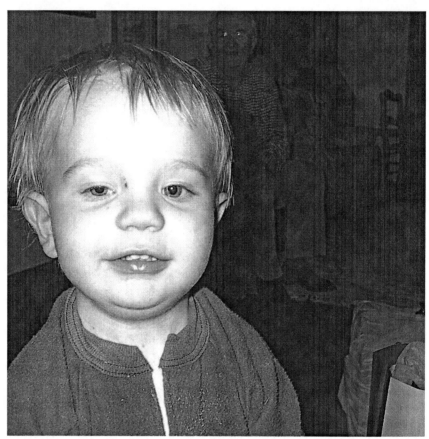

Figure 4.11A—Picture without Steganography

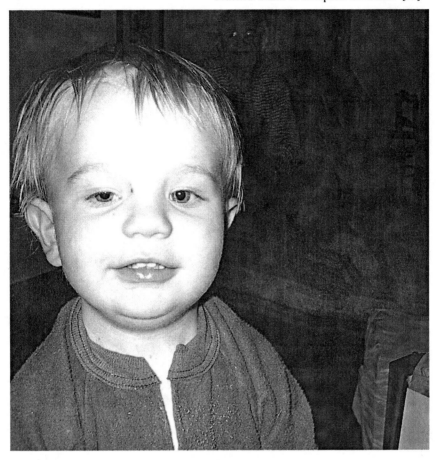

Figure 4.11B—Picture with Steganography, S-tools used in this Example

Steganography is used to embed one file into another. This process hides one file into another, and example is a word document into a picture file. There are hundreds of steganography tools on the market, some are very good and are free. When a file is embedded into the picture file the color scheme is changed slightly, so slightly that it is normally not detectable to the human eye. This makes detecting files that have been embedded with a file very difficult. It is also possible to use encryption and steganography on the same file. Take a secret document and encrypt it. Then take the encrypted files and embed it into a picture file.

Figure 4.11C—File with an embedded document using S-Tools® with pop-up screen for encryption

Anti-Forensics

Evidence Eliminator®, www.evidence-eliminator.com, by Robin Hood Software Ltd. is one of the anti-forensic software programs available. This product is one of many that claim to defeat forensic tools such as EnCase and FTK. Products like this will delete the Windows SWAP file, application logs, temporary files, recycle bin, browser related data, email items, slack space, unallocated space and many other items. What these programs will delete and when they delete them depends on how you configure them. From what I have been told these programs can be quite effective, but usually leave little signs that they were there. This creates a situation where the items you were looking for are actually deleted, gone, not recoverable, but you can find items relating to the evidence eliminator program. Now you get to ask the other side or person why they have this software and what were they trying to hide?

Databases

Databases are used by applications to store large amounts of data for applications like SAP®, Oracle Financials®, Lawson®, and others. Databases are themselves applications and have many of the items like other applications, log files, configuration files, and tables of data in the database. If configured correctly, the database is another source of data that can provide investigators with a wealth of information. This is important because many people who commit financial fraud are financial people, some are even CPA's, and do not understand how computers work behind the scenes.

So a computer savvy accountant may understand that the financial application has logs that would capture their actions and decide to use a back door. With an application like Excel the accountant can use an open database connection (ODBC) to access the database and modify the financial data, bypassing the application. An accountant would know enough about journal entries and their effect on the financial data to not need the templates the financial application would provide so using Excel in this was would be easy. The application's preventive and detective controls would have been bypassed, the operating system's controls would probably not show anything because it is a valid and authorized user on the computer system, but the database controls should have the log entries and the modified data.

Security Software & System Utilities

Another source of information for an investigator may be items associated with system utilities or security software. This can include antivirus, antispam, web filtering, firewalls, and email encryption. System utilities include the remote access servers (RAS), backup utilities, and disk defragmentation. These applications have configurations logs that will tell you how they are configured and the exceptions to the standard configuration. These applications will have files that will detail who has access to the application. For applications like a firewall, a RAS, or web filtering the files associated with the application should also tell you the level of access a user has through them. The log files generated by these applications can detail what happened and when it happened regarding remote access or Internet access.

Chapter 5
Microsoft Office Products

In the late 1980s the personal computer began to permeate the business community. As the personal computer began its slow journey to replace the dump terminals, which were connected to powerful computers, the need immerged for a software package to fulfill an all in one office role. While the dump terminals were used to input data into highly specialized and customized computing platforms, the office typewriter was still the most common piece of equipment in the office. These typewriters were at the heart of the business community's communication. Highly skilled typists were the corner stone of many businesses units. Microsoft noticed the dominance of these machines and wanted to the top provider of a whole suite of products to make business more productive. In the beginning phases it worked with such companies as Tandy to produce an all in one office solution. This was called the Tandy/Radio Shack PC Model 100. This single machine could now create letters, spreadsheets and communicate with other. In September 1983 Microsoft launched Word 1.0. The word processor was the beginning of Microsoft's "What You See Is What You Get" (WYSIWYG) programs. This means that the program allowed the user to see on the screen exactly what would be printed on the paper. While in its infancy this meant little more than bold, italics and underline, these powerful programs allow users to create very complex documents, which can contain a multitude of functions. To bring the power of word processing onto the personal computer would make it an absolutely necessity for every employee to possess. This foresight gave rise to an entirely new suite of products, which later came to be called Microsoft Office. Microsoft Office 3.0 was released in August of 1993. This core group of products included Word, Excel, PowerPoint and Mail. Now by having essential business applications on a single platform Microsoft began cementing its lead the industry standard.

We will focus on the Microsoft Word applications as it is the one user are probably the most familiar with. All of the Microsoft Office applications have similar interfaces and features, making them easier to use. We will look at these features as they relate to computer forensics and only bring up items for other application if they are unique for the application and/or if they have not been discussed yet.

Microsoft Word

The most common used program in the Microsoft Office Suite is Word, one of the most used word processing programs in the corporate environment today. It can be used for tasks as simple as creating a letter to as complex as an automated batch job called mail merge. What has made Word the most used word processing program is its simple straight forward and user friendly format. A user can open the program and immediately begin typing his/her document, but this program should not be under estimated for its functionality. Fortunately for the forensic accountant and computer forensic specialist there can be a wealth of meaningful information obtained from its temporary files and considerable information can be picked up. These clues can lead the resourceful investigator to the goose that layed the golden egg if one is through and processes a certain level of expertise.

A Microsoft Word document will generally have the file extension of 'doc'. As we have discussed in the previous section, it is possible for an individual to attempt to hide data by changing the file extension. However this technique is very well known and is usually one of the first things a computer forensics specialist will look for.

Another item a computer forensics specialist will look for is the document's properties. Word document properties are commonly overlooked and can contain beneficial information. Depending of the version and installation of the application, this can provide very valuable insights into the history of a document. Here are some examples of the information which can be obtained from a document created by Microsoft Word 97. Most of these examples are true for various version of Word; however we are going to explore Word 97 and Word 2003 as these are the most common installed versions of the application.

User Information—This can be viewed by opening the tools menu and selecting options. This will bring up a window with a number of different tabs in it. One of the most interesting is called "User Information." This tab has information about the document's creator such as name, initials, and mailing address. This information, also known as Metadata, is stored by the operating system and is obtained by Microsoft Word when a document is created. It is automatically populated into every word document, which is created on this computer. In order to get ride of this information the user will need to select each of these boxes and place a few blanks in the fields and then save this information. It is interesting to note that previous documents take on the name of the current data owner. A good example would be if an individual is accused a fraudulent activity, and this activity was surrounding a product for sale. The suspect might produce a Word Document, which supports his side of the story with some screen shots from this document as proof that he created it long ago. However when the forensic examiner makes a forensic image of the hard drive and begins to examine the documents one fact will be quite curious.

When this property area is opened on the forensic examiner's work station—it could show that the forensic examiner's information in this area. This is because the information from this area is dynamically linked to the installation information on the current computer system. When the document is sent to a different user then the User Information is repopulated with the data from the new machine assuming there is an installation of Microsoft Word on the computer in the first place.

Figure 5.1, Screen print of the 'Options' window

Personal Summary Information—is perhaps the most commonly known of all of the Word metadata. This series of tabs can be accessed by selecting the file menu—then properties. A series of five tabs will be displayed. These tabs are the following

General—this tab provides the document name, its location, size, MS-DOS name and file attributes such as read only, archive, hidden and system. This information is common to most windows storage information.

Summary—this tab can provide some very forensically significant information. It contains the following: Title, Subject, Author, Manager, Company, Category, Keywords and Comments.

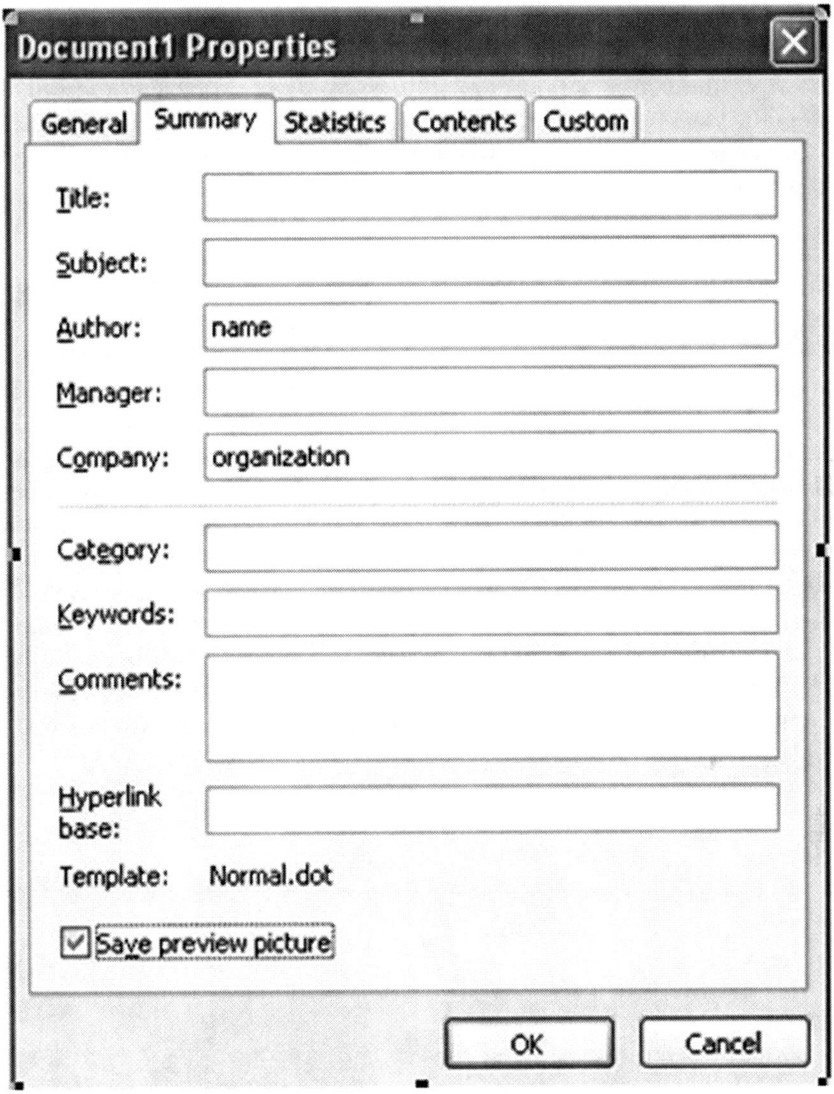

Document1 Properties ☒

General | Summary | Statistics | Contents | Custom

T̲itle: [   ]

S̲ubject: [   ]

A̲uthor: [name   ]

M̲anager: [   ]

C̲ompany: [organization   ]

Cat̲egory: [   ]

K̲eywords: [   ]

C̲omments: [   ]

H̲yperlink
base: [   ]

Template: Normal.dot

☑ Sa̲ve preview picture

[OK]   [Cancel]

Figure 5.2—Properties Screen Print

Statistics—this tab can provide some very significant information. Much of this information is the same as the file attribute information, which can be obtained from right clicking on the files from the windows explorer shell and then selecting properties. If the information from this area is changed, it will also be changed in the file attributes. When installing Microsoft Word the user is asked to provide their name and organization. This information is then embedded into Microsoft Office documents created using this computer. This can be a duel blessing and a curse. For example, a document is created by a user that has inserted their information during installation and then this document is emailed to second user. If a forensic examination is conducted on the second user's computer, this Word document can be conclusively linked to the original user.

However this can also be a curse. Let's say that the computer in question is reissued to another user, because the original user leaves the company. It is conceivable that the information provided in the original installation could be stamped into documents, which are created by the second user. Then the same forensic examination of the document would point to the original computer user and not the correct author of the document. The experienced computer forensic examiner should be able to make this distinction, provided that the reissue date of the computer is known. However if this is not known it can cause challenges to the case. This situation can change when you log onto a network, the network login information can appear in the Author edit box and in the last saved by field. It is interesting to note that removing all of the personal information may not prevent this from occurring. Some creative computer users may circumvent this by copying the data onto a USB thumb drive or floppy drive and working on the document from there. This will prevent the network from changing this information.

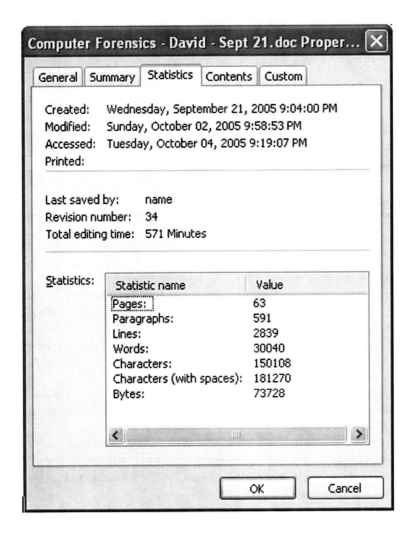

Figure 5.3—Properties Screen Print

Contents and Custom also allow additional information to be added to a document. Since this information is not auto populated, information found in this area can be very useful. However, because this information lacks auto population it is generally not created.

Document Comments—many Microsoft products allow the user to add comments to a document. When this is done, it can also contain the name of the person who entered the comments. Or should I say the name entered during installation of the operating system. When a user adds a comment, it generally appears as highlighted text. These can be removed by right clicking on the document and selecting 'Delete comment."

Headers and Footers—Microsoft Word has the ability for the user to insert repetitive information at the top and/or bottom of pages within a word document. This can contain information of significance.

Fast Save—is a feature that has been for the most part rendered useless, when Microsoft turned it off by default with release of Office 97 service pack 1. When this feature was released it decreased the time required to save a document, because it only saved the changes. This was forensically significant when information was deleted from the document by a user and then fast saved. Only the information was not actually deleted, it was just hidden. Since this feature is used so rarely anymore—it maybe useful to attempt to hide data there, however for the most part it can be ignored.

Hyperlinks—have greatly expanded the usefulness of Microsoft Word. It has allowed the ability to connect documents and other pieces of media in innovative ways. These links should be fully exploited during a forensic investigation, because they can provide additional clues to other information of investigative interest. For example an embedded link could point to a remote document, which could provide valuable information. Additionally the presence of these remote documents, images, spreadsheets could provide additional avenues for forensic exploitation.

Styles—is a special formatting option in Microsoft Word. This formatting may contains some additional metadata. Meta data is simply put is data about data.

Versions—is a feature, which has been added to later version of Word. It allows the author to save multiple versions of the same document within the same file. These older versions of the document can contain valuable information.

Code Fields—is a special formatting, which can link other images and objects within a document. You can view the field code by selecting options from the tools menus. Then you will need to locate the view tab and select the field codes option box. Now the field codes will appear in the document.

Templates—can provide some additional information regarding the origin of a document. Every new Microsoft Word document created using a template. These standard templates have the file extension of "DOT." The original name and path this template is stored within MS Word.

Routing Slips—can be useful when examining emailed documents. The routing slip feature allows MS Word to access your address book to obtain email addresses.

Authorship Information—is stored by MS Word by default. It automatically stores the last 10 authors from a document. This information can not be removed from the actual document itself, unless you change the formatting to a form, which does not support metadata as well. A good example would be rich text format.

In an investigation this information can be very useful. Ever had a contract modified from the original and you were trying to prove who made the changes? If the document was a Microsoft Word file there is a good chance you can find metadata that can help you prove who did it. If there was financial fraud at a company, the person(s) involved may use Excel to keep track of the fraudulent activities. If you find the Excel file(s) there is a good chance you can extract metadata that shows who created and modified the file. The reason I say there is a "good chance" or "may be able" is that this is electronic information and it is possible to remove it. Also, if the data fields on the computer are not filled in, like username, company name, etc. then the metadata fields will be empty as well.

There are several tools available from vendors like Microsoft and third parties that can identify, display and remove Metadata. One such tool is available from Payne Consulting Group, Inc. called Metadata Assistant.

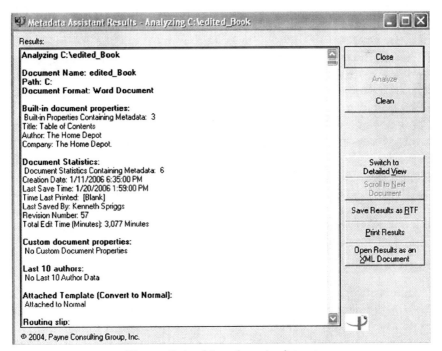

Figure 5.4—Metadata Assistant

Data Obviewscation

This section has been perhaps one of the most interesting to research. There are countless methods, which can be used to hide data within a Word Document. It should be noted that while this information may be hidden from the user on the surface, since the data exists in one form or another in the file as plain text—it can be easily located by programs such as Encase and Forensic Tool Kit. All of this completely changes if the user uses Encryption.

Coloring—perhaps one of the easiest ways of hiding data. This is done by selecting a group of data and changing its color to white—assuming that the document is white. Please bear in mind that while the data might not be apparent to the casual observer if the data contains keyword information then it will be really obvious to the computer forensic examiner.

Text Box—is another creative method of data hiding. This could be as simple as creating a text box at the end of the sentence, then changing the box line color to white or no line and shrinking the box to the size of a period. Another variation of this is to create a text box on top of another text box and then using ordering to place the "hidden" data underneath it.

Hidden Text—is a normal formatting option in Microsoft Word. While the word "hidden" in its name in and of itself conjures up images of a spy writing with invisible ink. This is really not the intent of this function. There are much more effective methods of "hiding" data than using this standard formatting option. This formatting option is just an editor's tool, which has been intergraded into a very powerful word processor. Less anyone thing that the importance of this issue is being downplayed—lets take a look at how easy it is to reveal the hidden truths. Open the tools menu and select options. Within this box select the view tab. Select hidden text check box and then select OK. This will display the hidden text inside of the document.

Text Images—is one of the hardest methods to detect. When a screen shot is created of text and this image is embedded into the word document. Since the actual words are not text, but are contained in an image any keyword searches would not actually locate it.

Encryption

Encryption is the methodology used to transform a regular MS Word document into cipher text. There are several different encryption possibilities within the later version of MS Word. In fact the encryption has gotten so good that for the educated MS Word user their data is pretty safe. Thankfully most users don't know about some of these very advanced features. The earlier versions of this encryption contained some significant security faults. This allowed for them to be easily cracked, even with a very strong password. These days, however, have long since passed. The encryption option is employed by selecting "save as" in the file menu. Then from within the "save as" menu box choosing tools and security options.

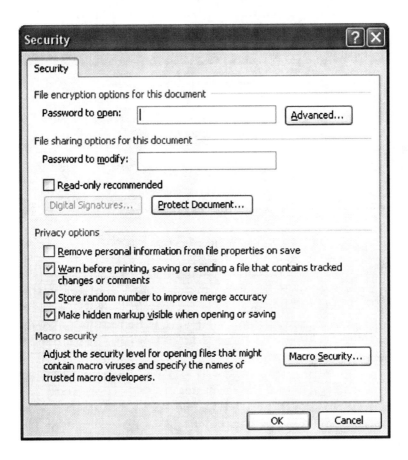

Figure 5.5—Security Screen Print

This security box contains several different features. The first is adding a password to the document. If someone wants to open the file, they will have to have the correct password. More will be discussed about this option in the next section. The next option is password to modify. This allows people to open and read the document, but to change the file the user must have the correct password. There is also an option to insure a digital signature.

Next are a series of privacy options. If the remove personal information box is checked then almost all of the previously mentioned metadata information will be lost. Also there are several other options such as warn before printing and make hidden information visible when opening or saving. Finally there is a security setting for macros.

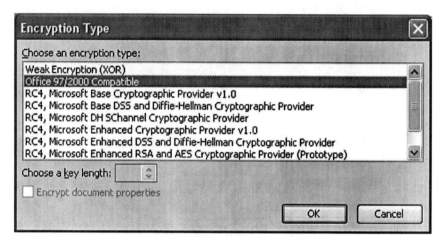

Figure 5.6—Encryption Type Screen Print

XOR is the first encryption option. This mathematical operation when bits are combined to form the encrypted value. An example is when two bits are added together—if the resulting operation is an even number then it produces one value and if the resulting operation is an odd number then it produces a different value. This is the weakest method of encryption.

Office 97/2000 is the second option. This is also a very weak option. There are several known flaws with this method of encryption.

RC4, Microsoft Enhanced RSA and AES Cryptographic Provider (Prototype) are the new kids on the block for encryption. The US government approved the use of Advanced Encryption Standard for unclassified government data. More information about this standard case can be found at http://csrc.nist.gov/encryption/aes.

Microsoft Excel

Microsoft Excel is similar to Microsoft Word in many of the options, formatting, and metadata available. For this reason we will not rediscuss these items, but will instead focus on items unique to Excel files that may be of use in hiding data or concerning computer forensics. Excel is a spreadsheet application that is basically a table of data that you can format and manipulate. Many people use Excel for small databases that can hold 65,536 rows of data per table (or per worksheet). The menu bar allows for a user to manipulate the data manually or they can create macros to automate this manipulation. This ability to manipulate data can provide some unique ways to hide data or other information in Excel.

Hiding rows or columns—Excel allows for a user to hide rows and columns within a worksheet. This allows for users to hide parts of the worksheet that may contain irrelevant data, formulas, lookup tables, etc. from view. This is also a simple way to hide data from others, if people do not know to look for data hidden like this it may never be found. Think about how many times you have sent or received and email with an Excel file attached to it. It is an easy way to move data, often undetected.

Formulas—Excel is often used for the presentation of financial data. The data that appear are numbers in the cells of the worksheet, but are they really numbers? Many times there are formulas in the cells that result in a number, so Assets minus Liabilities may equal Stock Holders equity or it might not. Formulas can force or plug numbers so that they always tie together. If you are auditing or investigating something that has printouts of Excel files, ALWAYS get the files. This way you can see what is behind the numbers.

Macros—these have grown to become basically a subset of Visual Basic (a programming language). Macros allow the user to manipulate data in the Excel file, other excel files, in databases, and other sources. Macros are also a way to introduce viruses or malicious code into a computer system. In the macro the user can add comments, another way to hide data or messages. The macro can also pull the data from an external source, like mainframe databases, manipulate it, and present in excel. If you want to know how the information was created, you would have to know there were macros and how to read them.

Links and Dependencies—users can link or make excel files dependent upon one another. This mean the data in a cell in one file may be actually pulled from another. So if you find the Excel file with the silver bullet, that bullet may be derived in another file and the linked or imported into the Excel file you are looking at. If you do not have both files, you only have part of the puzzle.

You may also find an Excel table in a word document. The information in the table is pulled from an Excel file, so if the Excel file is updated the table in the word document may be updated the next time it is opened. If you only get the printed version of the Word document you will never know about the Excel file. This Excel file may only have the data that you see in the Word document, but it probably has a lot more.

Hiding Data on the spread sheet—Say you have data in cell A1 that you would like to hide from the rest of the world. To hide that data, click on cell A1 and then choose Format/Cells. When the Format Cells dialog box opens, click the 'Numbers' tab and then select 'Custom' from the 'Category' list. Now, double-click in the 'Type' entry box and enter three semicolons ";;;". Then click OK to close the dialog box and continue. The data in cell A1 is still there and will work in calculations, but it isn't visible to the user.

Microsoft Access

Microsoft Access is a small database application that was designed initially for a single user on a personal computer. The maximum size of a database in Access is 2 GB. While it is better than Excel for storing and relating data, it is a far cry from the likes of Oracle, SQL Sever, or DB3. Microsoft Access supports macros like Microsoft Excel and has many of the items that are of interest to a computer forensic specialist as Microsoft Word and Excel. These items include metadata, file properties, formatting, links, macros, formulas, password protection, encryption, etc.

Microsoft PowerPoint

This application is great for presentations and slide shows. In a corporate environment you will generally find presentations on every computer, ones the individuals has created and the ones from meeting and training events they went to. Many people will jazz up their presentations with art work, photos, changing formats of the text, adding music, and other things. This can make for a presentation that people might actually stay awake for, and the neat thing is that all of these items are encapsulated in the Power Point file. Besides the methods for hiding data that has been previously discussed, here are a few methods that are unique to Power Point.

Hiding pictures—Users will paste pictures in the slides of a PowerPoint presentation. This will allow them to many times go undetected by corporate security software and provides a convenient viewing method. Many times I found inappropriate material in a PowerPoint presentation. While this has been images of individuals without proper (or any) attire, it could have easily been a picture of something that would give a competitor an advantage in the market place.

Another way to hide a picture is to layer it. This is where the person creating the presentation places the inappropriate picture in a slide and then places another picture on top of it. Viewers will only see the second picture, not the inappropriate one unless they edit the presentation and remove the second picture.

Audio Files—Have you ever seen a presentation with sound effects or music in the background? They make for more interesting presentation, but can also be used to send messages. Want to send a password via email without writing it down and get it past security? Send the person a normal presentation and on the agreed upon slide attach an audio file of someone saying the password. This can be used to send anything you want in an audio message, think of the possibilities.

Chapter 6
Policy and Standard Operating Procedures

Corporate Policy

A policy is used by an organization to establish clear and unambiguous guidelines for its employees to follow. Well written policies are very important, however following them is even more important. The first step after a policy has been established is training/awareness. If your information in the policy is locked away inside of a desk drawer, it does no good. Conversely if the policy is just dumped onto the organizations' intranet without anyone being told where it is—then its value is minimized.

Organizations need to be sure that their policies take a holistic prospective of their data concerns within the organization. This includes establishing intellectual property rights, defining fair use and outlines the expectation of privacy.

Have extremely granular policies, which define exactly who is allowed to monitor data, systems, and networks. It also might detail the level they are allowed to monitor. Then if unusual activities are noticed, they can define the scope of the investigative plan. It is also conceivable that these policies and procedures should detail the items that are to be documented, which departments in the organization need to be contacted along with the contact information, and under what circumstances external organizations, such as the police, are to be contacted. On the other hand some corporate counsels have chosen to only have their policies to define in only the broadest of terms what is expected of the employee. This allows the individuals within the management structure much broader range of options to deal with situations and still be within the scope of their policy.

At a minimum a corporate policy should provide some broad general guidelines for protecting the organization's computer resources and should define in broad terms how to handle an incident. The more detailed step by step procedures can be developed by the local divisions of the organization to ensure they are compatible with the local business environment, the corporate guidelines, and local legal requirements. This is because the detailed procedures will be different in a 20 person shop than it would be for a shop with 2000 people. The geographic location can make a difference as well. The laws concerning what needs to be done vary state by state and country by country. Crossing international borders has to be addressed because in today's business environment even a small organization can conduct international business.

Organizations can conduct business that cross into another country's jurisdiction and not even realize it or be broken into by someone in another country. Isn't the Internet wonderful? How many times have you heard or read about some person in Eastern Europe or Asia that steals or defrauds a company over the Internet. If something like this happens to your organization, would they know how to address it?

Some of the organizations' policies that can have an affect on internal and external investigations or computer forensic examinations include the following:

Expectation of Privacy—This should be one of the foundations of any organization's computer policy. It should be explained to the employee what, if any, expectations he/she should have when it comes to other people looking at the files on their work computer. This should also include information, which passes over the corporate intranet and internet. Many companies take this a step further by having the employees click on a banner message, when they log into the computer. The message will basically outline the company's information privacy policy. It has been my experience that companies take a "no expectation of privacy" on any company computer or network resources. This basically means that managers, network administrators and other Information Technology related people can look at their information to any degree with or without a need.

Incident Response—These policies should define what events can trigger the Incident Response procedures. These procedures need to define when a computer forensics specialist is to be brought into the process and what they are allowed to do. If these procedures do not specifically identify how the computer forensics specialist is to be used, then they will probably be called late or too late. This means they are called only after some of the potential evidence has been destroyed or they are not called at all. Since this document will be used by various people inside of the organization, it is not a bad idea to include your information on evidence handling. It is probably simplest to just keep a master document with your evidence policy; however some people like to include the verbiage in various documents. This increases the likelihood that other individuals will be exposed to the information. This becomes more and more important as your organization scales in size.

Internet Use—When someone uses company computer resources to go out on the Internet, does the company detail what they can and cannot do? This policy should provide guidelines for internet users and detail any actions or types of websites that are not allowed. This policy should also inform users that the company has the right to monitor and review internet traffic and usage on company resources. This would include laptops that may connect to the Internet without going through the company's network. This monitoring and review should include forensic review of the computer. This helps ensure that the person using the company's equipment has no expectation of privacy from a corporate review.

Internal Audit Access—If the company has an Internal Audit department then the Internal Audit Charter, signed by the Board of Directors, should clearly explain that Internal Audit has unrestricted access to all company resources and assets, including the computer resources. This ensures that if the Internal Audit team determined that the services of a computer forensic specialist is needed to aid with an investigation or audit that it is a simple matter of logics and not an authority issue.

Acceptable Use (of Computer Resources)—This policy is a general policy that sets forth the guidelines for using company computer resources. It should be read and signed by all employees, contractors, consultants, and vendors. This policy sets the tone for information systems security for the organization and should reference more specific policies like Internet Usage or Email as needed. A few items in this policy to look for can include:

- Corporate computer resources are to be used for conducting company business.
- Any computer that connects to company resources or that stores corporate data must adhere to the company's computer security standards. This needs to include cell phones, digital cameras, Personal Digital Assistants (PDA's), and other devices like thumb drives.
- The company reserves the right to monitor the activity and/ or review the contents of the storage media of any computer

owned by the company or that connects to the company's network.
- State that users have no expectation of privacy.
- Everything on the computer is property of the company.
- Only legal and authorized software can be installed on the computer.
- Detail who can authorize software to be placed on a computer.
- Detail that failure to comply with the terms of this policy can result in disciplinary action, including termination of employment.

Email Use—Email has become one of the most popular forms of communication in corporations today. Unfortunately most people are not as careful as they need to be with what they say in emails. People will often write an email stating things that they would never compose in a letter or say on the phone. Employees may want to put in a little extra time by working at home, and why not, all they need to do is email that report or document to their home email address. People usually do not stop and think about the risk they expose themselves or their organization to by their use of email. It does not require a great amount of sophistication to download a shareware tool and monitor a network connect. Also you should remember that many courts regard an email within the company the same as if it was written in a corporate memo. The areas to be addressed include:
- Appropriate use of Internal and Internet Email
- Prohibited use of email
- Encryption standards
- Transmission of company data standards
- Backup and retention standards
- Personal use
- Disclaimer of company liability
- Digital signatures
- Statement that the email system and any emails on company computers or computer storage media is the property of the company and the individual user has no expectation of privacy.

Instant Messaging (IM)—This can be included in one of the other policies like email or acceptable use or can be a completely separate policy. Some companies use IM internally for communication on their own networks. If the use of IM is not prohibited, then it needs to be addressed in the corporate policies and procedures. These policies need to determine the appropriate configuration of the IM software, the logging policies, as well as appropriate use. The logging policy can include logging by the servers (if the company has an IM server) and logging by the IM client on the desktop computer. The logging configuration of the desktops can be enforced with startup scripts; every time the computer is connected to the corporate network a script checks the configuration and resets it if needed. These logs can be very useful in an investigation.

Backup and Retention—Court cases have been won and lost on this policy. If the company has a backup & retention policy, do they follow it? Failure to adhere to your own policy can really sting you in this area. If you prematurely delete a backup it can be seen as destroying evidence. If you retain backups longer than the policy outlines then a court may ask why? Also, do you only keep the extra backup for selected computer systems, or all computer systems? If you only have the extra backups for a few selected systems, the court may view it as you had the extra backups for all systems. Then when it became evident that the backups may end up in court you magically began to follow your policies & procedures for selected computer systems and delete the extra backups. Was it because the selected system had the evidence on them?

If you are bringing in a computer forensics specialist as part of your investigation or for discovery these policies and procedures can be critical. A good policy will help the specialist determine what should be available for discovery and how to plan the acquisition process. The policies may bring to light data that should be available that you were told did not exist. An example is the company informs you that they only keep one week of backups for the email server, but in your review of the corporate policies you find that they are required to keep at a minimum one month of backups for all servers (including email). The difference of one week and one month would be a good question to ask about, especially in court. You can rest assured that should a company go to court, the other side will paint of bleak pictures of your actions and intents. By following these guidelines you prevent many of these cheap shots from being taken.

Some on the key points in these various policies that will aid a computer forensics specialist are:
- Computer resources are property of the organization and are to be used for the organizations business.
- The user has no expectation of privacy when using the organizations computer resources.
- The company has the right to monitor computer activity and/or review any computer storage media.
- Internal Audit has unrestricted access to all organizational resources, including computer.

- Defines roles and responsibilities so employees know when to bring in a computer forensic specialist.

Standard Operating Procedures for a Computer Forensics Lab

Now that we have discussed some of the ways that your corporate policies can insure that a forensic examination can provide maximum benefit to your organization, let's explore how a computer forensics lab should be run. I have been in numerous computer forensic labs throughout the United States and in some other countries. The level of professionalism ranges wildly from very carefully planned and executed to someone opening a closet and saying—"Ya we do that too." I have heard examiners give reasons for both of them, however I must say that at the end of the day—here is a good rule of thumb. He, who has the unambiguous documentation and carefully follows it, will win. This is not exclusively the case, however more times than not—it is correct. So the next question is exactly what should your policy cover? Let's look at some of these areas; however they are not in any particular order.

Role/Background—while there are lots of difference places to start, understanding exactly where computer forensics fits into your organization seems to be a logical place. I have read several policies which start with a background paragraph, however if your group is new, then you are making your own history. Unfortunately with most organization, a well defined computer forensics policy seems to be an after thought. The role of your computer forensics group will depend on where if fits within your organization. If you are a commercial enterprise rather than a unit set inside of a Law Enforcement Organization your computer forensics team is going to be different.

Authorization—this section will generally describe, who is allowed to start a case and by what authority. For example many computer forensics groups are just assistance units, meaning they do not organically start their own investigations. This basically means that they will have to wait until another organization comes to them and requests their assistance. On the other hand there are companies who are formed to do solely computer forensics or it maybe just one of many services provided as an investigative package. If you are you located inside of a large corporate or a one man show then it should be spelled out exactly, who the approving authority for starting a case is. This could be Human Resources, Corporate Security or a specific individual like the Chief Information Security Officer. If you are in a private investigator's firm or a Law Enforcement organization, then your authorization will probably depend on a search warrant. The judge will actually be the approving authority for your computer forensic examination. Keep in mind that a computer forensic examination is the digital body cavity search and is extremely invasive. You have to make sure that you have the legal authority to conduct your exploration, or your entire examination could be thrown out of court as "Fruit of the Poison Tree."

Principles—this section will establish the premise for how computer forensics is conducted within your organization. Understand that information recovered from electronic media is viewed by the courts in many cases as actual paper documents. This basically means that when items are seized and are to be presented in a courtroom—then they must be essentially the same documents no more or less than when they were seized. The tricky part with a computer is that every time that a computer is booted, multiple computer files, dates and times are changed. This means that information is altered every time that the computer is booted. This presents a challenge, because once it has changed when it seems to violate this most basic rule of evidence. The good news is that if you have good forensic preservation procedures and use write protection you should avoid most of the pit fall. However it has been my experience that if a mistake occurs and there is no intent to hide the change and it is well documented, and then courts (I should probably say the judge) can be fairly forgiving. However do not rely on the good nature of the court to save you from poor practices. If it appears that you are conducting your forensic examination in a sloppy manner then the chances of your evidence or personnel actually surviving cross examination are slim.

It may be helpful to discuss the methodologies and practices that are used in order to prevent writes to the computer evidence. The most common phrase is "highly specialized write protection devices." There devices are described in very broad and general terms. Remember this document is going to have to survive for a long period of time. It is probably sufficient to say that "write protection" is going to be used to the extent possible. There may be occasions where there are no write protection devices commercially available—for example with a blackberry. I don't know of a company that makes a blackberry write protection device. You might include a statement such as "write protection will be used to the greatest extent possible circumstances permitting." Also it may be helpful to talk about your methodologies in very broad terms. For example you might discuss that your methods will be repeatable and verifiable by an objective 3rd party.

Evidence—one of the primary reasons for having a computer forensics group is to be able to preserve digital evidence. This should be second nature to most police officers; however it is very different from a traditional Information Technology Team. While they may educate themselves by reading a book or manual, nothing can replace actual experience. Also, it is not a good idea for your first courtroom exposure to digital evidence to be your first case.

One of the most basic concerns with evidence is marking. There must be a uniform manner for the labeling of evidence. Generally this is done by affixing the case number to each piece of evidence. Just a note about your case number system, it really does not matter what sort of naming/numbering convention you use as long as you use one that is logical and makes sense for your organization. Most people seem to use some combination of the calendar or fiscal year, unit number or company name than a sequential number. Also it might be helpful to include the type of case involved although this is really a matter of personal preference.

Next is connecting the case number to the evidence. I have seen investigators who will write with a permanent marker on the outside of the computer. While this makes the computer easy to identify, it is sort of messy. It also does not work well if the outside case is black. This can be a problem, however then the evidence is transferred from one investigative organization to another—the case ends up looking like a white board. Also an investigator might write on the side panel of the computer. This is really not practical, because you have to open the case in order to see the case number. My preference is to use red electrical tape. This tape is easy to find at any local Home Depot and does not create an electrical problem. It makes the original evidence easy to identify. Also keep in mind that you should make provisions for the small evidence to be placed into a plastic bag and then the bag marked. Many organizations actually used small one time bags, which are numbered. Once the bags are sealed they must be torn open and the serial numbers from the bags listed on the evidence receipts. In a much larger forensics lab setting, it is very common to have an electronic bar coding and tracking system for evidence. For example in a traditional crime lab, there is a secured area for just police officers. While it is open 24 hours a day, generally there is only an evidence tech present during normal business hours. When the officer arrives he completed special evidence in processing form and stamps the evidence and the forms. Then he places the evidence and forms into a special one way locker. Once the evidence is locked inside then it can only be opened from the other side by the evidence tech. Each individual case's evidence would go into an individual locker. Each morning the evidence tech arrives and opens the locker one at a time and in processes all of the evidence. The very high volume labs use a bar coding system. This allows them to process a large amount of evidence at one time. As the evidence is moved from room to room then the bar code is scanned and the electronic evidence sheet is updated. This system is highly efficient; however it is cost prohibitive except in very high volume evidence processing areas.

The first rule of evidence is that it should be the same as the time or seizure. This means no changes. It also means that your evidence has been secured. This will go a long way in presenting an unbroken chain of custody. What does this mean? It means that your evidence has been in a control state since its seizure. Also it has been protected from unauthorized personnel. Someone will have to testify as to the integrity of the evidence. This means that you need to track every single person who has had access to the evidence. This is done with an evidence sheet. This document forms the backbone of your chain of custody. This document will sufficiently identify each piece of evidence and trace every person who took possession of the items in question. It is very important this document is correctly and completely filled out.

First I would like to point one of the most common problems that I see with amateur evidence handlers. Most evidence sheets have an area for a description of the evidence. A common problem is an inadequate description. Your description should be complete and through.

I was once working on a child molestation case. A detective which I commonly worked with was bringing one of the newer detectives to my former agency. When they arrived in my office, he left to catch up on old times with my boss, while the new detective and I unprocessed the evidence. She asked me for a cart to bring in all of the items. This happened from time to time so I didn't think anything of it. I gave her a cart and started filling out the paperwork. After several minutes she arrived back in my office with a cart full of items. One of the first things that I noticed was that there was a keyboard and mouse, mixed into the evidence. I explained that we didn't take these sorts of times—so we set them aside. The next step was to process all of actual digital evidence by completing my own evidence sheet. Her evidence was separated into 14 grocery bags. Each bag was labeled as "Bag A" "Bag B" and so on. The young detective explained that the bag was obtained in a different room and her notes told her what room each bag was from. I asked her for a copy of her evidence sheet. When I began reading over the document I discovered flaws. Each bag was listed as an item on the evidence sheet. The problem was the way that it was described. It appeared as follows:
Brown paper bag labeled "Bag A" containing various computer items.
I was so struck by how her evidence sheet was written; I quickly

scanned all of her documents. I asked her how many floppy diskettes she had. Her reply was very telling—"I don't know." While a police officer is not expected to know everything, they should know the exact number of items taken from a search warrant scene. I excused myself to the bathroom and walked into my boss' office and asked her to give me a hand. I was very fortunate to have a boss that did not mind getting her hands dirty.

We rolled the cart into our small conference room and began opening the bags. When the senior detective noticed that has happening and finally fully examined the evidence sheet, he was quite embarrassed. My boss and I quickly and efficiently sorted through several hundred floppy diskettes, compact discs, zip disks and almost every other type of media. We sorted everything into nice neat piles by bag and created another evidence sheet. Actually our agency policy required that we generate our own evidence receipt for each case. I listed this description on the lines on our property receipt.

Item 1, Bag A, Quantity 570, Description three and one half inch floppy diskettes.

Item 2, Bag B, Quantity 248, Description compact discs

Now I have also seen detectives go to the other extreme by listing each floppy diskette on a separate line such as the following

Item 1, Quality 1, Description black in color 3 ½ inch floppy diskette labeled "homework"

Item 2, Quantity 1, Description black in color 3 ½ inch floppy diskette labeled "my documents"

And so on

This would also be a good place to note that an audit of the evidence room should be conducted at least yearly and probably semiannually. This will insure there is a level of accountability in the evidence process. This audit should be done in writing, and it should be maintained in the evidence locker or in the SOP for a specified period of time.

Seizure and System Preparation is critical to maintaining proper custody of evidence. This often tends to be a very tricky area to compile, however it is also very interesting. I have seen several people who skip over this area all together just because it can be quite a chore to work all of the bugs out. There is often a great debate over the amount of detail that should be needed to describe a system seizure. There have been several very good manuals written about evidence seizure—so I'm not going to rehash that information in this area. I would personally suggest that you refer to Electronic Crime Scene Investigation: A Guide for First Responders, http://www.ncjrs.gov/pdffiles1/nij/187736.pdf. This manual describes in detail how to seize digital evidence.

System Preparation—this is really an important aspect of the how you are going to run your computer forensics lab. First you should understand this area will help your evidence survive cross examination. It should describe in detail how you are going to prevent contamination of evidence. Remember that one of your examiners is going to have to testify about exactly how to do this and how it was done. This is one of the reasons that it should be spelled out in detailed. Generally this involves requiring the "working media" of a forensic examination to be forensically sterile. What does this mean? Most people site the Department of Defense Cleaning and Sanitation Manual for this chart. Keep in mind when reading this standard there are two different levels. There is one standard for cleaning and one for sanitation. In most setting the standard for cleaning is much lower and meets the requirements for digital evidence. For example for a rigid media the cleaning standard is a single overwrite of every character on the media. The sanitation standard is much higher and requires multiple overwrites with different character sets. Just keep in mind that this standard was developed for classified media and was meant to safe guard classified data from foreign governments. It has been my experience that if you document the cleaning standard properly, then the courts will be satisfied. The other area of concern is the operating system. Some organizations require their forensic examinee's to have a virgin operating system on their examination computer. This is done by reinstalling the OS in-between each case. They argue this insures there is not cross contamination of evidence. On a practical level this is done by installing the OS once—then creating a Ghost image of the hard drive. After your forensic examination has been completed then all hard drives are wiped. The ghost image of the operating system is restored, and system updates are completed. Then an updated ghost image is made and the forensic examination begins. This method has many pros and cons, which need to be carefully considered before you make a determination of how this will be implied in your forensic lab.

Starting a Case—while every case is going to be different the procedures used to open each case should be very similar. Many organizations have very strict rules for opening a case and assigning it a case number. Most of the time once a case number is assigned it can not be changed. In fact some groups still keep the case number system in a physical book, which is kept inside of a locker container. Often only certain individuals are allowed to assign a case number. Other organizations have a computerized case management system.

While the computer assigns the case number only certain individuals are allowed to approve a case opening.

Forensic Procedures—there is a lot of debate in the forensic community about the level of detail, which should be present in the forensic procedures. Some require a great amount of detail and others do not. Some units have developed detailed case checklists as a beginning point and other forbid the use of any checklists. This is really up to the organization; however it will often depend of their experiences with the legal system they are involved with.

Case Reporting—this is a pretty standard paraphrase in most SOP manuals. The organization generally already has very precise guidelines of reporting. However let's just assume that you are starting from scratch. Most computer forensic reports are done on electronic media and in Hypertext Markup Language (HTML). I have seen reports that are extremely detailed and others that are not. In some organizations your computer forensics report is considered to be a single document, which is compiled at the end of the investigation. In others every single investigative activity is documented in summary format and placed into a case file. Once this investigation is completed then the entire case file becomes the final report. I have found since many of the procedures and processes and similar from case to case—it is often helpful to have a case template and then just fill in the blanks. It can have standard verbiage to cover imaging and other processes that at routine.

Security—is a critical area for evidence to be admitted into court. The burden is on the computer forensic examiner to show that the evidence is essentially the same as when it was seized. This is done by having access control on the computer forensics work area. This can be as elaborate as you feel is necessary to have your evidence admitted into court. It is pretty common to have an access control device with a security log. Some common locks used for access control are the high security locks from vendors such as Multi-Lock or Medico. However I have seen some attorneys vigorously attack very robust security, while other attorneys have raised no objected to very, very weak security. I think it is better to have more security than less, because in the event that your evidence is challenged on these grounds you want to make sure that you win and not the other side.

Conclusion

This outline of corporate policies and standard operating procedures will make it easier for the computer forensics specialist to do their job. This will also reduce the exposure they or the organization that hired them have to any invasion of privacy issues and can help them to weather the storm of cross examination. Without these policies and procedures companies may leave themselves exposed to lawsuits. Also, items found could be thrown out of court if they are not followed. Do not ever underestimate the need for well written, up to date policies and procedures.

Chapter 7
Legal Considerations

Disclaimer: Just to let it be known, I am not an attorney. I do not pretend to be an attorney. I am not an expert in the law, Federal, State or other. I did not sleep at a Holiday Inn Express last night (Ok, maybe I did—but this does not make me an attorney!) and thus pretend to be an attorney or legal expert. This chapter is merely the point of view of an accountant and computer forensics specialist regarding the laws that apply to computer forensics and electronic discovery. A great website to get more up-to-date information on court rulings and information on electronic discovery (and thus computer forensics) is www.kenwithers. com.

For attorneys or someone involved in a corporate investigation electronic discovery and computer forensics is becoming something that can no longer be ignored. Various studies are being published that are starting to show that people use email and instant messaging more than the telephone at work. Other studies reveal that 90% of all documents are electronic and never make it to paper. So the question becomes can your investigation afford to ignore the most popular means of communication in the office and approximately 90% of any potential evidence?

Would you consider and audit effective if 90% of the population was scoped out of the audit? This would leave only 10% of the population for the auditors to select their samples from for testing or to survey. I think this would be a hard sell to an audit manager reviewing the work papers and you should get review notes to go back and to do the audit test correctly, i.e. not scooping out that 90% of the population. If your investigation goes to court, how do you think the judge will view this scope reduction? Will it give the opposing attorney more chance to win as it can be claimed that the evidence that would clear the accused was in the emails and other electronic documents? Evidence that was ignored in the investigation may be spoiled (unusable) by now.

In the initial stages of the investigation or the discovery stage of a case is on which computers need to be considered. As early as possible the scope of potential electronic evidence needs to be defined. This can include identifying contacts to assist in obtaining the computer storage media, the computer systems, applications on the computer systems, any backups, and any network connections. Once these items are identified the computers that need to be forensically reviewed can be identified and steps taken to preserve them. If this is a case that could go to court, then this would be the time for opposing attorneys to discuss cost allocation.

If the investigation results in charges being filed against someone, then there are several things the attorneys need to do in the pre-trial stage. There needs to be a 'meet and confer' session. In this session all aspects of electronic discovery, including computer forensics, should be discussed. This includes the discovery process, data format, cost involved, use of a neutral 3rd party (to reduce expenses), any court guidelines, the use of electronic evidence, and any expert witnesses. If the case is going to use electronic evidence, then the court should be notified. Should there be any issues concerning discovery process involving computer forensics, have a pre-trial meeting to resolve them. Also, before the trial starts the person making the presentation(s) to the court needs to go and inspect the courtroom to determine the equipment they need to bring. You do not want to show up to court and find out you cannot give your wonderful PowerPoint presentation because you lack the proper equipment.

During the trial the computer forensics specialist may be asked to give a presentation to the court on the tools they used, basic computer forensics, how the evidence was found, or even find the evidence again in court. Can the computer forensics person you are working with do this? They may be the best technical person around, but can they communicate this to the Judge? Can they explain what they did to a jury of their peers (Ok, peers that are potentially computer illiterate)? Can they qualify as an expert witness or will you only be able to use them as a fact witness, thus not able to express opinions.

If you want the computer forensics specialist to be able to qualify as an expert, what are the standards they must meet? This will vary from judge to judge and can be very different between state and federal judges. While you may not know the judge before you hire a computer forensics specialist, you should know the venue the case will be tried in and the case law associated with it. In years past some courts used the Guild test to determine if the person was an expert in their field. This is where several people from the same professional association relating to the field would agree or disagree that the person was an expert. This later evolved into the Frye Standard, Frye v. United States 293 F. 1013 (DC Cir. 1923). The Frye standard basically looks for 'general acceptance' in the related field. The court's gatekeeper role was to be conservative in nature. This gate keeping function was to keep unproven 'science' out of the courtroom. This works well until a case came before the court that involved a scientific issue that was new, thus there had not been enough time to gain 'general acceptance'. This was becoming an issue in the courts and then finally there was Daubert.

The Daubert case, Daubert v. Merrell Dow Pharmaceuticals, 509 U.S. 579 (1993), finally set precedence for a new standard. Daubert evaluates 'scientific knowledge' by the method it was derived, the support it has, and it reliability. Many times a Daubert motion is raised in pre-trail or during the trail in an attempt to disqualify a person as an expert witness. This would exclude the person from making a presentation to the judge and/or jury of any potential evidence. If your computer forensics specialist wants to present 'unqualified' evidence or used questionable procedures in the examination you could be in trouble. If the computer forensic specialist fails to qualify it can cast a cloud of doubt on the entire case.

The Daubert standard is based on the Federal Rules of Evidence, Fed. R. Evid. 702. This rule does not even mention the 'general acceptance', instead if focuses more on the ability of the person and the procedures they use. Rule 702 broadly governs the admittance of someone as an expert witness. If you are interested in more information on the Federal Rules of Evidence a good website is Law School at Cornell University, http://www.law.cornell.edu/rules/fre/.

While the Courts realized the need for a standard for qualifying someone as an expert, they also realized that Judges need some flexibility. Daubert basically looks at four things to a person trying to qualify as an expert; their credentials and experience, testimony based of fact, is it relevant and reliable, and are there any other factors regarding admissibility. Likewise there is no checklist for Judges to follow when considering the tools and methods used in the testing, but instead some guidelines:

- Have the theories and procedures used by the scientific expert been tested;
- Have these been subjected to peer review and/or publication;
- Do the techniques employed have a known error rate;

- Are subject to standards governing their application; and
- Do the theories and techniques used have widespread acceptance.

It is important to remember that Daubert is a Federal Court decision. This means that the individual state courts may or may not adopt this standard.

Beside Daubert, there are many other cases that are notable in providing guidance in the area of computer forensics and electronic discovery. Zubulake v. UBS Warburg, LLC, 217 F.R.D. 309 (S.D.N.Y. 2003) was one of these cases, which had 5 reported decisions before it went to trail. In this trial one of Europe's largest banks lost a discrimination suite vs. a former employee and the jury awarded about $29.3 million for damages. In the discovery process, the attorney's for Zubulake had requested the emails from UBS's computers relevant to the case. They were unable to get these emails because they no longer existed (Zubulake V, 2004 WL 1620866 (S.D.N.Y 2004)). The court basically had two thoughts on this, (1) the Court found that USB had a duty to preserve email evidence since USB should have known that they might be relevant to the case and (2) the Court found that USB did not comply with their own retention policy, which would have preserved the emails.

Either of these two items can be damaging to your case. A client company may be able to lessen the damage concerning the first one by claiming ignorance or blaming inter-company communications (or lack of it). The damage done to a case by the second one could be fatal. If a company has policies and procedures on how they operate and the time period of your request just happens to be the time period they did not follow these for some reason, then this has guilt written all over it (in my personal opinion). UBS's inability to produce the emails in this case resulted in the jury being told that they were to assume that the missing emails would have hurt UBS's case. The attorneys for Zubulake must have been jumping for joy (at least inside) when they heard the judge say that. Can you imagine what 12 jurors would say about this when they are discussing the case behind close doors? Many time people in this situation will gravitate towards the worst-case scenario and their resulting conclusion may be worse than the truth.

Zubulake is also highly referenced because of the decisions concerning cost allocation and providing for the sampling of backup tapes. The cost shifting issues came up because UBS claimed that complying with the plaintiff's request to produce all documents concerning the plaintiff between UBS employees would be an undue burden and expensive since this would involve recovering emails from archival media. The court came up with a 7-factor test (Zubulake I, 217 F.R.D. 309 (S.D.N.Y. 2003)):

I. The extent to which the request is specifically tailored to discover relevant information,

II. The availability of the information from other sources,

III. The total cost of producing the evidence compared to the amount being disputed,

IV. Total cost compared to the resources available to each side,

V. Ability of each side to control cost and their incentive to do so,

VI. The importance of the issue at stake, and

VII. The relative benefits of obtaining the information to each side.

In the Zubulake case the court decided that UBS must produce everything as directed by the plaintiff at its own expense. Then after the contents of the archival media were reviewed and the cost quantified a decision would be made regarding cost shifting. One of the steps both sides in the case agreed on to control cost was a sampling of the archival media, or backup tapes, so that all of them would not have to be restored.

American Bar Association standards

There are several American Bar Association (ABA) standards that relate to e-discovery and thus computer forensics. These standards cover electronic information, using technology to facilitate discovery, discovery conferences, work product and privileges, and technological advances. The ABA Civil Discovery Standards concerning E-discovery standards (see www.abanet.org/litigation for more information) include:

Standard 29—Electronic Information

Is designed to help counsel identify the types of electronic data that might be available and how the duty to preserve applies to these. It provides a checklist on where the electronic data may be found and that some of the relevant data may be deleted. It reminds counsel that the duty to preserve may apply to the deleted data as well. It reminds counsel they have the option of specifying the format they would like to receive the data and that they may want inquire about how the data is stored and where. Then standard 29 also contains wording concerning cost allocation and how that may be resolved.

Standard 30—Using Technology to Facilitate Discovery

This standard is short and sweet. It states that the data sought in discovery may be obtained in electronic format even if it is not stored in an electronic format. It addresses how the cost of producing everything in electronic format may be allocated. Lastly it states that the requesting party should provide all request and responses in electronic format, unless they two sides agree to something else.

Standard 31—Discovery Conferences

This standard addresses what should be discussed in the initial discovery conference concerning electronic discovery. How this is implemented varies by district (Federal courts) and by state (State courts), but it is prudent to have a discovery conference as early as possible, whether it is compelled or not. This standard is designed to assist counsel and the court by providing a list of potentially relevant items to consider. This is where both side begin to define the scope of the discovery in regards to the subject matter, time period covered, where the electronic data is located, key contact people, computer platforms, types of computer storage media, software, accessibility issues, data retention policies, preservation issues, and key words to be used in searching the electronic data.

This standard also brings up the idea of the two parties using a single or single set of technology consultants, either retained by them or appointed by the court. This is actually a good idea for a computer forensics specialist because they will, or should, report what ever they find without bias. This ethical standard is similar to an auditor's independence issues. Just as an auditor needs to remain independent of the client they are auditing, so a computer forensic specialist also needs to remain independent. The use of mutually agreed upon consultants can reduce the cost associated with e-discovery and computer forensics. The standard also addresses cost allocation, as rarely people want to pay 50-50 on the bill. After the initial meeting there will probably be several more and this is covered by this standard.

Standard 32—Attorney-Client Privilege and attorney Work Product

This addresses the concerns when dealing with consultants, especially a third party that is not employed by the producing party, regarding privilege and the work product. This would be the situation if the computer forensics specialist was appointed by the court or a neutral third party agreed upon by both sides.

Standard 33—Technological Advances

The ABA realized that it was impossible to keep the standards up with the latest technology, so they created standard 33. This basically suggests that standards 29 to 32 be consulted regarding discovery of data and use common sense to make modifications.

The ABA's standards of civil discovery are not the laws or rules developed by the Federal or various State governments, but are a guide for attorneys and others on the subject. The ABA's website is a great place to learn more. Another great place to learn more on the rules of discovery for electronic evidence is the Federal Rules of Civil Procedure

(FRCP). You can anticipate some changes in the Federal Rules of Civil Procedure that are likely to take effect in December 2006 (full text is at www.uscourts.gov/rules/Reports/ST09-2005.pdf). There are important changes to several of the rules. One of the most important to computer forensics and electronic discovery is the proposed changes to rule 26. If the changes to Rule 26 are accepted it will require both parties to identify the sources of electronically stored information they intent to access in discovery up front. A proposed new Rule, 37(f), would provide protection to parties that accidentally destroy electronic information if they have a good electronic management system in place. A few of these rules are listed below.

Federal Rules of Civil Procedure

Rule 26—General Provisions Governing Discovery; Duty of Disclosure
A.   Required Disclosures; Methods to Discover Additional Matter.

This is basically setting the rules in place for the disclosure of information needed to plan for discovery. This is where the computer forensic specialist can help you scope out the need, if any, for computer forensics. You can get key contact information, network layouts, listing of the computers with their applications and data, data retention and backup policies and procedures, and other information that is helpful.

B.   Discovery Scope and Limits

Defines the scope of what can be discovered and the limitations that the court can place on them. Pretrial preparations concerning experts, materials, and claims of privilege or protection are covered.

C.   Protective Orders

Discusses what can be done to protect someone from annoyance, embarrassment, oppression, or undue burden or expense in the discovery process.

D.   Timing and Sequence of Discovery

Define the timing and sequence of the discovery process and what can alter this, such as a motion from the court.

E.   Supplementation of Disclosures and Responses

F.   Meeting of Parties; Planning for Discovery

The two sides need to meet as soon a practicable possible to discuss discovery. This is important with data on computer storage media as it can be here today and gone tomorrow.

G.   Signing of Disclosures, Discovery Request, Responses, and Objections

Talks about the items that must be documented and signed.

Rule 33—Interrogatories to Parties

Rule 33 deals with interrogatories and written depositions, how they can be used in court, and the option to produce business records. In e-discovery and computer forensics you may want to get a written deposition from the other side's computer forensics person, information technology people, or other people that were identified in previous meetings.

Rule 34—Document Productions

Do you want to know what the other side has in the form of documents and other evidence? This rule allows you to serve the other side a request to find out. In the world of computer forensics it means that you can get active and deleted data from the computer storage media. You can get the business data, and compilations the other side used in their conclusion and assertions, and normally an image of the other side's personal hard drive. This can be nice. This is also one of the reasons some attorneys will specifically ask for a report not to be written by the computer forensics specialist. Because once it is written it is discoverable.

Rule 30(b)(6)—Depositions

In the deposition of the designated technology person(s) at a company or organization you should have a list of questions. These questions are tailored to the investigation you are involved in, but should include question about personnel, computer systems, network information, email systems, applications, preservation of the electronic data, third party sources, computer storage media & backups, passwords, decommissioned hardware, any Legacy data, and other legal actions. The computer forensics specialist can help you develop these questions and evaluate the responses you receive.

In recent years the Federal government has passed several laws that in one way or another touch computer forensics. Some of the current laws that companies must deal with are Sarbanes-Oxley (SOX), Health Insurance Portability and Accountability Act (HIPAA) and Gramm-Leach-Bliley Act (GLBA). These laws make good internal controls a must, not just a good idea. Laws like SOX were born out of the massive fraud cases in the United States like WorldCom, Tyco, Global Crossings, Enron, and others that saw investors lose billions of dollars and some employees lose their life savings, including their retirement. While these laws cover much more that computer forensics, we will look at some of the ways these laws touch the world of computer forensics.

The Ad Hoc Committee for Electronic Discovery of the United States District Court for the District of Delaware has developed a default standard for the discovery of electronic documents. This default standard is available for use by the Court and by parties engaged in litigation in the District of Delaware. The Ad Hoc Committee includes the following members:

Chief Judge Sue L. Robinson

Kevin F. Brady, Esquire, Skadden, Arps, Slate, Meagher & Flom

Mary B. Graham, Esquire, Morris Nichols Arsht & Tunnell

Richard K. Herrmann, Esquire, Blank Rome

William F. Lee, Esquire, Hale and Dorr

Michael A. O'Shea, Esquire, Clifford Chance

George F. Pappas, Esquire, Venable LLP

Matthew D. Powers, Esquire, Weil Gotshal & Manges

Paul A. Ainsworth, Law Clerk to Chief Judge Robinson

Janet A. Gongola, Law Clerk to Chief Judge Robinson

The Judges of the Court express their gratitude to the Ad Hoc Committee members for their work on this project.

The Ad Hoc Committee for Electronic Discovery of the United States District Court for the District of Delaware has developed a default standard for the discovery of electronic documents. This default standard is available for use by the Court and by parties engaged in litigation in the District of Delaware.

Default Standard for Discovery of
Electronic Documents ("E-Discovery")

1. Introduction. It is expected that parties to a case will cooperatively reach agreement on how to conduct e-discovery. In the event that such agreement has not been reached by the Fed. R. Civ. P. 16 scheduling conference, however, the following default standards shall apply until such time, if ever, the parties conduct e-discovery on a consensual basis.

2. Discovery conference. Parties shall discuss the parameters of their anticipated e-discovery at the Fed. R. Civ. P. 26(f) conference, as well as at the Fed. R. Civ. P. 16 scheduling conference with the court, consistent with the concerns outlined below. More specifically, prior to the Rule 26(f) conference, the parties shall exchange the following information:

a. A list of the most likely custodians of relevant electronic materials, including a brief description of each person's title and responsibilities (see ¶ 6).

b. A list of each relevant electronic system that has been in place at all relevant times1 and a general description of each system, including the nature, scope, character, organization, and formats employed in each system. The parties should also include other pertinent information about their electronic documents and whether those electronic documents are of limited accessibility. Electronic documents of limited accessibility may include those created or used by electronic media no longer in use, maintained in redundant electronic storage media, or for which retrieval involves substantial cost.

c. The name of the individual responsible for that party's electronic document retention policies ("the retention coordinator"), as well as a general description of the party's electronic document retention policies for the systems identified above (see ¶ 6).

d. The name of the individual who shall serve as that party's "e-discovery liaison" (see ¶ 2).

e. Provide notice of any problems reasonably anticipated to arise in connection with e-discovery.

To the extent that the state of the pleadings does not permit a meaningful discussion of the above by the time of the Rule 26(f) conference, the parties shall either agree on a date by which this information will be mutually exchanged or submit the issue for resolution by the court at the Rule 16 scheduling conference.

3. E-discovery liaison. In order to promote communication and cooperation between the parties, each party to a case shall designate a single individual through which all e-discovery requests and responses are made ("the e-discovery liaison"). Regardless of whether the e-discovery liaison is an attorney (in-house or outside counsel), a third party consultant, or an employee of the party, he or she must be:

a. Familiar with the party's electronic systems and capabilities in order to explain these systems and answer relevant questions.

b. Knowledgeable about the technical aspects of e-discovery, including electronic document storage, organization, and format issues.

c. Prepared to participate in e-discovery dispute resolutions. The court notes that, at all times, the attorneys of record shall be responsible for compliance with e-discovery requests. However, the e-discovery liaisons shall be responsible for organizing each party's e-discovery efforts to insure consistency and thoroughness and, generally, to facilitate the e-discovery process.

4. Timing of e-discovery. Discovery of electronic documents shall proceed in a sequenced fashion.

a. After receiving requests for document production, the parties shall search their documents, other than those identified as limited accessibility electronic documents, and produce responsive electronic documents in accordance with Fed. R. Civ. P. 26(b)(2).

b. Electronic searches of documents identified as of limited accessibility shall not be conducted until the initial electronic document search has been completed. Requests for information expected to be found in limited accessibility documents must be narrowly focused with some basis in fact supporting the request.

c. On-site inspections of electronic media under Fed. R. Civ. P. 34(b) shall not be permitted absent exceptional circumstances, where good cause and specific need have been demonstrated.

5. Search methodology. If the parties intend to employ an electronic search to locate relevant electronic documents, the parties shall disclose any restrictions as to scope and method which might affect their ability to conduct a complete electronic search of the electronic documents. The parties shall reach agreement as to the method of searching, and the words, terms, and phrases to be searched with the assistance of the respective e-discovery liaisons, who are charged with familiarity with the parties' respective systems. The parties also shall reach agreement as to the timing and conditions of any additional searches which may become necessary in the normal course of discovery. To minimize the expense, the parties may consider limiting the scope of the electronic search (e.g., time frames, fields, document types).

6. Format. If, during the course of the Rule 26(f) conference, the parties cannot agree to the format for document production, electronic documents shall be produced to the requesting party as image files (e.g., PDF or TIFF). When the image file is produced, the producing party must preserve the integrity of the electronic document's contents, i.e., the original formatting of the document, its metadata and, where applicable, its revision history. After initial production in image file format is complete, a party must demonstrate particularized need for production of electronic documents in their native format.

7. Retention. Within the first thirty (30) days of discovery,

the parties should work towards an agreement (akin to the standard protective order) that outlines the steps each party shall take to segregate and preserve the integrity of all relevant electronic documents. In order to avoid later accusations of spoliation, a Fed. R. Civ. P. 30(b)(6) deposition of each party's retention coordinator may be appropriate.

The retention coordinators shall:

a. Take steps to ensure that e-mail of identified custodians shall not be permanently deleted in the ordinary course of business and that electronic documents maintained by the individual custodians shall not be altered.

b. Provide notice as to the criteria used for spam and/or virus filtering of e-mail and attachments; e-mails and attachments filtered out by such systems shall be deemed non-responsive so long as the criteria underlying the filtering are reasonable.

Within seven (7) days of identifying the relevant document custodians, the retention coordinators shall implement the above procedures and each party's counsel shall file a statement of compliance as such with the court.

8. Privilege. Electronic documents that contain privileged information or attorney work product shall be immediately returned if the documents appear on their face to have been inadvertently produced or if there is notice of the inadvertent production within thirty (30) days of such.

9. Costs. Generally, the costs of discovery shall be borne by each party. However, the court will apportion the costs of electronic discovery upon a showing of good cause.

10. Discovery disputes and trial presentation. At this time, discovery disputes shall be resolved and trial presentations shall be conducted consistent with each individual judge's guidelines.

Ad Hoc Committee for Electronic Discovery of the U.S. District Court for the District of Delaware (http://www.ded. uscourts.gov/Announce/AdHoc-Disc.pdf)

Sarbanes-Oxley

SOX is about companies managing their exposure to financial fraud through sound controls. There are preventative controls such as separation of duties and detective controls like internal audit. Any weaknesses in these controls are to be reported to investors. Part of the detective controls is being able to investigate possible incidents of fraud. In the majority of companies in the United States this means accessing data stored on computers. One of the effective ways to investigate financial fraud is with computer forensics. If an audit or a hotline tip uncovers possible fraud how are you going to investigated it? Most of the time a person that is involved in fraud will have tell-tell signs on their computer. These signs can include emails, Excel files, Word documents, and Instant Messaging.

A computer forensics specialist can image the hard drive of the suspect's computer at night without anyone knowing it. Then in the comfort of a lab the contents of this hard drive can be examined and evaluated. Without a computer forensics specialist the investigation would take more time, involve more people, and the investigation may become known to the suspected employee and their co-workers. If the suspected employee's co-workers know the investigation the organization may face some legal issues if nothing is found. Under SOX, failure to investigate a whistleblower complaint quickly and completely could show a failure to comply with sections 302 and/or 404 of SOX. This can be bad news for the organizations C-class executives (CFO, CEO, etc.) as they have to attest to the organization's internal controls and could be personally liable. Failure to comply with section 301 of SOX could result in the organization being de-listed.

Section 802 of SOX has some pretty severe penalties (up to 5 million and/or 20 years in jail) for the destruction of evidence. Electronic data is here today and gone tomorrow, so how can you preserve the electronic evidence and make sure you comply with SOX? Computer forensics can help. As soon as practically possible have a computer forensics specialist image the computer storage media in question. This will preserve it and help show that the company was not negligent in their duty to preserve electronic data.

Gramm-Leach-Bliley Act

This act deals with the information security policies and procedures for the financial institutions in the United States. The computer security of a financial institution is a major part of this. Think about how many people bank on-line, trade stocks on-line, and conduct other financial business over the Internet today. How many times in the last month have you gone over the Internet to conduct some sort of financial transaction? Chances are you have. Now think about all of the computer crimes you have heard about in the news. How many of these involved a financial institution? Probably most of them did because that is where the money is!

The part of the information security standards under GLBA that touches computer forensics deal with incident response and internal investigations. Computer forensics is a critical part of any incident response plan. The imaging of the computer storage media on the affected computer preserves any evidence that may be there. The analysis part of computer forensics can help an organization determine what happened. For internal investigations computer forensics in critical as most work is done on computers. This includes emails, word processing, spreadsheets, databases, financial software, and almost all other data in an organization is stored on a computer. If someone wants it on paper, you print it on a computer. How else are you going to investigate inappropriate financial activity? While computer forensics is not the entire investigation, an investigation without it is incomplete.

Health Insurance Portability & Accountability Act

This act deals with a person's medical records and data. Computer forensics comes into the picture when you are investigation inappropriate access to this data. A hospital or other type of company could be facing lawsuits if someone gains unauthorized access to a person's medical records. If adequate controls are not in place to track this, how do you prove or disprove this? Electronic discovery may be able to provide you with all the answers you need, especially if you are looking at a large number of computers or large amount of computer storage media. Computer forensics may also be needed to retrieve log files, emails, and other items relating to the inappropriate access from one or more of the computers.

Other legal issues the computer forensic specialist needs to be aware of include spoliation and chain of custody. The spoliation of evidence on computer storage media can happen in a number of ways. Simply booting up the computer can cause several hundred writes to a hard drive with one of the Microsoft Windows operating systems. Once this is done everything on the hard drive is spoiled. This is because it is impossible to determine which files were added, deleted, or modified. While the time stamps on the files offer some guidance in this, they can be easily changed. Time stamps are created using the computer's system clock. The computer's system clock can be changed very easily by a user or script to be what ever date you desired. Then anything created, deleted, or modified would have this incorrect date. Once you are done making modifications just set the computer's clock back to the correct date and know one is the wiser. So, poking around on a computer to determine if you want to perform computer forensics on it will almost always lead to one answer—NO. By poking around you have spoiled the potential evidence and anything found would not be admissible in court. A review of the computer's hard drive may be useful in finding leads that yield evidence that can be admitted though.

There are other ways the evidence on computer storage media can be spoiled, remember you are dealing with volatile storage media most of the time. The spoliation of evidence on computer storage media could also be damaging to a court case. Not only did you lose the evidence, you now have to explain this in court. Then you get to deal with the assumptions a Judge and possible jury of your peers will make. Even if the items found on the computer storage media would have had no negative impact on your case, spoil this evidence and you probably will have a negative impact. Another issue that can get evidence on computer storage media thrown out is chain of custody issues.

The chain of custody is very important, if there is a break in the chain, then the evidence may be thrown out. A break will occur when there is a time period that the evidence can not be accounted for. To counter this, the computer forensic specialist uses inventory sheets and access logs to track the movement of evidence. When the evidence is stored, it is kept in a secure location that is locked. The people with a key to access this are strictly controlled. All this to ensure the chain is not broken. The chain of custody and the procedures used to maintain it are usually the first place the opposing side will attack evidence found on computer storage media. If they find a weak or missing link, then the evidence may be thrown out. Larger firms that provide computer forensic services will generally have more procedures than a single person firm. This is because the larger firm has to worry about employee turnover, sometimes in the middle of a case. Also in a larger firm many people may have a key to the evidence locker, while in a single person firm only one person has a key. What ever the procedures are to ensure the chain of custody, just be comfortable that they can be defended in court.

The legal issues surrounding computer forensics is often more than people realize. This is why many computer forensic specialists are former law enforcement or attend continuing legal education events to learn about these issues. Rarely will ignorance be an acceptable defense should you make a mistake. If you are providing computer forensic services or contracting for these services it would be prudent to make sure someone on the team understands the legal aspect.

Chapter 8
Finding a Specialist

Since the discipline of computer forensics is fairly new many wonder how to go about finding a well qualified computer forensic examiner. For many this may be a completely foreign experience. It is also conceivable this is the first litigation, which they have been party. This is further exacerbated by the fear of intrusting their company's secrets to someone else. For many small and medium size companies a single intellectual property theft could destroy their business. Add the factor of how do they determine if the person charging the fee is truly a qualified computer forensics specialist or some novice want-a-be? In the computer security community, a novice hacker is often referred to as script kiddie. This is someone, who has no knowledge of how a tool works—they just blindly use a tool in a shotgun approach in an attempt to get results. In the undernet being called a script kiddie is like being called a string of four letter words in the average workplace. So how can you differentiate from a qualified and paper specialist?

With the proliferation of electronic discovery, season litigators should carefully consider the ramification of leaving the electronic door open for a lawsuit if they do not at least document that they considered a forensic review of computers in question. If the decision is made to forensically review computer storage media for an investigation, where can you find someone?

As with any 'new' field of expertise there are a lot of questions and misunderstandings. Many people will say "Cool, I can do that" and hang out their shingle as a computer forensic specialist. How can you tell a PC technician or a system administrator from a qualified specialist? This chapter is designed to help you separate fact from fiction.

First we need to consider the question—why can't the IT staff be our computer experts? After all, these skilled individuals are intimately familiar with the equipment, operating systems, and day to day functions of the equipment. While all of this information can be helpful during a computer forensic examination, it simply does not provide the intimate knowledge of how the internal working of the operating system functions and quickly loses its luster. This knowledge is critical. Next a computer forensic examiner will many times have a membership in the professional organization with a vetting process. This might require the individual to have sponsors in order to join. Or as in the case of Infragard require that its applicants submit to a FBI background investigation. Would you want to take the chance of finding out that someone in your IT staff was convicted of a felony, while he/she is being cross examined as your expert witness? Another factor worth considering is objectivity. By hiring a third party from outside of your organization, it will give you a different prospective on the information in question. Several years ago—I was talking to a good friend of mine at the Federal Bureau of Investigation. I asked him how his case load was going. He then proceeded to explain to me that members of the FBI's CART (Computer A———- Response Team) don't actually investigate cases. He said their investigators are required by policy to bring the computers to a CART certified examiner. He emphasized that many times an investigator would get very close to the case and might have his judgment bent from one perspective to another. By having another individual look at the electronic evidence, then it would often provide a much more balanced investigation. Now that we have established why it's really important to obtain an outside expert the next question is how?

First it is helpful to determine what a true blue computer forensic examiner is and should know. It is far too easy to read a few chapters from the latest computer forensics book at Borders and get the entire lingo down. However does that really qualify a person be able to provide you with the expert advice and these often very complicated cases. The answer is obviously no.

The field of computer forensics requires a mix of skills including computer expertise, legal knowledge, and auditing. You may have the best technical person in the world, a super geek if you will, but is this enough? Does he/she understand the legal issues surrounding computer forensics, such as the chain of custody or the concept of the tainting of evidence? Also how will this person stand up to cross examination and redirect? If the best laid case is cut to shreds on cross examination, your "expert" could end up doing much more harm than good. Do they understand the necessity for documentation or the 'art' of report writing? It is not out of the question to ask for a list of references. Then actually call these references, ask about the forensic examination, and how was it conducted. If the person you hire as a computer forensics specialist does not have all the skills needed you may be in trouble. When you want a good accountant, you look for the Certified Public Accountant (CPA) designation first. While this does not make the person an expert in accounting it does show a minimum level of ability and knowledge. It also means that this person has agreed to abide by a code of ethics.

In computer forensics a standard certification like the CPA has not emerged yet. There are several that are available to people in the computer forensics field and a couple are starting to gain credibility. Just like the CPA, none of these certifications will make someone an expert; they just give assurance that the met the criteria set out in the certification. In addition to certifications there are several other items to look for, including:

- Have they ever testified in court or qualified as an expert witness. While not previously qualifying as an expert in court does not disqualify a person, it is nice to know they have done it. Outside of law enforcement, many computer forensic specialists have never even been in court. It is also helpful to ask the prospective examiner, what type of testimony have they provided? If they have only testified about a giving traffic tickets, this does not count as computer forensic testimony. Also many experts can go years without testifying in a case. This is because most cases never make it to court. So if the computer forensic specialist has never qualified as an expert, there are other items to look for. If the computer forensics specialist has attempted to qualify and failed, be careful. However you will need to actually look at the testimony to determine what was the cause. It is also not uncommon for a forensic examiner to not be qualified as an expert the first couple of times in court. There are several online services that are available where you can verify an examiner's court experience, such as Verdict Search, http://www.verdictsearch.com.

Even if they have not testified in court, you can still ask about previous cases and examinations. While a computer forensic examiner may not be able to discuss the specifics of a case with you due to confidentiality, I would ask about courtroom testimony. Once the matter is presented in court, it generally becomes public record. The examiner should be able to freely share with you material that he has provided testimony about. It has been my experience that generally it takes between 1—3 years for a matter to reach a courtroom. Also of the computer forensics cases that I have worked less than 10% actually make it to the opening statements. Many people find this information very hard to believe, however it is absolutely true. If the evidence is very convincing, most legal professional do not want to argue a losing case. This means it is critically important to insure that you are getting good advice; you have to do your homework.

- How long has the person been working in the computer forensics field? How long in related fields? As a good rule of thumb the computer forensics field began to really grow from isolated pockets of professionals in 1997 and 1998 to the fully developed discipline of today. If you are talking to someone, who says they have been doing computer forensics prior to 1997, I would careful check their background. You could have stumbled onto one of the grandfathers of computer forensics or you could have a snake oil salesman on your hands. Remember, there is no substitute for actual experience in any profession. Does the person have experience in related fields? I mentioned above that computer forensics was part audit. Financial auditing may be a stretch for some when you try to relate it to computer forensics, but how about information systems (IS) auditing. Many IS auditors are already familiar with computers and their behind the scenes workings. They are familiar with preparing work papers and writing reports on technical computer audit findings for very non-technical people. These skills are very helpful in conducting a forensic exam of computer storage media. It should be noted that computer forensics and IS auditing are two very different but related fields. So being a highly qualified IS auditor does not qualify someone to do computer forensics. Other related fields are IS security or system administration positions. These professions will provide someone with the computer knowledge needed, but not necessarily the forensics skills they need. Additionally, many computer people have aversions to creating documentation like work papers or to writing formal reports.

- Training classes are always good. Until very recently it was difficult to find a university or college that taught computer forensics. The best and sometimes the only training available was through seminars, conferences, or continuing education type classes. If the expert conducted computer forensics while working in Law Enforcement, they will probably have taken at least one if not several courses by the National White Collar

Crime Center. Their website is http://www.cybercrime.org. In fact this is one of the primer computer forensic training organizations. While their primary training facility is located in West Virginia, they conduct classes all over the United States and various other countries. On the west coast the SEARCH organization was one of the first groups dedicated to computer forensics. There website is http://www.search. org/. Just like an accountant, a computer forensics specialist needs to attend training classes on a regular basis to help maintain their abilities. If you are talking to a computer forensics specialist that claims they do not need continuing education to stay current, keep looking this is not the person for you. Think about it, if you were interviewing someone for a financial auditing position and they boosted that they did not need any continuing education to stay current on accounting and auditing matters what would you think? Do they really understand the profession if they say this? Also consider the rate at which new computer technology comes out; this makes it scarier in computer forensics.

- Has the person ever presented at any conferences relating to computer forensics or taught classes on the subject? It would be the exception and not the rule to find a qualified expert, who has not presented a presentation or two on computer forensics. Many times people are allowed to present at these conferences based on their reputation with their peers. Basically the person is respected enough by their peers in the profession that they believe the person is qualified to teach others, at least the subject(s) presented. Not having presented does not mean the person is not qualified, but having presented does make a case that the person knows what they are talking about.

- Is the person published? Have they had any articles published in a respectable publication like a trade journal or professional paper? Not only do you learn a lot when you write something for publication, if it is published it means that at least one publisher thinks so as well. It also puts the person's thoughts and opinions out for public scrutiny.

- Is the person a member of any professional groups that relate to computer forensics? Involvement in professional groups is very important. It shows a commitment to the profession and is a great way to network with peers. This is one of the easiest and most cost effective ways to learn about new items in the profession. If a specialist is not a member of any professional groups, I would wonder why and how serious are they about their trade. In fact I would suggest that membership in a single organization is not a favorable sign. Many computer forensic examiners are members of several different ones. This is also refereed to as Association Clustering. Next you should discover their level of involvement. This is usually very easy to check by just contacting one of the current officers and ask about the person's participation. The officers are generally very open to discussing who attends meetings and who does not.

- Can the person provide you with any references? This can be previous clients or reputable peers in the profession that vouch to their ability.

Since the profession is so new, what certifications can you look for that are worth more than the paper they are printed on? That is a very good question, since there is several certifications that nothing more that a piece of paper someone paid too much for. As with professional associations, I would look for certification clusters. The average examiner will have more than one computer forensics certification. One of the oldest computer forensic certifications that I know of is the Certified Forensic Computer Examiner (CFCE), but this is only available to law enforcement and is not available to the general public. There are several certifications available to non-law enforcement computer forensic specialist that you can look for. These include the CCE (Certified Computer Examiner), EnCE (EnCase Certified Examiner—if using EnCase), CIFI (Certified Information Forensics Investigator), and the CCFT (Certified Computer Forensic Technician). Most of these certifications require a criminal background check and require people that are certified to follow a code of ethics.

- The CFCE is by the International Association of Computer Investigative Specialists. Generally individual who has this certification has been in law enforcement at one point in time. It should also be noted that most law enforcement agencies will not allow their computer forensic examiners work on civil cases on the side. There are some notable exceptions but generally this holds true. There is an external certification program; however I am just going to provide the requirements for the traditional program. In the traditional plan the applicant is required to attend a two week course, which had been held in Orlando for the past several years. At the end of the first week—the students are given a pass/fail test over the course materials presented. If the student successfully completes this test—then they are allowed to continue onto the second week. At the end of the second week the student is given a password to open an encrypted file. This file contains an executable, which will place a forensic image back onto a floppy diskette. The student is provided a case scenario and told to conduct the forensic examination. Also the student is assigned a coach to help them with the process. The coach/mentor was a novel concept at the time it was created. The coach provides help and assistance and also grades the initial reports by the student. Each report can be quite in depth. After the student successfully completes seven floppy diskettes, then the student is mailed a compact disc and then a hard drive. While the size of the hard drive is small, it is very, very challenging. After this is completed, the student has to complete a large take home test, which has several very detailed essay questions. This was very, very channeling. After all of this has been completed then you are allowed to join the rates of other CFCE examiners. You can obtain more information on this certification at http:// http://www.cops.org.

Figure 8.1—www.cops.org

- The CCE is by the International Society of Forensic Computer Examiners, http://www.isfce.com, and requires that a person pass a written examination and a practical examination consisting of three different media, have met the training requirements, and have adequate experience as determined by the certifying board. The ISFCE also does a criminal background check on the applicant to ensure that they do not have a criminal record. A list of certified individuals is at http://www.certified-computer-examiner.com/list.htm.

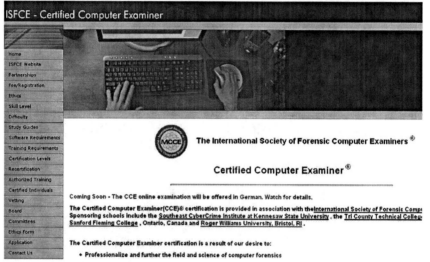

Figure 8.2—www.certified-computer-examiner.com

- The EnCE is a vendor certification sponsored by Guidance Software, http://www.encase.com. To become an EnCE the person has to pass an online exam and a practical exam. EnCase software must be used to complete the practical part of the exam. A list of certified individuals can be found at http://www.encase.com/training/ence/referrals.asp.

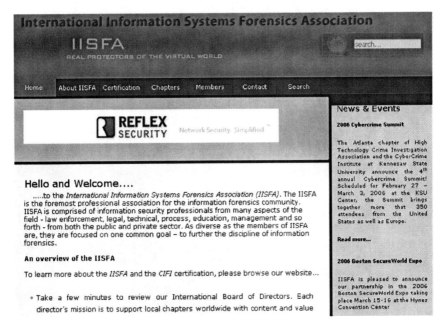

EnCE Referrals

EnCE certification recognizes that an investigator is a skilled computer examiner with at least 18 months of investigative experience. Certification also requires extensive proof of qualifications through both written and practical examinations. Below is a list of EnCE certified individuals who have agreed to list their contact information. Please contact them directly if you would like to use their services.

Country	State/Province	Name	Email
Australia	NSW	John Simpson	simp1joh@police.nsw.gov.au
Australia	NSW	Nigel Carson	Nigel.Carson@syd.fh.com.au
Australia	NSW	Norman Napiza	norman.napiza@au.pwc.com
Australia	QLD	John Boggon	john.l.boggon@transport.qld.gov.au
Australia	VIC	Michael Cerny	michael.cerny@au.pwc.com
Australia	VIC	Roger Clay	roger.clay@au.ey.com

Figure 8.3—www.encase.com/training/ence/index.asp

- The CIFI is sponsored by the International Information Systems Forensic Association, http://www.iisfa.org, and requires an individual to pass the CIFI exam and adhere to the IISFA code of ethics. For more information about the CIFI check out the association's website, http://www.iisfa.org/certification/certification.asp.

Figure 8.4—www.iisfa.org

- The CCFT is sponsored by the High Tech Crime Network, http://www.htcn.org, and requires an individual to have adequate training and experience, and to document a number of cases they have completed. More information is at their website, http://www.htcn.org/cert.htm.

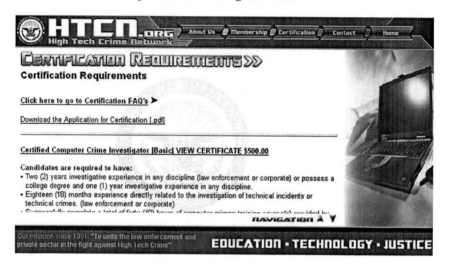

Figure 8.5—www.htcn.org/cert.htm

- The ACE, AccessData Certified Examiner, is a vendor certification sponsored by AccessData, http://www.accessdata. com. The ACE credential provides corporate and law enforcement agencies with recognition of AccessData tool-centric knowledge and practical application of the Ultimate Toolkit.

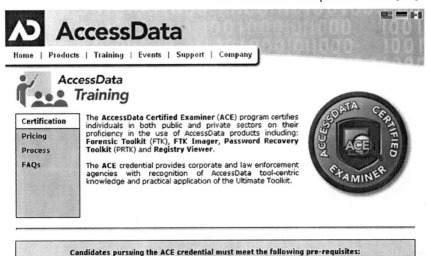

Figure 8.6—www.accessdata.com/training/ace

On this note I would also like to point out a disturbing trend. I have noticed that more and more computer security professionals are jumping onto the computer forensics bandwagon. For example I have seen more than one individual have a certification such as the Certified Information Systems Security Professional (CISSP) and proclaim they are a computer forensics expert. You should know that the CISSP has a single domain dedicated to covering Law, Investigations and Ethics. These three areas are in a single common body of knowledge. As part of this domain, computer forensic imaging is covered. While this certification does provide an introduction to computer forensics, if this is the only certification that your expert has—then I would seriously examine his/her background.

There are several types of training classes available in computer forensics. These include vendor classes, conferences, professional groups, and recently several colleges and universities have added this to their class schedule. For vendor training it is generally only relevant if it relates to the software the specialist is using. So if the specialist is using SMART, make sure they have gone to at least one training class from the vendor (ASR Data). Most vendors offer several levels of classes, beginning, intermediate, advance, or special topics (such as email recovery), so you may want to inquire as to the level of the classes the computer forensic specialist has completed. There are several annual conferences around the country that are hosted by various companies and professional groups that help specialists keep their skills up to date. In the southeast some of the more popular ones are the Techno-

Security conference, http://www.techsec.com/html/Techno2006.html, the Cybercrime Summit, http://www.cybercrimesummit.com, and the GMU conference, http://www.rcfg.org. The latter two are sponsored by local chapters of the High Tech Crime Investigation Association (HTCIA), a professional group.

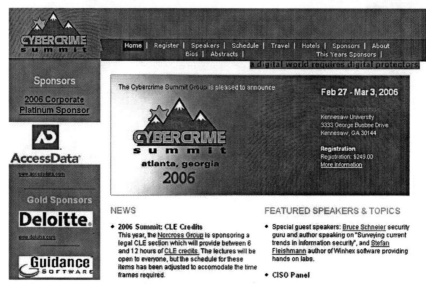

Figure 8.7—www.cybercrimesummit.com

The HTCIA is one of the oldest associations for computer forensics and computer crime, but its members are strictly prohibited from criminal defense work. There are several other professional groups such as the International Information Systems Forensic Association (IISFA) whose membership is open to all professional. IISFA members are required to adhere to the organizations code of ethics. There are other professional groups forming around the country, but aside from the HTCIA these are newer and are still forming their reputation. In accounting the similar groups would be the various state associations of CPA's and the AICPA. Just imagine these accounting associations when they were one or two years old and most people had never heard of a CPA. This is where most of these computer forensics associations are today. My experience is that active participation in these groups is not only a great way to learn what's new, but members tend to talk about the tricks and tools of the trade.

Some computer forensic specialist may try to convince a potential client that they are experts because of the tool(s) they use. I have heard some speakers say that only tool X will be accepted in court or if tool

X is not used then the person is obviously not an expert and just a chiphead hobbyist. This is akin to saying only accounting firm X knows how to properly do audits because they have a special methodology. In computer forensics there are now several tools that a specialist may use; some of the more popular ones are EnCase, New Technology Inc (NTI), Forensic Tool Kit (FTK), SMART, Mareware®, ProDiscover®, Datalifter®, and P2®. It is also helpful to note that many forensic examiners will use different tools to cross check their results. Any of these software tools used correctly can get the job done. However if sound forensic procedures are not followed then it does not matter which tool is used, any findings may end up being useless. If a computer forensic specialist is relying on a point and click tool to magically get the job done, my advice is to keep looking for a specialist. Typically a specialist will use several tools and depending on what needs to be done will select the best tool. The specialist will also be able to explain how the tool works and be able to perform the same test with several tools and get the same end result if needed.

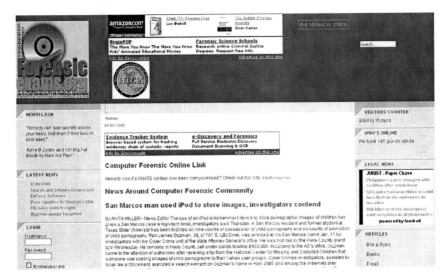

Figure 8.8—www.forensicexams.org

Now that we have covered several of the items to look for in a computer forensic specialist, where do you start looking to find them? You can always do a Google search or use a site like http://www.dogpile. com to search for someone. This way will yield results, but what kind of results will you get? Will the person actually be competent or just have a cool website and take your money. There are legal websites such as http://www.law.com that have expert listings associated with them. Remember these websites make money by selling listings to people. The more listings they sell the more money they make, so they are generally not real particular about whom they sell a listing to. There are website more focused on the computer forensic community like http://www.forensicexams.org that allow specialist to list for free and there are referral websites associated with some of the certifications. The referral websites, such as those mentioned in this chapter, would be a better place to start looking for someone if you do not know any one. At least the people listed on these sites usually have a minimum level of ability and knowledge. Again you could also locate your local HTCIA chapter and contact one of their officers. These individuals could probably point you in the right direction and are generally eager to help.

Chapter 9
The ToolKit

In the course of this book we have mentioned several items that a computer forensics specialist may use. There are software application, hardware tools, and forms that they should have, but what should you look for? In the past decade computer forensics tools have evolved from home grown to several major commercial packages. There are also hardware write blocking devices, hardware imaging tools, portable workstations, and other items that a computer forensic specialist can use.

Also be weary of the computer forensic specialist, who only uses one tool or only has one certification for that matter. Despite what all of the marketing hype would have you believe there is no one all inclusive computer forensics tools. I remember when I was a boy, every Saturday I would watch a Kung-Fu Theater. Around November I remember seeing a commercial for the wonder wrench. You see my father had been an auto mechanic for almost 20 years in our small town. Our shed was full of auto tools. The wonder wrench claimed to be the perfect tool for every use. I was so excited because I wanted a Go-Cart, which would have never fit in the shed with all of the tools. I figured that I could buy my Dad the wonder wrench for Christmas and he could get rid of all of those other tools. This would make just enough room for a Go-Cart.

Well Christmas came around I gave my dad the wonder wrench and Santa brought me the Go-Cart in spite of the space problem in the Shed. How he got it in the living room, and we got it out—I just don't remember. However around the New Year my father was working on his truck. I noticed that he had his trusted assortment of tools scattered around him. I remember being so sad that he was not using the "wonder wrench." When I asked him about it—he told me to go and get it and he wanted me to help him remove some bolts. I remember digging it out from the other gift in the guest bedroom and running outside. He asked me to remove two bolts for him, while he got a drink of water. I remember being as proud as I put the wonder wrench on the bolt. I pulled and twisted and pulled. The bolt didn't move—then when I really put my weight into it—the marvelous wonder wrench slipped off, and I cracked my knuckles on the engine block. I was so angry, plus the grease was making the cuts burn. My dad came out and handed me a box end wrench and asked he to give it another try. I worked the bolt all of the way out. I was so let down that the wonder wrench didn't cut the mustard. I will never forget what my Dad said. "You have to use the right tool for the right job. If you don't then you just end up with bloody knuckles."

In computer forensics I would encourage you to take my Dad's advice—use the right tool for the job. Do not get all caught up in all of the marketing hype around different tools, try them out, and test them over and over and over. Remember that just because the word forensics is in the product's name does not mean the court is going to accept it. In computer forensics just like in life—there is no magic bullet.

Common Forensic Software

Some of the software in the tool kit may include imaging programs, viewers, unerase tools, wiping tools, CD/DVD analysis tools, and/or a forensic suite of programs. Each of these tools plays a part in the process. Some of the more common tools are listed below with a brief description:

- CD/DVD Diagnostic®—This software is for the analysis and extraction of data from CD-R, CD-RW and DVD media. It has a number of analysis tools specifically designed for CD's and DVD's and reporting tools as well. CD/DVD Inspector is a product of Infinadyne.

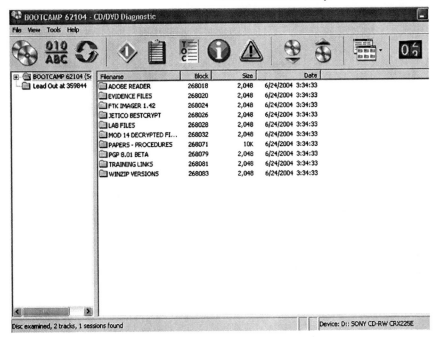

Figure 9.1—CD/DVD Diagnostic

- DataLifter—This program is a set of carving utilities that is that does an excellent job of carving files from an image or a file. This is a nice suite of tools, though it does not have an imaging tool and also lacks many of the functions found in a suite line EnCase, FTK, or SMART. Many times a computer forensics specialist will use DataLifter in conjunction with a tool like EnCase, FTK, or Ghost®. DataLifter is a product of StepaNet Communications, Inc.

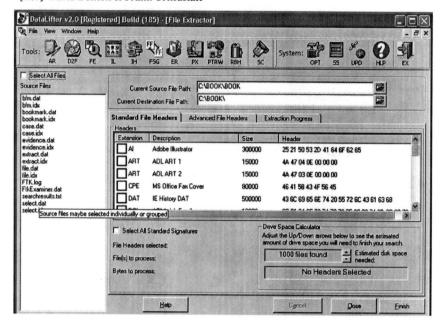

Figure 9.2—DataLifter

- EnCase—Is considered to be one of the better forensic software suites available. The various tools the examiner will need during the course of the review are included in one neat GUI front end. While this product does not have every software tool an examiner will need, it is one of the most comprehensive tool sets on the market. EnCase is one of the more complex forensic software suites and has a longer learning curve. The Enterprise edition allows for the imaging of computer storage media over a network. EnCase is a product of Guidance Software.

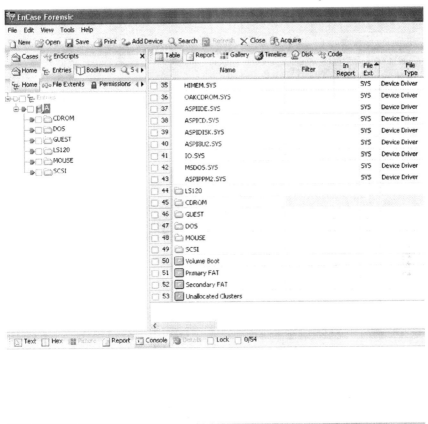

Figure 9.3—Encase

- Forensic Tool Kit (FTK)—This software suite is newer to the market than EnCase, but is still a very good software suite. It has a very well thought out GUI front end and work well with AccessData's other software tools, Registry Viewer®, Password Toolkit®, and Wiper utility. One difference is that FTK does a lot of pre-processing, so before an examiner starts reviewing the images, the software has already created indexes of every word on the image, hashed the files, and compared these files to various hash sets. FTK is a product of Access Data Corporation.

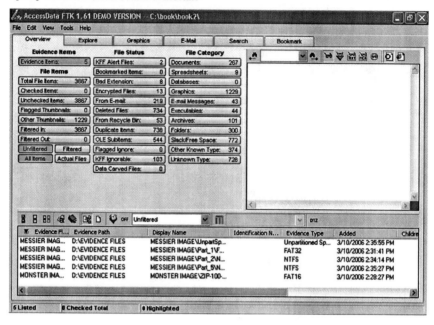

Figure 9.4—Forensic Tool Kit

- Ghost—Ghost was developed as a backup and replication tool for system administrators, not for use in computer forensics. Despite this, Ghost can be configured to make forensically sound bit stream images of a hard drive. Ghost is a product of Symantec Corporation. The main problem with using Ghost as a forensic utility is not in the actual product itself but is a licensing issue. The standard license of ghost, which you purchase off the shelf, is good for one computer. This means that you are allowed to use ghost on only one computer. Some could argue that by putting a suspect's hard drive into your computer, this does not constitute a licensing violation. I will leave the lawyering and wordsmithing up to the attorney's.

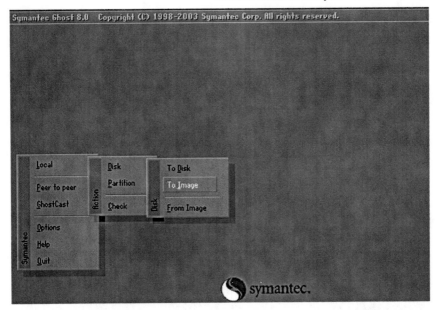

Figure 9.5—Ghost

- Maresware—This is the only suite of forensic software tools that does not have a GUI front end, but the people I know that use this suite do not seem to mind. This vendor has a suite of forensic tools for Windows/DOS and Linux operating systems. The Maresware suite of software is now available through our distributor, the Norcross Group.

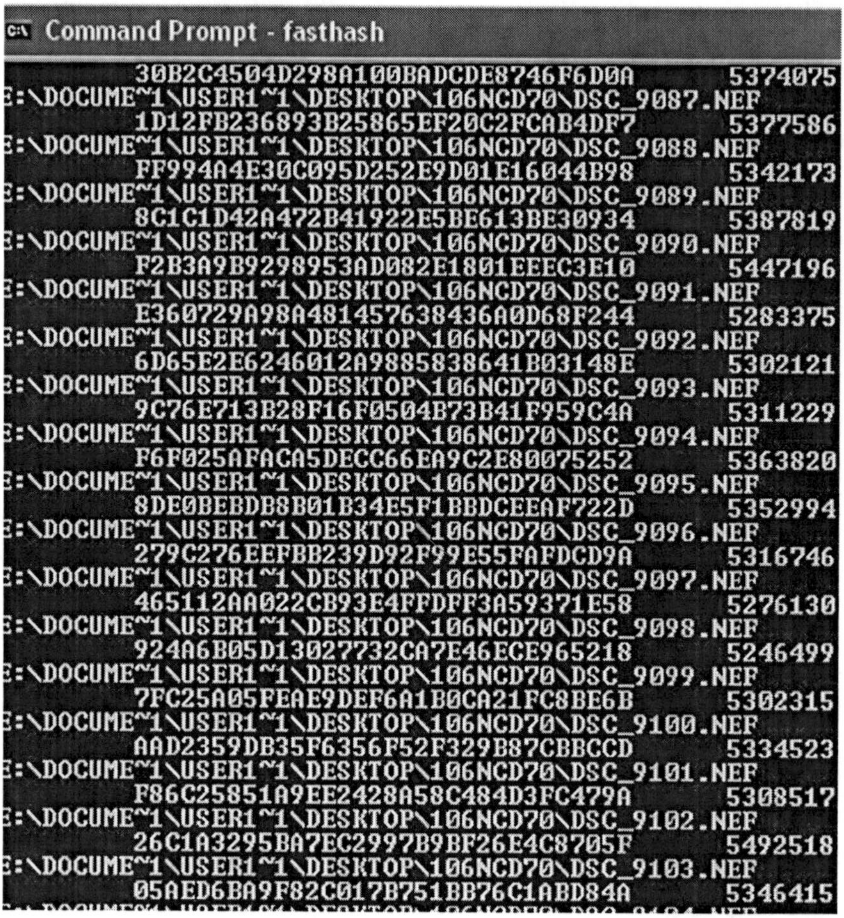

```
Command Prompt - fasthash
        30B2C4504D298A100BADCDE8746F6D0A        5374075
E:\DOCUME~1\USER1~1\DESKTOP\106NCD70\DSC_9087.NEF
        1D12FB236893B25865EF20C2FCAB4DF7        5377586
E:\DOCUME~1\USER1~1\DESKTOP\106NCD70\DSC_9088.NEF
        FF994A4E30C095D252E9D01E16044B98        5342173
E:\DOCUME~1\USER1~1\DESKTOP\106NCD70\DSC_9089.NEF
        8C1C1D42A472B41922E5BE613BE30934        5387819
E:\DOCUME~1\USER1~1\DESKTOP\106NCD70\DSC_9090.NEF
        F2B3A9B9298953AD082E1801EEEC3E10        5447196
E:\DOCUME~1\USER1~1\DESKTOP\106NCD70\DSC_9091.NEF
        E360729A98A481457638436A0D68F244        5283375
E:\DOCUME~1\USER1~1\DESKTOP\106NCD70\DSC_9092.NEF
        6D65E2E6246012A9885838641B03148E        5302121
E:\DOCUME~1\USER1~1\DESKTOP\106NCD70\DSC_9093.NEF
        9C76E713B28F16F0504B73B41F959C4A        5311229
E:\DOCUME~1\USER1~1\DESKTOP\106NCD70\DSC_9094.NEF
        F6F025AFACA5DECC66EA9C2E80075252        5363820
E:\DOCUME~1\USER1~1\DESKTOP\106NCD70\DSC_9095.NEF
        8DE0BEBDB8B01B34E5F1BBDCEEAF722D        5352994
E:\DOCUME~1\USER1~1\DESKTOP\106NCD70\DSC_9096.NEF
        279C276EEFBB239D92F99E55FAFDCD9A        5316746
E:\DOCUME~1\USER1~1\DESKTOP\106NCD70\DSC_9097.NEF
        465112AA022CB93E4FFDFF3A59371E58        5276130
E:\DOCUME~1\USER1~1\DESKTOP\106NCD70\DSC_9098.NEF
        924A6B05D13027732CA7E46ECE965218        5246499
E:\DOCUME~1\USER1~1\DESKTOP\106NCD70\DSC_9099.NEF
        7FC25A05FEAE9DEF6A1B0CA21FC8BE6B        5302315
E:\DOCUME~1\USER1~1\DESKTOP\106NCD70\DSC_9100.NEF
        AAD2359DB35F6356F52F329B87CBBCCD        5334523
E:\DOCUME~1\USER1~1\DESKTOP\106NCD70\DSC_9101.NEF
        F86C25851A9EE2428A58C484D3FC479A        5308517
E:\DOCUME~1\USER1~1\DESKTOP\106NCD70\DSC_9102.NEF
        26C1A3295BA7EC2997B9BF26E4C8705F        5492518
E:\DOCUME~1\USER1~1\DESKTOP\106NCD70\DSC_9103.NEF
        05AED6BA9F82C017B751BB76C1ABD84A        5346415
```

Figure 9.6—Maresware

- P2—This is a suite of tools that can be purchased individually or in a package. This vendor is known for having a very good program for handling emails and excellent tools for PDA's and cell phones. P2 is a product of Paraben Corporation.

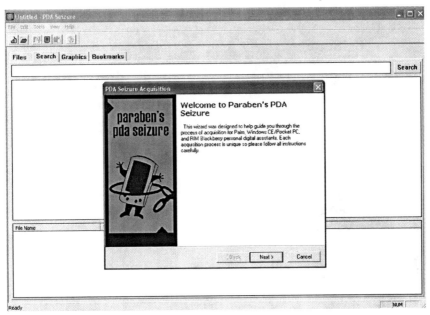

Figure 9.7—P2

- ProDiscover—Is a powerful computer forensic tool that enables examiners to remotely investigate the disk contents of systems throughout a corporate network. This is a newer suite of forensics tools than EnCase, and does not have the same level of refinement and support as EnCase, but is a very good software suite. This tool allows for the imaging of computer storage media, such as hard drives, across a network. While EnCase Enterprise also has this feature, but ProDiscover cost significantly less. ProDiscover is a product of Technology Pathways, LLC.

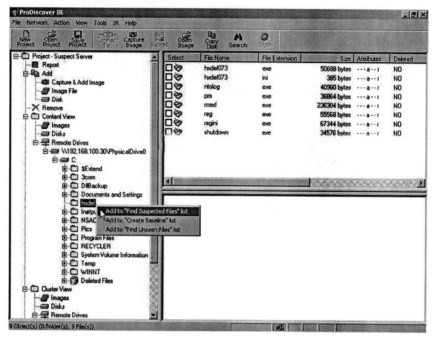

Figure 9.8—ProDiscover

- SMART—SMART is a software utility that has been designed to support computer forensic specialist in their duties. This is a forensic software suite that was developed with the intention of integrating technical, legal and end-user requirements. One difference between SMART and other software suites like EnCase or FTK is that it is based on Linux and not Windows. Many in the field of computer forensics see this as an advantage as Linux tends to be a better operating system for forensics. SMART is a product of ASR Data. For more information on ASR Data's first product, Expert Witness, go to the following site: http://www.asrdata.com/store/store.html.

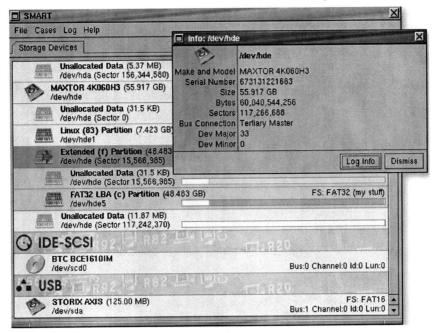

Figure 9.9—SMART

- QuickView Plus®—This viewer allows the user to view files created by more than 225 applications without having to have the application on the computer. This is a very handy tool as it saves the user considerable amount of money when compared to having to buy each of the individual application programs. The platforms supported by QuickView Plus includes Windows, DOS, Macintosh, and Internet formats including text, spreadsheet, graphic, database, presentation, and compressed files including PKZIP, as well as HTML and UUE. QuickView Plus is a product of Avantstar, Inc.

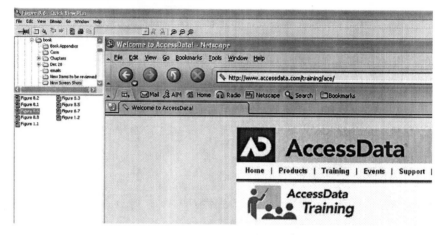

Figure 9.10—QuickView Plus

- WIN HEX®—This software allows you to open a view and view it in hex. They also produce a forensic version of the software, which allows quit a lot of functionality. It is hard to imagine that you would look at a computer forensic examiner's computer without at least one hex editor installed.

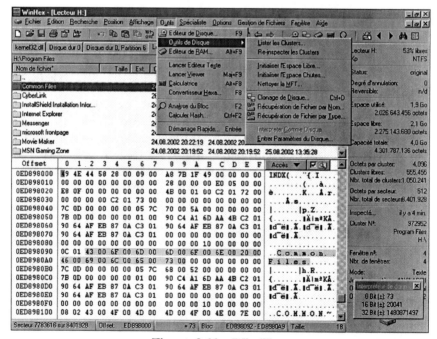

Figure 9.11—Win Hex

- Gargoyle®—This software can be used to scan a hard drive for malware. This can include Trojans, Rootkits, Keyloggers, Spyware, Encryption, Steganography, Surveillance tools, Botnets, and more. This is useful to examiners to ensure their examination machine is clean and to review suspect's hard drives to determine if they were infected with any of these. We have had cases where people claim malware is on their computer and it did the bad things. While this could be true, often it is not and this is one of the tools that will help an examiner in this search. Gargoyle is a product of WetStone Technologies., Inc.

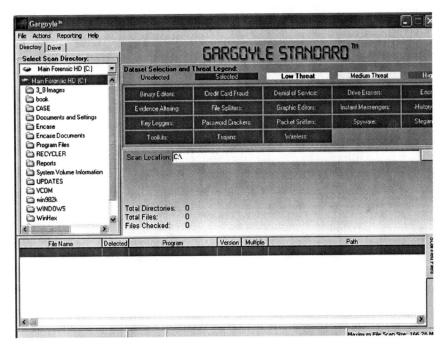

Figure 9.12—Gargoyle

- LiveWire® Software Suite—These tools are from WetStone Technologies and can be used in network discovery, live acquisitions (even remote computers), and Malware identification with Gargoyle. These tools can allow examiners to scan a corporate network to identify the computers or storage media that needs to be imaged, image the items found across the network, and does some analysis work on the acquired images.

Most computer forensic examiners will have some combination of the previously mentioned tools within their toolkits.

Write Protection (hardware and software)

When computer forensics was starting there was no such thing as write protection. All too frequently an investigator would sit down at the keyboard and look at the computer; however this made numerous changes to the media. This presented a problem because an essential part of evidence preservation is it should be no more or less than at the time of seizure. This required a whole new class of software tools to be created. While I have yet to be able to discover, who was the first company with a software write protection—currently they are sold throughout the profession. One of the most fundamental items is some sort of write protection. Write protection insures that the forensic examiner does not place information onto the suspect's computer hardware. Software write protection consists of a highly specialized computer program used in conjunction with a modified boot diskette. This is critically imported to having the evidence admitted into any court. These write blockers blocks the interrupt 13, which prevents any write instructions from being executed. These include the following:

- PDBlock® by Digital Intelligence
- Encase for DOS
- Many Linux boot CDs are available that mounts the hard drives as read only.

Just as a computer forensic specialist has several software tools, they can have an assortment of hardware tools as well. Some of the hardware tools are designed to work in conjunction with other software tools and some are not. The forensic images of a hard drives are made with a GUI (Graphical User Interface) software tool, then the process may require a hardware write blocker. A write blocker can be combined with a laptop computer to make a portable imaging system. Several tools like FTK Imager and EnCase for Windows need to use a hardware write blocker to make forensically sound images. Some common examples of hardware write blockers are the following:

- Fast Block® by Encase
- Firefly® by Digital Intelligence
- ICS Drive Lock®

A common configuration of a portable imaging setup using a laptop with a hardware write blocker to connect the original hard drive to and an external hard drive case for the target hard drive. The target hard drive is the one that has been sterilized and will receive the image of the original hard drive. Some specialists prefer to just carry a computer workstation with them in the field and yes there are workstations designed to be portable. These are sometimes called 'Lunch Boxes' and are full workstations in a portable case that when it is folded up resembles a large lunch box. These are nice, expensive, and can eliminate the need to buy a laptop and separate forensics workstation for the lab.

If the computer forensic specialist does not want to spend the money on a hardware imager, then they may use a write blocker in conjunction with imaging software. This option is usually a couple of thousand dollars cheaper and will still provide the used with a forensically sound image and a verification hash if desired. Many times a computer forensic specialist will chose a write blocker over an imaging device if they do limited field acquisitions.

Figure 9.13—Firewire/USB Drive Lock from ICS

It is important to remember that each type of write blocker is designed for only one or two different types of interfaces. The most common hardware write blocker is for an IDE or EIDE hard drive. This is generally because they are the most common. However you can't forget that there are many other types of hard drives and devices on which digital evidence can reside. The include:
- Thumb drives
- Serial ATA Hard Drives
- SCSI Hard Drive (and there are many different types of SCSI drives)

These One of the most comprehensive set of write blockers is produced by Digital Intelligence. It is called the Ultra Kit®, and I rarely go into the field without the handy kit.

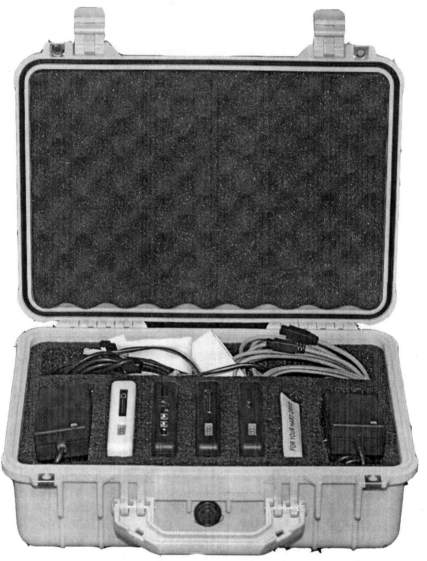

Figure 9.14—Utlra Kit

Forensic Imaging (hardware and software)

There are hundreds of pieces of equipment a person may need in a forensic review of computer storage media and acquiring them all can be cost prohibitive. For this reason many computer forensic specialist buy the equipment as they need it. Just as there is software imaging tools, there is hardware imaging tools as well. Some of these imagers are small enough to be held in the hand of the examiner. This makes getting as much of the details as possible in the initial meeting important. Some of the more common pieces of hardware include:

- Imaging Device—While there are several software imagers such as Ghost and DD there are also several hardware imagers available. These are normally a little faster than their software counterparts but are also expensive. These will make a bit by bit copy of the original media without changing a single bit and many will also provide a verification hash to the user such as a MD5 hash number. The main advantage of these is when acquiring hard drives in the field as oppose to the lab.

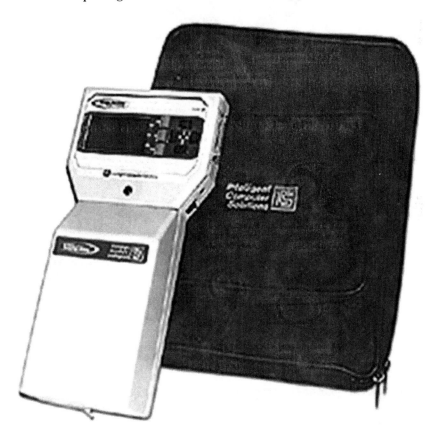

Figure 9.15—Image MASSter Solo2 Professional Plus by ICS

- External Hard drives—These are wonderful devices to use in the field when the computer forensic specialist is away from their forensic workstation(s). Usually the forensic workstation will have several removable hard drive bays that are available for hard drives to be placed in them. So if the computer forensic specialist takes a laptop into the field, they can add all the hard drive storage they need with these.

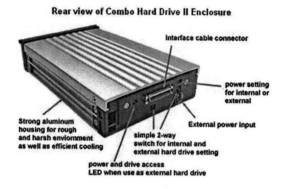

Figure 9.16—Combo Hard Drive II enclosure

Figure 9.17—Connection Options for the Combo Hard Drive II enclosure

External Hard Drive enclosure and accessories by Addonics®, Inc., www.addonics.com this is only one example, there are many vendors with external cases on the market.

Forensic Workstations

- Forensic workstations—This is where most of the analysis work will be done, and often all of the work for a case. One common attribute of forensic software is that they are resource hogs. To accommodate this, the forensic workstation will normally have a good motherboard, top of the line processor(s), and as much random access memory (RAM) as possible. This workstation should also be able to be configured to handle many different configurations to accommodate almost any computer storage media encountered.

Figure 9.18—FRED workstation by Digital Intelligence

Figure 9.19—Forensic Computers.com

- Portable computers, "Lunch Boxes"—Sometimes the computer forensic specialist may want to take their workstation into the field with them. The traditional tower configuration of a workstation and a big monitor may not be practical. Luckily there is a middle ground with portable computers often called lunch boxes. These are full blown workstations with a LCD display and keyboard that fold up so that it can be carried like a lunchbox. This can be an advantage in the field as workstations are normally more powerful and have more configuration options than a laptop. The down side is these are heavy and are expensive, often more expensive than a similarly equipped tower computer.

One of my personal favorite mobile computer systems is by www.bsicomputers.com. These all in one system is extremely portable and very, very rugged. These systems place the functionality of a full time computer system board inside of a very rugged case. While I was in the military I noticed these cases were very common in the various tactical operations centers (TOC). One of the distinct advantages of this case is the monitor is placed in the interior of the case. Some other portable systems place their monitor on the exterior of the case. This design increases the lightly hood of the monitor being damaged by a blow to the outside of the case. The BSI design uses the keyboard to protect the monitor. This means dramatically increases the likelihood that the monitor could survive a blow to the exterior case.

Figure 9.20- FREDDIE by Digital Intelligence

Figure 9.21—BSI Computer

Miscellaneous

- Flash/Smart Card Readers—Ten years ago who would have thought that your camera and cell phone are computers. Today these are routinely included in an engagement by computer forensic specialist. Think of all of the information that is stored on the average cell phone; call history, address books, appointments, personal organizers, etc. If the cell phone is Internet ready then there may be emails, web history, and other items associated with web browsers. Cameras are can be important because of the pictures that their storage media contains, which some may be deleted pictures. It still holds true, delete does not normally mean delete. Also, it is relatively simple for someone to photograph a document or other sensitive material. A neat way to smuggle items out of an organization.

Now that we have looked at some of the computer forensic hardware required—let's look at some of the more specialized tool kits.

- Hard Drive adapters—most standard hard drives in desktop computers meet a 3.5 inch form factor. In a laptop computer the hard drive is considerably smaller and usually conforms to a 2.5 inch form factor. <<add more>>

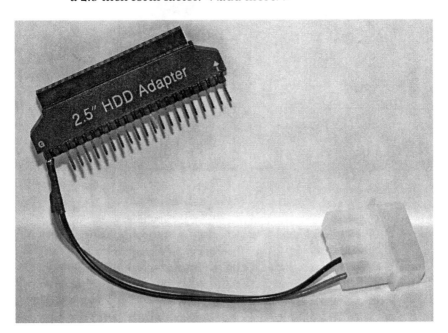

Figure 9.22—Hard drive adapter

- Tools—a good traditional computer tech's set of tools is very important.
- Evidence Bags—one of the most important aspects of any forensic examination is properly securing the digital evidence. A simple way to do this is to use a traditional evidence bags. There are many manufacturers, who sell these items in various shapes and sizes to include
- http://www.evidentcrimescene.com
- http://www.securityandsafetysupply.com
- http://www.crime-scene.com

Figure 9.23—Evidence bags

- Security Bit Sets—these are used to remove the non traditional types of screws from the backs of computer cases. Several years ago using specialized computer screws was a great way to secure your case. This could provide someone from opening up the case and resetting the jumper on the motherboard to clear the BIOS password. However these screws have become pretty common and can be purchased in almost any major computer store.

Conclusion

The advantages of commercial tools kits are readily available and supported. I have heard over and over that it is cheaper to build a forensic computer yourself. In many cases this is correct; however some people seem to forget the commercial software and warranties, which are bundled with these packages. There is something to be said for when any device in an all in one kit fails being able to sent it back to a single place. Keep in mind that if you build it yourself then you are forced to deal directly with the manufacturer and must provide your own support.

In addition to having hardware, you need to make sure that you have the proper software tools necessary to get the job done. Some packages can come bundled with forensic software. While you are considering these packages keep in mind that it is very important that any software tool has been subjected to peer review, analyzed by professional publications and had articles published about them. Also it may become necessary for the opposing side to have access to the same tools for the court case so they can use it to verify/disprove any findings. If you are taking to a computer forensics specialist that claims to have the best software available because they wrote it, you may want to keep looking. There are only a handful of computer forensics examiners who are also programmers. These people are generally well known in the industry, sale their tools and provide training. If this is the case, and the tools have done well in the peer reviews, etc. the computer forensics specialist is probably very good. You don't want to get onsite only to discover that you have to make a trip to the local computer store.

Chapter 10
Computer Lab

Have you ever wondered what a computer forensics lab looks like? Voice recognition access control on the doors, or is it the retinal scan like the one you saw in the James Bond movie? Will it be managed by "Q" or some guy in a white lab coat? Will it be similar to the clean room they use to manufacture chips? Will it be just a good ol' boy in the basement with a Dungeons & Dragons poster on the wall and a beer by their side? The truth may be more the later than you need to know, but the basement will be one that meets some pretty good standards for security and environmental controls. In the preceding chapter we discussed some of the tools that a computer forensics specialist may use. Now let's see how they may fit into a lab.

Access Control

Physical access to the lab needs to be restricted to as few people as possible, generally only the people that are actually doing the forensic work. In large corporations this may ruffle the feathers of some of the higher level of management, but it a court case it could save them. If possible the door should have some sort of auditing feature that will keep a record of who is coming and going with time stamps. Once inside the lab you may find monitoring cameras on the door, but not the forensic workstations. The cameras are kept off the workstations to maintain the confidentiality of the items being reviewed. Then inside the lab is an evidence locker or safe that is locked. This provides another level of physical access control to the evidence. It should be noted that the locks should not be the standard sort of every day house lock. These provide very little assurance, since any one with a lock picking set and quickly open the standard lock. I would highly recommend that all of the locks be "high security." This generally means that you will be using one of two major manufacturers—Multi-lock® or Medico®.

You may ask—is a high security lock really important? The answer is absolutely YES!! Here is a quote from the Multi-Lock website—

> Most locks are made with inferior material, which can be drilled, pried, and tampered with using minimal efforts to force open almost door. Most cylinders are not made to resist picking. With specialized pick sets readily available through mail order catalogs and the internet, just about anyone can get specialized tools and instructions on how to pick open almost any lock cylinder.3

If you don't properly protect your information then are you asking for trouble?

Figure 10.1—Click Interactive by Multi-Lock

One of the newest features in the lock market is called "clix interactive." This combines the auditing features of full blown access control device and the protection of a high security pad lock into a wide variety of device. The clix technology allows the user to have a level of audit control, which is highly configurable and very secure.

When you go into court, it is quite conceivable about that you will be asked to describe your lab's access control system. If you explain that you have logging, a security system, a combination safe and/or high security locks then chances are you can show that you have done due diligence.

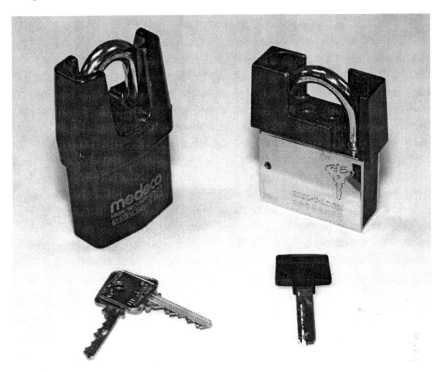

Figure 10.2—Image of locks

However if you have decided to go with only one of the above then don't be surprised if you face strong objections to the admissibility of the evidence into state or even federal court. This can be further complicated it the forensic examiner or company that does not have a reputation for testifying in court. However let's just say that you left the evidence in the trunk of your car for weeks at a time without any other information assurance system in place. Then you could run into trouble if you don't take some special measures.

Another method of providing a level of assurance is to use an evidence bag. These bags can have a serial number and are very tamper proof. No there is not some sort of James Bond super bags. They are little more than zip locking bags with serial numbers and very strong glue. An item can be placed inside of a bag and then the serial number is recorded on the evidence sheet. When it comes time for trial, a simple visual inspection could show that the evidence has not been tampered with. These bags can be purchased for several different police supply houses.

Network Access

Network access is another issue that needs to be dealt with. The examiner needs access to the internet to update software, get updates for the anti-virus software, or possible to do research. Being on the Internet also could potentially expose the forensic workstation to malicious software or viruses that could compromise an examination. So the examiner needs access to the Internet at the same time they do not really want it, what to do? One option is to access the Internet at the beginning of an examination to update everything that is needed and then physically disconnecting the Internet connection. This minimizes the forensic workstation's exposure to the Internet and is the cheapest solution. In a larger organization they may have the forensic lab on its own network or subnet behind a separate firewall. It is generally a good idea to keep the forensic lab off the normal corporate network because of the research they may have to do. They may need to access the webpages that the person they are investigating accessed. These may be sites that violate corporate policies, and thus may be blocked or monitored by the organizations security team.

Evidence Identification and Storage

One of the fundamental components of computer forensics is the proper handling of evidence. Evidence is "anything that may be presented to determine the truth about a fact in question, or a fact from which another fact may be inferred."4 Evidence should be collected and marked in accordance with common accepted protocols and procedures. Once it arrives at the computer forensic lab it must be handled caution.

The first step in this process is the marking/labeling of evidence. Each forensics lab should have a prescribed manner for this process. For example, some computer forensic labs use a digital bar coding system. They can use specially designed evidence sheets along with a traditional bar coding software. There are two major evidentiary concerns—chain of custody and cross contamination. This means that you must properly mark each individual piece of evidence and keep it separated from evidence of a different case. This can be implemented in a variety of ways. They can range from extremely complex to rather simple.

The more complex implementation is the triple or double bar coding system. This is traditionally implemented in larger forensic labs. In this situation a series of labels are created using a traditional three column label sheet. Across each row the same identical bar code is printed into each of the three columns. When a piece of evidence arrives at the lab, each row is assigned to an individual piece of evidence. The bar code from each column is affixed to different components. For example one bar code would be affixed to the actual piece of evidence such as a floppy disc, compact disc or hard drive. A label from the same row would then be affixed to the corresponding item on the evidence sheet, and the final bar could be affixed to an evidence log. Some labels use a digital evidence log, which requires that all of the information from the evidence sheet be typed into the digital evidence log. The advantage of this sort of a tracking system allows a bar code reader to be connected to each doorway or evidence locker. As evidence is moved to various parts of the lab for processing, it can be simply scanned at the doorway. This allows for very accurate reports to be created on exactly where a certain piece of evidence is located at a particular time. Also these reports can be created by the crime lab for the court room and is very persuasive to a judge and jury.

However what if you are working in a one or two person computer forensics shop is all of this really necessary—probably not. Remember everyone in the chain of custody could be required to testify at trial. In the large forensic labs 20 or more people could handle the evidence. Many large forensics labs have full time evidence receiving technicians. The totality of their jobs is the in processing of evidence, however in a smaller shop this could be preformed by the computer forensic examiner or some combination of the two.

Next is the internal marking/labeling of the computer evidence, this varies wildly from person to person and reflects their particular training. My personal favorite is Home Depot's red electrical tape. Each piece of original evidence is marked with this red tape. The case number is written onto the tape, and a copy of the evidence sheet is attached to it. This allows each piece of evidence to be quickly identified. It also insures that evidence is not commingled.

Evidence storage will vary from lab to lab, but they should have a few things in common. Evidence should be stored in such as way as to prevent someone from modifying it without someone's knowledge. For example labs store their evidence inside of a safe at night. Others allow the evidence to only be outside of a locked container when someone is directly working on it. The original evidence and the image(s) then need to be stored in a secure place until they have been examined and the case is over. The case and evidence files may be stored on a server and then achieved to DVDs.

Environmental Controls

The forensic lab or workroom should be in an environmentally controlled condition. I remember listening to the stories of a friend of mine—Mike Toto with the Atlanta Federal Bureau of Investigation. Mike is part of the Computer Analysis Recovery Team (CART). He volunteered to assist with the Gulf War. He told stories about doing computer forensic examinations on the hood of a HUMVEE in full chemical protective suits. While there can be extenuating circumstances, it is very important to conduct your examination in the proper environment. Also keep in mind that computer can generate a lot of excess heat. If the computer system is not keep within the specified operating range than it can experience a much higher rate of failure.

The technical concern in any computer forensic lab is Electrostatic Discharge, which is the movement of electricity between two objects of dissimilar charges. While working on a computer forensics team in Atlanta, we noticed that our hard drives were failing quite often. One of my coworkers joked that the manufacturer's RMA team knew her by name, because of the sheer number of drives that we returned to them. Whenever we walked from one office to another it was not uncommon for us to be shocked when touching the door knob. This was caused by ESD. While we realized what was happening, we implemented a very aggressive ESD protection program. This program consisted of specially designed mats, workbenches and wrist bands. Once this program was fully implemented the rate of hard drive failure was greatly reduced. More great information can be obtained about electrostatic discharge at http://www.esda.org.

The room may have a dehumidifier if the local climate warrants it, as humidity and electronic equipment have a history of not playing nice together. The computers should have surge protectors and backup power supply for the forensics workstations

Forensic Computer Workstations

A good forensics workstations will typically cost between $5,000 to about $25,000 if it is pre-built, depending on the options. This is why many computer forensic specialists will build their own, and why not. They take apart and re-assemble computers in their normal days work. If the machine is built by the specialist it will generally only have the hardware the specialist has needed for past examinations and will generally be a more powerful machine than the pre-built models. This would be similar to comparing a standard production model Corvette to one an enthusiast has customized. The customized model will normally have more power, and may not be street legal. Personally

I have built my machines because I enjoy it, it is more cost effective, and mine are normally more powerful that the off the shelf forensic workstation. Another thing, do not be surprised to see the side panels missing from a forensic workstation. I typically keep mine off to allow better access to the internals incase I need it and to help the machine run cooler. On larger examinations the workstations may be running one or two days at near capacity preprocessing a case or performing complex procedures. During this time they will run hot. A couple of examples of computer forensic workstations that you can buy are the FRED® by Digital Intelligence and the Forensic Tower II® by Forensic computers.

It would be great if the forensic workstation was the only forensic computer we needed, but unfortunately it is not. It works great as long as the computers or computer storage media can be set to the specialist at the forensic lab. These forensic workstations do not work as well when you have to travel, especially if you have to fly with them. The contents of a travel kit will vary from examiner to examiner, but I will use my own as an example. Instead of lugging a workstation around with me I use a laptop computer. While I give up some power, I gain mobility. This is ok because most field work is making images of the computer storage media, not actual analysis work. Instead of a write protected drive bay that can be found on the workstation I have a write-blocking device that plugs into a USB or Firewire port on my lap top. I attach the hard drive to the write-blocker and I am safe from altering the original evidence. Then instead of a destination drive bay I have an external hard drive case that plugs into a USB port on the laptop. I also carry the tools to handle SCSI hard drives, floppy disk, CD's, DVD's, card media, RAID's, and other computer storage media as needed.

The travel kit will also have other items. When the specialist travels into the field to make an acquisition they usually have to open the computer up to document what is inside the box and then remove the hard drive. For this a tool kit is needed. In addition to the basic computer tool kit, I like to carry a Leatherman® folding scissors. A digital camera is a must; a picture is the easiest way to document a computer in its natural environment and the acquisition process. A few boot floppy disks and CD's are always nice to have just in case something unexpected happens. On one assignment I fly to the client sight to make the images, I was told just a few personal computers. When I get there they inform me that I needed to image a server with a RAID5 array of disks. Because I had the needed bootable CD's and a cross-over cable I was able to accommodate this request.

In addition to a cross-over cable, the traveling kit will have a variety of cat5 and other cables. A clock that sets its self to the atomic clock is nice as it is a good reference when taking notes and to compare to the computer's system time in case there is a difference. Various software manuals, software dongles, and restore CD's for the specialist's computer. These restore CD's are just in case something happens to corrupt the specialist's computer while they are in the field. And last, but very important is change for the Coke machine! Caffeine is very important, especially when you consider more field acquisitions take place during the night, early morning hours, or the weekend.

Chapter 11
Case Studies

Since the year 2000 there has been an increased awareness of what computer forensics can do and the need for this in legal cases. One of the headliners is the Enron and Arthur Anderson cases that brought down one of the largest international accounting firms and one of the largest international energy companies in the world. Then there were the much publicized trials of Michael Jackson and Scott Peterson. Each used computer forensics to attempt to prove or disprove allegations in their respective trials. In the Peterson trial a computer forensic "expert" stated that based on web surfing habits it was possible that Laci was on the Internet the morning she disappeared after Scott had already left.

The role of the computer forensics examiners plays a major role in growing number of investigations. In order to have a better understanding of this role it is necessary to understand the overall process. While this process may very to a degree in the hardware and software, the general stages actually are fairly well defined. To help explain this in very practical way, we would like to use several case examples.

These examples are not intended to represent any single case we have worked, but they are compilations of our experiences, training, imagination, past court cases that we have read about, and stories we have heard others tell. In each case we have tried to make sure several things were done incorrectly, because if everything was perfect it would be a boring case to study. These few cases do not include all possible scenarios nor do they include all possible mistakes that can be made. They are a few examples that are designed to get you to think about computer forensics.

Whistle Blower Case

Auditor uncovers company's senior executives are getting kickbacks from suppliers in the form of cash contributions to their 401K accounts. This was uncovered in a regular audit of the company's payroll. Using automated testing, all employees were reviewed for a selected month. This included re-calculating all deductions, including 401K, and comparing them to a third party. For the 401K part of this test the vendor provided the auditors with a count of all 401K monies received for the month and the total dollar amount for the month. This resulted in 1 more payment into the 401K program than expected and $300,000 more that what the company records had showed it had sent to the 401K vendor. The auditor in charge of the audit discussed this with the Director of Internal Audit, while this was a nice finding for the audit report, why would the company overpay its 401K? This would reduce earnings (though not noticeably) and could potentially lower the bonuses employees received.

The audit director decided to expand testing in two ways. First they would request the 401K vendor to provide a list of all money sent into the company's 401K plan from any source with the date received, amount, who sent it, and who received it. Second the audit team would review the company's 401K activity with the vendor to determine if there were any unusual or unexpected items. The review of the company's transactions showed that they were valid, appropriately documented, and properly recorded. The list from the vendor of payments received showed 4 payments, one every 3 months, from an offshore bank. While this was odd enough, it was discovered that the money from these payments went into the 401K plans of several of the company's executive officers. The Director of Audit was concerned by this and met with the chairperson of the company's Audit Committee to discuss the next steps. It was agreed that external legal counsel would be retained to investigate the matter.

The external law firm first set up a meeting with the auditors that had uncovered this to help determine the scope of the investigation and an action plan for the investigation. After reviewing the auditor's work papers they came up with a simple plan, to work with local state law enforcement to follow the money trail back to the source. Law enforcement was able to trace the money, with help of the off-shore bank's security team, through a series of accounts to a foreign company that proved to be nothing more than a facade.

In investigating what little could be found on this foreign company, one of the auditors recognized the name on the foreign company's incorporation records. The name was the same as one of the contacts at a major supplier for the company. This was the same name some confirmation notices were sent to for verification in another audit. Could the two people be the same person? It was a finding that warranted further investigation, and the auditors knew just how to do it. First the financial auditor began an audit of the vendor selection process. The information systems auditor scheduled a meeting with the corporate computer security officer (CCSO) to discuss what could be done.

In the meeting with the CCSO the situation was explained and a game plan was developed. The employees receiving the extra money in their 401K were discussed and the computer that they use (in this case their personal computers and a single email server) were identified. The CCSO immediately took the email server backup tapes out of the backup rotation and replaced them with new tapes. These backup tapes were then bagged up and locked in the CCSO's desk. Next the CCSO copied the contents of the identified employees to a new hard drive using Windows Explorer, creating a separate folder for each employee. This captured all of the items that the operating system could see, which is all the IS auditor & CCSO figured they would need, besides that is all there was.

The IS auditor began reviewing the copied items from the employee's hard drives and did not find the smoking gun they had hoped for. They did find some emails that referred to the vendor and their 401K accounts and some excel files that an employee was using to calculate their retirement. The retirement calculations included a contribution column in the Excel worksheet titled 'Other'. The amounts in the 'Other' column matched the contributions made from the off shore account, which the auditor figured made these files relevant to the investigation.

The financial auditors were finding a few oddities in their audit, particularly with the vendor in question. It seems that this vendor wins all of the contracts it bids on and is always the lowest priced bidder. Further review of these past contracts indicates the vendor has never missed a deadline and has never gone over budget. While this appears to be great, it is also unusual. The audit team then decided to confirm the losing bids for a few of the recent contract, and found something interesting. Of the three contracts selected to confirm that the losing companies actually bidded on the contract, none of the losing companies had any records of bidding on the contracts. They all stated that they could have done the job for less though. It appears that the contracts were awarded without and bidding taking place and then fake documentation was created to make it appear that it had.

These audit findings were discussed with the law firm's investigation team and law enforcement at their next meeting. Based on this they decided to bring in the computer forensics specialist to image the computers over the weekend and review them. The CCSO meets the computer forensic specialist that Friday night about 9:00 PM to start the imaging of the computers. They image 5 desktop computers and one email server. The specialist makes two images of each hard drive and the about 7:30 AM Saturday morning the imaging is done. About two weeks later the computer forensic specialist is ready to discuss preliminary finding with the investigation team.

In this meeting the computer forensic specialist details what was found so far. The IS auditor was interested in how deleted items were recovered, after all once a file is deleted it is gone for good, right? Besides, most of the items the forensic specialist found the IS auditor had found several weeks ago just poking around on the copy he and the CCSO had made. The IS auditor was quite proud of himself and then explained the process he went through. The Excel file he had found in the executive's personal directory the computer forensics specialist found in the unallocated space of the hard drive (it had been deleted) with a reference to the file in a deleted INFO2 file. The computer forensic specialist also found more emails and file fragments in the hard drive's unallocated space.

Although the forensic review of the five desktops and one email server did not find a smoking gun, it did help the investigation piece together enough information to exonerate two of the suspects and identify several employees that should have some knowledge of what was going on. These employees were more than willing to work with the investigation team to provide enough information to where the investigating law firm could build a strong case against several of the suspects.

Questions:

1. Was the computer forensics specialist brought onto the team at the best time?
2. What are the consequences of the IS auditor's 'poking round'?
3. Did the computer forensic specialist bring any value to the investigation?
4. Can anything else be done?

Last Minute Examination

A major international accounting firm was finishing up its annual audit for FY 2004 of a company and noticed that the numbers did not add up. Accounts receivable had increased each of the past two years, but cash collections had not increased. Further review began to reveal that accounts receivable has been tampered with. Accounts were not aging as they should and so would never make it to bad debt, thus over stating the amount in account receivable. Suspicions were furthered raised when one of the staff auditors found a printout of an email asking if Accounts Receivable had been "fixed" for the auditors, who were arriving next week. The email was from a former CFO, Thomas Fowler, who retired almost 2 year ago and was sent to an accounting supervisor, George 'G-Money' Mahoney, that left 3 years ago. The email dated July 4, 2004 was copied and placed in the audit work papers. The dollar amount was significant enough to delay the issuance of the audit report and could possible put the company in violation of their loan covenants. If the company was in violation of the loan covenants, bankruptcy could follow. This question of the company's ability to continue as a going concern had to be resolved. At this point an investigator was brought in on February 1, 2005 to examine the situation to determine what exactly had happened. If it was just one person doctoring the numbers or was there collusion among the executives.

The lead investigator was a very capable attorney, Petrovich 'Pete' Maddox, that knew the industry well. On his investigation team were former F.B.I. agents Certified Fraud Examiners (CFE) and Certified Public Accountants (CPA) that were experience in corporate fraud and investigations. As they began their investigation the external auditor strongly suggested that the computers used by the 'C' class executives, certain accounting managers, and the email server they used be forensically reviewed to see if there was in electronic evidence. This evidence could include spreadsheets, word documents, instant messages, emails, or other files that could relate to the irregularities and to determine if there was collusion. The investigators agreed, but the attorney in charge refused. Maddox view was that a forensic review of the computers would be expensive and useless. After all, items on a computer are volatile and if it related to the investigation would have been deleted and not recoverable, especially items like email.

The investigation continued for almost a year, nine months into the investigation the external auditors met with the attorney to discuss preliminary findings. When they discovered that the computers they suggested had not been reviewed, they were upset. They then informed the attorney leading the investigation and the company's general counsel that they would not sign off on the audit report until this was done. The attorney leading the investigation argued that he had never need to do this in an investigation and saw no reason why this on should be any different. The investigating attorney did have a backup plan just incase he needed it. A few weeks after the investigation started Maddox on February 14, 2005 had the IT staff at the company copy all of the Microsoft Office files (Excel, Word, Access, & PowerPoint) on the C-class executives to a separate hard drive. This was done over the network with Windows Explorer. This was nice, but did not satisfy the external auditors. This argument between the external auditors and the Maddox continued until two weeks before the investigator's report was due to the company and external auditors. At this point Maddox gave in and reluctantly agree to the forensic exam of the computers.

This put the forensic review of the computers on a tight schedule. The findings from the computer forensic specialist had to be delivered to the investigators within one week so the information could be reviewed and if needed included in the report. The scope of the examination was determined to be seven personal computers, one email server, and one backup tape of the email server. Considering that the examination of a single computer hard drive can take 40 hours or more, the examiner in charge of the computer forensics work did not have much time.

The best time to image computers in a business environment is on the weekends, for corporate servers it is after the Friday night backups are finished. Due to the Maddox's refusal to include computer forensics in the investigation until the last minute, there was only one weekend to complete the imaging.

Soon the computer forensic specialist was meeting with the CIO of the company to discuss the scope of the work. During this meeting we discussed the backup and retention policy and procedures of the company and how we were going to image the computers. The computer forensic specialist also verified that the personal computers that were to be imaged had not been replaced within the past year and that their hard drives had not been replaced. The email server was a different story. About 6 months ago the company had migrated from a legacy email system to Microsoft's corporate email solution. The forensic specialist secured the last known back-up tapes from this legacy email system as well as the latest back-up tapes from the current email system.

When a computer system is replaced in this situation it could be a problem, a very big problem. Most of the items computer forensics specialist typically finds that bring value to an investigation are the items someone is trying to hide or delete. When the computer hard drive is replaced, you normally lose all of the deleted items because only non-deleted files are copied over to the new hard drive. Since it had been over a year since the fraud being investigated had taken place, deleted items were probably the best bet in finding something. The investigators and the computer forensics specialist came to this conclusion because it had been over a year since the events in question. This gave people a year to delete anything they want to hide or destroy.

During the examination of the computers nothing was found that would support collusion among the employees in questions or anything else that indicated inappropriate activities had taken place. The computer forensics specialist did notice a couple of the hard drives had a folder called "Old C Drive" with a creation time stamp about 3 months after the attorney started the investigation. This type of folder is common when a new operating system is installed on the computer or the computer is replaced. When this happens, the selected work and personal files and folders are copied to the new hard drive. The items on the old computer that are not selected or that had been deleted would not be copied over. Then once the computer is sent to the junkyard it can be almost impossible to find.

The Maddox was not worried about the "Old C Drive" folder. He had a copy of everything he needed from the hard drives, the Microsoft files. He had reviewed the files and found an Excel spread sheet that appeared to be a schedule showing the company's accounts receivables, write-off to bad debt, bad debt recoveries from the collection agency, and how close they were to making the 'Numbers'. The attorney had then inserted a worksheet to the Excel file to create a sheet that compared these 'Numbers' to the covenants associated with the Bonds. He thought he could easily prove someone was 'cooking the books' with this. The searches by the forensic specialist had not found this Excel file, or any part of it.

The CIO was asked about the "Old C Drive" folder and started to do a little more research. He discovered that Sanchez and Mahoney had acquired new computer by expensing them and not ordering them through the IT department. The IT Help Desk then configured them and copied the files they wanted to keep to a folder on the new computer called "Old C Drive". These old computers had been reformatted and were in the help desk's staging area to be used as loaners. The CIO immediately took the 2 computers to his office so that no one else could use them; this was on June 19 or 20, 2005.

The forensic review of the personal computers, the current email server, and the back-up tapes associated with the current email server was completed. The review of the personal computers did not produce any evidence that would indicate fraud or collusion among current employees. The review of the email server did find the email from the former CFO that the external auditors had found. It was dated 6 months after he had retired, thus it was doubtful that he had actually sent it. The back-up tapes associated with the legacy email system have not been reviewed as there have been some problems with restoring them due to the old email system they had used.

The external auditors had the forensic specialist image the 2 computers that were secured by the CIO on June 28, 2005—prior to the issuance of the audit report. After the computers were imaged the computer were returned to the Help Desk and securely wiped, reformatted, and re-issued to Company employees. The external auditors are not happy with the results of the investigation and refuse to issue an un-qualified audit opinion. The auditors point to the hard copy of the email they found, the delay in imaging the computers, that no one at the company can explain how accounts receivable got messed up in the first place. Then there were the 2 computers found late in the game that had not been analyzed yet.

The audit report was issued on June 30, 2005 with a qualified audit opinion and the external auditors than resigned from the account. This action caused the company's stock to lose 45% of it value in one day. The company then filled a lawsuit against the former external auditor on July 8, 2005.

The company's executives state that the anomaly in accounts receivable was cause by a computer glitch and has been corrected. Management also asserted that this 'glitch' did not cause a material misstatement of the company's financials.

Potential Evidence Items

The email

A review of the email system did find this email. Both the sender and recipient were no longer with the company and there was no evidence found that could associate these former employees to the email. They had no known physical or virtual access to the company since they left. The email system did not keep any logs or other information that could be used to identify the sender and receiver of the email. IP addresses are assigned dynamically, so these were of no use in identifying who was using these email accounts. The forensic specialist did create a log sheet and chain of custody form for this.

The Excel spreadsheet from the Attorney

This seemed to prove that the books were being intentionally altered to make sure the bond covenants were not broken. It was copied to a hard drive by the IT staff under Maddox's supervision. These files had been validated with an MD5 Hash after being copied. Maddox then worked on this copy and even inserted a new worksheet to the Excel File. The original worksheet with the account receivables on it was 'protected' by Maddox so that he would not make any changes to it. Maddox did make an extra or back-up copy of this, when he first opened it he saved it as "Original—Bonus Ins.xls". On July 1, 2005 the forensic specialist imaged this hard drive. He could sense a lawsuit and wanted his work validated with a MD5 hash. The forensic specialist created a log sheet for this item on July 1, 2005, the day he imaged it. There are no chain-of-custody forms.

The Excel file has a creation date of February 14, 2005

The legacy backup-tapes

These tapes have yet to be recovered due to time constraints and difficulties recreating the needed environment for the Legacy system. The tapes are being stored by the forensic specialist. These tapes may be of some value as this email system was active while some of the alleged fraud was being committed. The forensic specialist kept a log sheet & chain of custody on these.

Two computers found in the Help Desk area

These were imaged by the forensic specialist just prior to the issuance of the external auditor's report. These images were not analyzed by Maddox and his investigation team. The hard drives with the images were taken by the external auditors for save keeping right after the image was done. There are log sheets but no chain of custody for these items.

Initial Statements

Ben Kenton, Computer Forensic Specialist used by Maddox during his investigation

Is very irritated that his bill, beyond his retainer, has not been paid yet and only agreed to testify after consulting his attorney. Mr. Kenton testified that he imaged the email server at the Company using EnCase over a cross-over cable. The server was booted with a special EnCase boot CD into a server mode; this was to ensure that the integrity of the data on the email server was preserved. The two computers that the CIO seized towards the end of the investigation were imaged using Ghost. Mr. Kenton explained that this request came to him while he was meeting with the external auditors and Mr. Maddox to discuss the findings and what else could be done, thus he did not have his imaging tools with him. The Company had an enterprise license for Ghost, so he used this tool to image the two computers. Mr. Kenton went into great detail to explain how a forensically sound image could be made using Ghost and the steps he took to ensure the images were good ones. Mr. Kenton admitted that due to time considerations, and at the request of the external auditor (Mr. Sisenburg), he did not validate these images. Normally he would validate an image with a MD5 hash.

Mr. Maddox esq. the investigating attorney

Admitted the he and Sisenburg attended the University of Georgia and were member of the same fraternity, though Sisenburg graduated 2 years before him. Mr. Maddox explained the procedures he and one of the system administrators took to copy the files from the executive's hard drives. He admitted that he did not image the files like the expensive forensic specialist did, but under the circumstances Windows Explorer worked just as well as any forensic tool. The desired files were copied to a spare hard drive the Company had (New, just out of the box—Maddox added). After this was done Maddox testified that he just attached the hard drive to his laptop with an external enclosure to a USB port. Once this was done Maddox carefully examined each file in it native environment (Word, Excel, etc.) to determine if it had any relevance to the investigation. When he found the "Smoking Gun" Excel file he used Excel to protect the worksheet that had the information on it and created a new worksheet to create his worksheet that tied the accounts receivable to the fraudulent scheme. Mr. Maddox saw no value in the two computers imaged on June 28. His investigation was done and he had more than enough evidence to make his case.

West Sisenburg—Managing partner for the external auditor

Sisenburg mentions that he had met Maddox while he was at UGA, but that the two never really spent much time together. They traveled in different social circles. Sisenburg testified that he had always had a good working relationship with the Company, up until this year. This year the Company's management became more difficult to work with and claimed that the audit tests were becoming an undue burden and should be minimized. Mr. Sisenburg also testified that he refused to reduce any of the audit test citing professional standards from the AICPA. Mr. Maddox stated that Company executives were almost in a panic when he showed them the email they found during field work and they took it stating they would get back to the auditors about this. Mr. Maddox stated that he kept the email and made copies for the work papers and one to show Company management.

Additionally Mr. Maddox testified that he believed the investigation was professional done and he was happy with the integrity of the findings. He admitted that he would have been happier if the computer forensic specialist was brought in sooner in the investigation.

Questions:

1. How could the use of a computer forensics specialist been more effective?
2. Did the investigating attorney leave himself open to any potential problems?
3. Are there any issues that could prevent the printed email that the auditors found from being admitted as evidence?
4. How could the investigation process concerning the Excel file, Original—Bonus Ins.xls been improved? What issues could keep this out of court?
5. Could the two computers found by the CIO be of any value to the case?

Appendix A
Annotated Case Law on Electronic Discovery

Kenneth J. Withers
Updated August 1, 2005

> Kenneth J. Withers works at the Federal Judicial Center in Washington DC as a Senior Judicial Education Attorney. His responsibilities include developing educational programs for federal judges and attorneys employed by the United States Courts, concentrating on Internet-based distance learning and information resources. Programs include electronic discovery, technology in the criminal justice system, and advanced uses of technology in the administration of justice. For more information about Kenneth please see his website, http://www.kenwithers.com/about/index.html.

I.   Data Preservation and Spoliation

Anderson v. Crossroads Capital Partners LLC, No. Civ. 01-2000, 2004 WL 256512 (D. Minn. Feb. 10, 2004). In a sexual harassment and whistle-blower suit, the defendant requested and obtained access to the plaintiff's personal computer. The defendant's examining expert reported that the hard drive found in the plaintiff's computer was manufactured more than two years after the alleged events and that the plaintiff had recently installed and used a file-wiping program called "CyberScrub." In response, the plaintiff claimed that she had been using the same computer throughout the litigation, despite changing the hard drive; she also disclaimed any intent to use CyberScrub to destroy potential evidence. The judge found that although the plaintiff's "exceedingly tedious and disingenuous claim of naïveté...defies the bounds of reason," her behavior was not egregious enough to warrant dismissal of the case. But since "[she] intentionally destroyed evidence," the court instead would give the jury an adverse-inference instruction during trial.

Arista Records, Inc. v. Sakfield Holding Co. S.L., 314 F. Supp. 2d 27 (D.D.C. 2004). In a copyright infringement suit, the central question was jurisdiction. The court ordered discovery limited to the jurisdictional issues, particularly discovery of the Internet servers that would presumably contain copies of the copyrighted works, Internet transaction histories, and subscriber information. When the plaintiffs' expert examined these servers, he found that the defendants had intentionally destroyed most of the data by running a "data wiping" program fifty times from a remote location after receiving notice of copyright claims. The court admonished the defendants for arguing that "it destroyed crucial evidence to prevent further transfer of music files" because the defendants "could have disconnected its website from the Internet in any number of ways without destroying one single file." But the court declined to "impose any particular sanctions as a result of these actions but instead grant[ed] plaintiffs the right to file appropriate motions for sanctions or otherwise in the future." On the jurisdictional issue, the court accepted the plaintiffs' expert's extrapolation from the fragmentary data recovered that approximately 241 users in the District of Columbia had downloaded approximately 20,000 copyrighted musical works. The defendants' claim, that plaintiffs' evidence was inadequate, lacked merit because "[d]estruction of evidence raises the presumption that disclosure of the materials would be damaging." Therefore the court held that the plaintiff had established "continuous and systematic contacts" between the defendant and the District of Columbia.

Capricorn Power Co. v. Siemens Westinghouse Power Corp., 220 F.R.D. 429 (W.D. Pa. 2004). In a liability case stemming from the failure of electric generator equipment, both the plaintiff and the defendant filed motions for data preservation orders. The court noted that the case law on the standard for issuing such orders is "scant" and that attempts to borrow the four-part test for injunctive relief are inappropriate. The court announced a new three-part test for data preservation orders:

1.   the level of concern the court has for the continuing existence and maintenance of the integrity of the evidence in question in the absence of an order directing preservation of the evidence;

2.   any irreparable harm likely to result to the party seeking the preservation of evidence absent an order directing preservation; and

3. the capability of an individual, entity, or party to maintain the evidence sought to be preserved, not only as to the evidence's original form, condition, or contents, but also as to the physical, spatial, and financial burdens created by ordering evidence preservation.

Applying this new test, the court concluded that the defendant's motion for a data preservation order was not justified or necessary. Likewise, the court denied the plaintiff's counter-motion, which appeared to have been filed as a "tactical, quid pro quo response to the [d]efendant's motion" rather than out of necessity.

Coleman (Parent) Holdings, Inc. v. Morgan Stanley & Co., No. CA 03-5045, 2005 WL 679071 (Fla. Cir. Ct., 15th Cir. Mar. 1, 2005), 2005 WL 674885 (Mar. 23, 2005). In a lawsuit alleging accounting fraud and misrepresentation in the sale of stock, the plaintiff filed a motion for sanctions, including an adverse-inference jury instruction for the defendant's destruction of e-mails. The defendant had a practice of overwriting e-mails after twelve months, although it was required by the SEC to retain e-mails for two years. The court had ordered the defendant to review backup tapes, conduct searches, produce e-mails and a privilege log, and certify compliance with discovery obligations. The defendant certified discovery as complete despite having failed to review more than 1,400 backup tapes. In its order dated March 1, 2005, the court granted the adverse-inference instruction sanction, noting that "the conclusion is inescapable that the defendant sought to thwart discovery" and "[the defendant] gave no thought to using an outside contractor to expedite the process…[knowing] it lacked the technological capacity to upload and search the data…and would not attain that capacity for months." In addition to the adverse-inference instruction and disqualification of counsel, the court made findings that shifted the usual burden in a fraud case onto the defendant to demonstrate that it did not commit the fraud alleged. Two weeks later, it was disclosed that the defendant had not informed the plaintiff or the court of thousands of additional backup tapes that existed but had not been secured or reviewed. In its order on March 23, 2005, the court revoked the pro hoc vice license of the defendant's trial lawyer and disqualified the law firm, forcing the defendant to seek substitute counsel two weeks before trial.

Convolve, Inc. v. Compaq Computer Corp., 223 F.R.D. 162 (S.D.N.Y. 2004). In a patent infringement suit involving disk drive technology, the plaintiff moved for an adverse inference jury instruction, alleging spoliation of e-mail messages and laboratory test results by the defendant. In considering the circumstances surrounding the destruction of the e-mail messages, the court noted that the duty to preserve potentially discoverable e-mail had clearly arisen, since the messages were composed and sent after litigation had commenced. However, the court found that the plaintiff had failed to establish that the e-mail messages in question had been destroyed intentionally, or that the e-mail messages had any significant bearing on the facts of the case. Regarding the laboratory test results, the court found that the "results" consisted of visual observations of waves displayed on an oscilloscope as disk drives were subjected to electrical variable currents. Since these "results" were ephemeral, "the preservation of the wave form in a tangible state would have required heroic efforts far beyond those consistent with [the defendant's] regular course of business." Citing the recently published proposed amendment to Fed. R. Civ. P. 37, the court held that absent a violation of a preservation order, no sanction was warranted.

Danis v. USN Communications, 53 Fed. R. Serv. 3d (West) 828 (N.D. Ill. 2000). The plaintiffs filed a motion for sanctions against the defendants for misconduct. The court found that the plaintiffs had demonstrated inadequate document maintenance on the part of the defendants, but the plaintiffs failed to establish either that the defendants intentionally destroyed documents or that the missing documents were "critical." While insufficient to compel a default judgment, the failure to take reasonable steps to preserve data at the outset of discovery resulted in a personal fine levied against an inside director of USN.

GTFM v. Wal-Mart Stores Inc., 49 Fed. R. Serv. 3d (West) 219 (S.D.N.Y. 2000). The defendant initially claimed that computer records the plaintiffs requested were not easily accessible and would place an undue burden on them. A year later the plaintiffs discovered that statement was false and that the defendant could have retrieved the desired information without difficulty, but since the elapsed time it would no longer be possible. The court ordered the defendant to pay attorneys' fees and costs expended to litigate the sanction motion and recover the data.

Harrison v. Jones, Walker, Waechter, Poitevent, Carrere & Denegre, L.L.P., 2004 WL 2984815 (E.D. La. Dec. 9, 2004), 2005 WL 517342 (Feb. 24, 2005). In a trade secret theft/unfair trade practices case filed in state court, the plaintiff obtained an ex parte "Order for Expedited Discovery to Preserve Evidence" under which the plaintiff entered the defendant's home business, accompanied by sheriffs, and imaged computer hard drives. The defendant filed this civil rights action in federal court. In December 2004, the federal court held that the civil rights claim, though yet unproven, would survive a motion to dismiss for failure to state a claim. Three months later, the federal court dismissed with prejudice the section 1983 conspiracy claim against the state court judge and the law firm, but dismissed without prejudice the civil rights claims against the remaining individuals, pending further proceedings in state court.

Hypro, LLC v. Reser, No. Civ. 04-4921, 2004 WL 2905321 (D. Minn. Dec. 10, 2004). In a theft of trade secrets/unfair business practices case, the plaintiff requested and obtained a temporary restraining order enjoining the defendant from engaging in a number of allegedly unfair business practices. In addition, the court granted the plaintiff's motion to preserve "all evidence, including electronic documents and electronic mail" during the pendency of the litigation because of the belief that the defendant had "previously attempted to destroy computer files regarding his involvement with other [d]efendants."

Keir v. Unumprovident Corp., No. 02 Civ. 8781, 2003 WL 21997747 (S.D.N.Y. Aug. 22, 2003). In an ERISA class action suit, the parties agreed to a data preservation order after several conferences. The order was very narrowly drawn and concentrated on preserving six days of e-mail records on the defendant's backup media and hard drives. However, the defendant's upper management did not communicate the order to its information technology (IT) staff for nearly two weeks, and most of its data-management functions had been outsourced to IBM, which failed to implement the required preservation. Although the court found that the defendant's failure to preserve the data was unintentional, it criticized the defendant's poor compliance with the preservation order. The court recommended that further action be taken to determine the feasibility of retrieving the lost data to which the plaintiffs were prejudiced, in order for the court to fashion an appropriate remedy.

Landmark Legal Foundation v. EPA ("Landmark II"), 272 F. Supp. 2d 70 (D.D.C. 2003) (mem.). In a civil suit stemming from a Freedom of Information Act (FOIA) request, the court issued a preliminary injunction ordering that the EPA refrain from "transporting, removing, or in any way tampering with information responsive" to the plaintiff's FOIA request. Subsequently, the hard drives of several EPA officials were reformatted, backup tapes were erased and reused, and individual e-mails were deleted. The plaintiff filed a motion for contempt. The court held that under the strict standards of Fed. R. Civ. P. 65, the order was sufficiently specific and the data destroyed went "to the heart" of the plaintiff's claims. The court found the EPA in contempt and ordered it to pay attorneys' fees and costs, but the court declined to hold several individuals and the U.S. Attorney's Office in contempt. Cf. Landmark I, under "Records Management" at III.

Lewy v. Remington Arms Co., 836 F.2d 1104 (8th Cir. 1988). In a product liability suit alleging defective design of rifles, documents concerning past consumer complaints relevant to the suit were destroyed. The trial court issued an instruction that the jury could infer that the destroyed documents would have provided evidence against Remington "as to whether the overwriting of drafts by the expert violated any duty of preservation of obligation under Fed. R. Civ. P. 26(a)(2)(B)." Remington appealed, claiming that the document destruction was routine, pursuant to the company's three-year records retention schedule. The appeals court remanded the case to the trial court for a determination of whether a three-year records retention schedule was reasonable in relation to the importance of each document, "whether lawsuits concerning the complaint or related complaints ha[d] been filed, the frequency of such complaints, and the magnitude of the complaints," and finally whether or not the policy was instituted in bad faith.

Linnen v. A.H. Robins Co., 1999 Mass. Super. LEXIS 240 (Mass. Super. Ct. July 15, 1999). In a wrongful death suit, the defense was initially enjoined from destroying evidence. The defendant succeeded in having the injunction vacated, but subsequently destroyed e-mails relevant to the plaintiff's case. The court could not issue monetary sanctions because the injunction had been vacated. However, the court held that a spoliation instruction to the jury was a reasonable sanction.

MasterCard International Inc. v. First National Bank of Omaha, Nos. 02 Civ. 3691, 03 Civ. 707, 2004 U.S. Dist. LEXIS 2485 (S.D.N.Y. Feb. 23, 2004). In a trademark infringement suit, the defendant moved in limine to exclude the testimony of the plaintiff's expert witness on the grounds that the expert destroyed e-mail correspondence with counsel and previous drafts of his report. The plaintiff, however, claimed it did not have e-mail correspondence with the expert, and the defendant did not produce evidence to the contrary. While the plaintiff's expert did overwrite prior drafts, the defendant's expert did as well. Since both parties followed the same practice, and neither provided drafts to opposing counsel, excluding testimony was not merited. In coming to its decision the court explicitly avoided the question as to overwriting's legitimacy under Fed. R. Civ. P. 26(a)(2)(B).

MasterCard International, Inc. v. Moulton, No. 03 Civ. 3613, 2004 WL 1393992 (S.D.N.Y. June 16, 2004) (mem.). In a trademark infringement suit against a website featuring a "fairly tasteless parody" of MasterCard's "Priceless" ad campaign, the defendants failed to take any measures to preserve e-mails until five months after the suit was filed, despite knowledge of the lawsuit and a discovery request. The plaintiff moved for spoliation sanctions. The court found that the defendant did not act in bad faith in deleting the e-mails, but that such actions were "grossly negligent." As simple negligence is the threshold of culpability, sanctions were therefore appropriate. The court denied the plaintiff's request to have key issues in the case "deemed conclusively established," because plaintiff did not make a compelling case as to likely significance of the e-mails. The court concluded that the appropriate sanction was an adverse-inference jury instruction.

McGuire v. Acufex Microsurgical, Inc., 175 F.R.D. 149 (D. Mass. 1997). In a sexual harassment lawsuit, the human resources director removed a paragraph of a report of an internal investigation of the sexual harassment allegations. Although normally removing a paragraph would qualify as destruction of evidence, the court held removing the paragraph was not misconduct because it was edited for accuracy. Corporations have an obligation to maintain truthful records, therefore the defendant had an obligation to remove the "false" statement, making sanctions inappropriate. The court appeared to limit its holding to the facts of the case.

In re Merrill Lynch & Co. Research Reports Securities Litigation, No. 02-MDL 1484, 01 CV 6881, 2004 WL 305601 (S.D.N.Y. Feb. 18, 2004). In a suit under the Private Securities Litigation Reform Act (PSLRA), the plaintiffs moved for an order lifting the PSLRA's automatic stay of discovery, claiming that discovery was necessary to preserve and restore deleted e-mails. The court held that part of the PSLRA's stay of discovery was a duty imposed on the parties to preserve all relevant evidence "as if they were the subject of a continuing request for production of documents," 15 U.S.C. § 78u-4(b)(3)(C), and therefore lifting the stay of discovery for the purpose of preserving such evidence, absent unusual circumstances, was unwarranted.

Metropolitan Opera Ass'n, Inc. v. Local 100, Hotel Employees & Restaurant Employees International Union, 212 F.R.D. 178 (S.D.N.Y. 2003). The plaintiff sued the defendant for improperly involving it in a labor dispute to which it was not a part. Contrary to counsel's representations, the defendant had failed to conduct a reasonable investigation in response to discovery requests, failed to prevent the destruction of documents, failed to adequately instruct the person in charge of document collection, and shortly before a scheduled on-site inspection allowed computers subject to discovery to be replaced with new computers. The court found that the defendant's behavior was in bad faith and constituted a "combination of outrages," and ordered judgment against the defendant and payment of attorneys' fees.

Morris v. Union Pacific Railroad Co., 373 F.3d 896 (8th Cir. 2004). In a case superficially resembling Stevenson v. Union Pacific Railroad Co., 354 F.3d 739 (8th Cir. 2004), decided by the same court just a few weeks earlier, the court held that Union Pacific's destruction of tape-recorded conversations between the train engineer and dispatcher at the time of an accident did not constitute spoliation, and that the plaintiff's motion for an adverse-inference jury instruction should have been denied by the trial court. The appellate court distinguished the two cases, stating that in Stevenson, the trial court made a specific finding that Union Pacific acted with requisite intent to destroy the tape recording for the purpose of suppressing evidence, while in the Morris case, the trial court found that the destruction was unintentional. The appeals court went on to state that the standard announced in Lewy v. Remington Arms, 836 F.2d 1104 (8th Cir. 1988), that a finding of spoliation could be sustained if the accused "knew or should have known" that the destroyed evidence would be relevant to pending or anticipated litigation, was to be replaced by a new standard requiring a trial court to find "intentional destruction indicating a desire to suppress the truth" before an adverse inference jury instruction could be issued.

New York State National Organization for Women v. Cuomo, No. 93 Civ. 7146, 1998 WL 395320 (S.D.N.Y. July 14, 1998), dismissed on other grounds sub nom. New York State National Organization for Women v. Pataki, 261 F.2d 156 (2d Cir. 2001). In a class action against the governor of New York and others alleging inadequate enforcement of discrimination laws, the plaintiffs sought sanctions for the defendants' failure to preserve a computer database of discrimination complaints and annual summaries of the data prepared for the governor's review. The court held that while a duty to preserve such relevant evidence arose long before an explicit document request was issued, "[d]efendants' counsel treated that obligation cavalierly. Counsel have a duty to advise their client of pending litigation and of the requirement to preserve potentially relevant evidence." However, absent any evidence of bad faith on the part of the defendants or prejudice to the plaintiffs' case, no sanction for spoliation was appropriate.

Propath Services, LLP v. Ameripath, Inc., Civ. A. 3:04-CV-1912-P, 2004 WL 2389214 (N.D. Tex. Oct. 21, 2004). In an unfair trade practices case, the plaintiff sought a temporary restraining order (TRO) enjoining the defendant from engaging in a number of allegedly unfair business practices. Included in the proposed TRO, however, was a clause prohibiting any act of the "[d]efendants deleting or destroying any documents or e-mails containing any ProPath related information and requiring such material to be segregated." The court's analysis focused exclusively on the other proposed clauses dealing with the use of trade secrets, customer lists, and other materials claimed by the plaintiff in the defendant's course of business. An amended TRO was granted by the court containing the following clause: "Defendants shall not delete, destroy, or alter any document, e-mail or computer drive containing any ProPath or ProPath related information, but shall segregate said items into a confidential file not to be used in their business."

In re Prudential Insurance Co. of America, 169 F.R.D. 598 (D.N.J. 1997). In a class action suit alleging deceptive sales practices by insurance agents, the defendant agreed to suspend its usual records retention schedule for sales literature nationwide in response to a document preservation order. Each field office had a detailed records-management handbook, which was updated often in the usual course of business, but the order to suspend destruction of sales literature was communicated by bulk e-mail, which was routinely ignored by the field agents. This finding and the defendant's pattern of failure to prevent unauthorized document destruction warranted a $1 million fine, reimbursement of the plaintiff's attorneys' fees for the motion for sanctions, and court-ordered measures to enforce the document preservation order. Also, the court stated it would draw an inference that the destroyed documents would have aided the plaintiff.

Pueblo of Laguna v. United States, 60 Fed. Cl. 133 (Fed. Cl. Mar. 19, 2004). In one of several cases against the United States for alleged mishandling of Indian land trusts, the plaintiff filed a motion for a document preservation order that would affect computer data as well as paper documents. The Court of Federal Claims, although an Article I court, held that it had the same scope of inherent powers as an Article III court to issue either a document preservation order or a preliminary injunction against the destruction of documents, if appropriate. The court also held that a document preservation order does not constitute an injunction and need not meet the strict requirements for injunctive relief. However, the court held that it should exercise its inherent powers with restraint and require that a party seeking a preservation order demonstrate that the order is necessary and not unduly burdensome. The plaintiff relied on the many acts of document destruction reported in Cobell v. Norton, a related pending class action involving many of the same organizations as this case, to establish the need for a protective order, which the court granted. However, the court narrowed the plaintiff's proposed document inspection, identification, and indexing protocol and adopted instead a protocol closer to the defendant's counterproposal.

Residential Funding Corp. v. DeGeorge Financial Corp., 306 F.3d 99 (2d Cir. 2002). Remanding the trial court's denial of a spoliation instruction, the court held the trial judge has the discretion to consider "purposeful sluggishness," resulting in denial of access to e-mail that may include discoverable data, an equivalent to spoliation for the purposes of Fed. R. Civ. P. 37. Conduct need not be willful and need not result in the physical destruction of the evidence to be sanctionable.

Sonnino v. University of Kansas Hospital Authority, 220 F.R.D. 633 (D. Kan. 2004). In an employment discrimination suit, the court overruled the defendant hospital's objection to an interrogatory seeking information about its computer and e-mail systems. The court also ruled that the brief response proffered by the defendant in a supplemental answer was inadequate, and it gave the defendant twenty days to provide a complete and full answer.

Strasser v. Yalamanchi ("Strasser II"), 783 So. 2d 1087 (Fla. Dist. Ct. App. 2001). In a breach of contract dispute, the appellants' employee threw a computer hard drive away after lightning damaged it. The appellee was not notified that the hard drive, an important piece of evidence, had been thrown away until almost a year later. Because of the critical nature of the hard drive to the appellant's case, the appellate court held that the trial court did not err when it allowed evidence to establish negligent destruction of evidence or spoliation. Cf. Strasser I, under "Scope of Electronic Discovery" at II.

Thompson v. United States HUD, 219 F.R.D. 93 (D. Md. 2003) (mem.). In a suit against the Department of Housing and Urban Development, the court entered an order under Fed. R. Civ. P. 37(b)(2) precluding the United States from calling certain witnesses until it either answered certain outstanding requests for the production of e-mail or demonstrated to the court's satisfaction that responsive e-mail did not exist. Later, after the deadline set by the court and on the eve of trial, the United States produced approximately 80,000 responsive e-mails. The court acknowledged that electronic discovery is expensive and a cost-benefit analysis under Fed. R. Civ. P. 26(b)(2) is appropriate when the burdens alleged are supported by facts, but when no such facts are presented, sanctions for failure to respond to discovery requests are appropriate. In determining an appropriate sanction, the court applied a five-part test:

1. surprise to the party against whom the evidence would be entered;
2. ability of that party to cure the surprise;
3. extent of possible disruption to the trial;
4. importance of the evidence; and
5. explanation for failure to produce the evidence in discovery.

Applying these factors, the court ordered that the United States be precluded from entering any of the e-mails into evidence and that U.S. attorneys be forbidden to use any of the e-mails in preparing witnesses. The plaintiffs were allowed to use the e-mails as evidence if they so chose and were invited to move for costs and attorneys' fees necessitated by last-minute review of the e-mails for trial. In addition, if evidence from the trial regarding the nonproduction of these e-mails justified it, the plaintiffs could move for contempt of court against the United States.

Trigon Insurance Co. v. United States, 204 F.R.D. 277 (E.D. Va. 2001). In a corporate taxpayer suit against the United States, the United States hired a litigation support firm, which in turn hired experts to act as consultants and testifying experts. The litigation support firm had a policy under which all e-mail communications with experts and draft reports were destroyed. The court held that under the facts of this case, those communications and drafts would have been discoverable, and the United States was responsible for its litigation support firm's intentional spoliation. The court found that adverse-inference instructions regarding the content of the destroyed electronic documents were warranted along with paying attorneys' fees. The court noted that "the degree of culpability, and the quantum of prejudice" must be taken into account to determine the "least severe, but most effective sanction."

United States v. Philip Morris USA Inc., 327 F. Supp. 2d 21 (D.D.C. 2004). A blanket data-preservation order was entered early in this national tobacco products litigation. The defendant, however, for at least two years continued its routine practice of deleting e-mail messages more than sixty days old. After discovering this apparent violation of the order, counsel for the defendant delayed informing the court about it for an additional four months. The United States moved for sanctions against the defendant. The court found that eleven of the company's highest placed officers and supervisors violated not only the court order, but also the company's stated policy for electronic records retention. The court fined the defendant $250,000 per employee, for a total of $2,750,000, and precluded the defendant from calling any of the eleven employees as witnesses at trial.

Welch v. Wal-Mart, No. 04 C 50023, 2004 WL 1510021 (N.D. Ill. July 1, 2004). In a personal injury suit involving the collapse of a display in a Wal-Mart store, the plaintiff included separate counts for the negligent spoliation of evidence, and alternatively, for the intentional spoliation of evidence, based on Wal-Mart's destruction of surveillance videotape that the plaintiff claimed had recorded the entire incident. The court, applying Illinois law, found that the count for negligent spoliation could only survive the defendant's motion to dismiss if the plaintiff could show that Wal-Mart had a duty to preserve the videotape. The court found that Wal-Mart could not have reasonably foreseen that the videotape was material to a potential civil action. Therefore the negligent spoliation court was dismissed. However, the court held that the plaintiff's count for intentional spoliation, which did not depend on the element of a duty to preserve the evidence, could survive the motion to dismiss.

Wiginton v. Ellis ("Wiginton I"), No. 02 C 6832, 2003 WL 22439865 (N.D. Ill. Oct. 27, 2003). In a putative class action alleging sexual harassment, the plaintiff's counsel notified the defendant's counsel by letter to halt all destruction of potential paper and electronic evidence. The court held the letter did not create a duty to preserve data, but it did put the defendant on notice of the type of data that would be sought during discovery. The defendant had a duty to preserve documents that might be relevant at trial and by ignoring that duty and destroying e-mails the defendant acted in bad faith. Using backup tapes, it would be possible to determine the importance of the missing e-mails. Sanctions should be proportional to the degree of harm to the party, therefore the motion for sanctions was dismissed without prejudice. If the plaintiff's expert discovered important information on the backup tapes sanctions might be appropriate.

Wm. T. Thompson Co. v. General Nutrition Corp., 593 F. Supp. 1443 (C.D. Cal. 1984). In an antitrust lawsuit, the defendant destroyed documents that were critical to the case. The defendant, knowing a lawsuit might be pending, destroyed business records that would have been relevant to the plaintiff's case. The practice continued even after a special master twice ordered the defendant to preserve its business records. The court held a default against the defendant was appropriate because the defendant "purposefully undertook a program [that] impede[d] and obstruct[ed] the litigation process." Plaintiff was awarded $453,312 for costs in addition to attorney's fees with interest.

Zubulake v. UBS Warburg ("Zubulake V"), No. 02 Civ. 1243, 2004 WL 1620866 (S.D.N.Y. July 20, 2004). In this opinion, the fifth published in this employment discrimination lawsuit, the court considered the plaintiff's motion for sanctions against the defendant UBS Warburg for deleting e-mails the plaintiff claimed would support her allegations of sex discrimination. The court found that, contrary to instructions from both outside counsel and in-house lawyers, certain UBS employees deleted relevant e-mails. UBS counsel failed "both in terms of its duty to locate relevant information and in its duty to preserve and timely produce that information." In addition, the defendant failed to preserve backup tapes on which copies of the destroyed e-mails might have been found. The court held that an adverse-inference jury instruction and an award of costs were appropriate, based on the apparent willful misconduct of certain UBS employees in destroying the e-mails. In a footnote, the court stressed that the sanctions were not based on the negligent failure to preserve the backup tapes; the defendant was sanctioned for its employees' willful destruction of e-mails.

II. Scope of Electronic Discovery

Anti-Monopoly, Inc. v. Hasbro, Inc., No. 94CIV.2120, 1995 WL 649934 (S.D.N.Y. Nov. 3, 1995). The plaintiff made a motion to compel the defendants to provide certain data-processing files. The defendants contended that they had provided duplicate information in hard copy and that the motion would force the company to create new documents. Relying on National Union Electric Corp. v. Matsushita Electric Corp., 494 F. Supp. 1257 (E.D. Pa. 1980), the court rejected both of the defendants' arguments. The court stated that the plaintiff was not precluded from asking for electronic data that it already had in hard copy or electronic documents that would have to be created. However, the reasonableness of creating new documents may depend on the plaintiff's willingness to pay the costs to do so.

Bethea v. Comcast, 218 F.R.D. 328 (D.D.C. 2003) (mem.). In an employment discrimination suit, the defendant stated that after making a diligent search, it had no documents responsive to one of the plaintiff's requests for production. Dissatisfied with the result, the plaintiff made a motion to allow it to inspect the defendants' computer systems believing relevant data existed on them. The court rejected the motion because the plaintiff was relying on mere speculation and could not demonstrate the relevance of compelling discovery.

Byers v. Illinois State Police, 53 Fed. R. Serv. 3d (West) 740 (N.D. Ill. June 3, 2002) (mem.). The plaintiffs in a sex discrimination case requested discovery of e-mail backup tapes going back eight years. The court distinguished paper discovery from electronic discovery, noting the sheer volume of electronic documents available. Given the substantial cost in retrieving electronic documents, a cost-benefit analysis was necessary. The plaintiffs failed to prove that any of the e-mails from the past eight years would support their case. The court held that if the plaintiffs wanted to retrieve the e-mails they would have to bear the costs of licensing the defendant's old e-mail program.

Compuware Corp. v. Moody's Investors Services, Inc., No. Civ. 03-70247, 2004 WL 2931401 (E.D. Mich. Dec. 15, 2004). The defendant in this unfair trade practices case requested "[a]ll documents, including but not limited to internal memoranda, internal e-mails, and correspondence with [IBM] or any other entity or person, referring or relating to actual or potential effects on Compuware's business of any past, present, future, or contemplated conduct by IBM." After initially objecting that the request was overbroad, the defendant responded by producing all of the requested documents, estimated in the "tens of millions," on compact disks. Arguing that the production was overbroad, the defendant asked the judge to narrow the scope of its own request and order the plaintiff to index the documents on the

CDs and designate those that were relevant to the subject matter of the dispute. The court denied the request.

Cumis Insurance Co. v. Diebold, Inc., No. Civ.A.02-7346, 2004 WL 1126173 (E.D. Pa. May 20, 2004). In an insurance recovery action against an armored car operator stemming from the misappropriation of funds intended to be used to replenish the cash of the insured credit union's automated teller machines, the court ordered the defendant to produce requested computer data. The plaintiff sought additional electronic documents from the defendant. The court briefly touched on the relative burdens of the parties in discovery—the requesting party's burden of demonstrating relevance, and the responding party's burden of demonstrating why the requested discovery should not be permitted. The requesting party in this case went beyond showing relevance and countered the defendant's argument that it had already produced all relevant computer data by bringing into court relevant electronic documents and e-mails obtained from other sources that the defendant had not produced.

Fennell v. First Step Designs, Ltd., 83 F.3d 526 (1st Cir. 1996). In a lawsuit alleging wrongful termination, the district court denied the plaintiff's motion for further discovery under Fed. R. Civ. P. 56(f) and granted the defendant summary judgment. On appeal, the court held that the district court had not abused its discretion. The court noted there would be great costs involved if it granted the plaintiff discovery of the defendant's hard drive without any demonstrable benefit. Also, the plaintiff's motion was not sufficiently specific, giving the district court reasonable concern that further discovery would be a "fishing expedition."

In re Ford Motor Co., 345 F.3d 1315 (11th Cir. 2003). In a design-defect suit against Ford, the district court granted the plaintiff's motion to compel direct access to Ford's extensive dealer and customer contact databases without a hearing and before Ford had responded to the motion. Granting a writ of mandamus to vacate the district court's discovery order, the court of appeals held that the district court had abused its discretion. No findings were made that Ford had failed to comply with previous discovery orders, and the district court did not offer an explanation for its order. Further, the district court granted access to Ford's entire database, much of which was beyond the scope of discovery.

Hagemeyer North America Inc. v. Gateway Data Sciences Corp., 222 F.R.D. 594 (E.D. Wis. 2004). In a commercial dispute between two corporations, deposition testimony of one of the defendant's "top executives" indicated that computer backup tapes might contain e-mail files and accounting records. The plaintiff moved for production of the backup tapes, which had already been made available as part of a larger production of all of the defendant's business records, and upon which the plaintiff had already performed some cursory searches, resulting in no relevant documents. The court refused to compel production of all the backup tapes without a more substantial showing of a likelihood that responsive documents would be found. Adopting the approach of McPeek v. Ashcroft, 202 F.R.D. 31 (D.D.C. 2001), the court ordered the defendant to restore three sample backup tapes and for the parties to make additional submissions on the benefits and burdens of the proposed discovery, based on the results. The court also announced that it would adopt the factors set out in Zubulake v. UBS Warburg, 217 F.R.D. 309 (S.D.N.Y. 2003), to consider whether costs for any further production should be shifted to the plaintiff.

Marcin Engineering, LLC v. Founders at Grizzly Ranch, LLC, 219 F.R.D. 516 (D. Colo. 2003). In a construction-engineering suit, the defendant's motion for an extension of time for discovery of the plaintiff expert's computer drafts and preliminary work was denied. The motion came five days before the deadline for expert disclosure and the defendants had for five months delayed reviewing paper materials originally produced to them. The court stated that delay and carelessness in requesting electronic discovery are not compatible with the showings of diligence and good cause necessary to extend discovery deadlines or delay summary judgment under Fed. R. Civ. P. 56(f). Furthermore, the defendant had been repeatedly advised by the court that its proposed discovery, "when considered in the light of the amounts claimed as damages, made no economic sense."

McPeek v. Ashcroft ("McPeek I"), 202 F.R.D. 31 (D.D.C. 2001). In a sexual harassment lawsuit, the plaintiff sought a motion to compel discovery of backup tapes that might contain deleted e-mails. The court noted electronic discovery can be prohibitively expensive if left unchecked, and only discovery that justified the cost of retrieving electronic data should be granted. To determine the costs and possible benefits of allowing discovery for backup tapes, the court granted limited discovery of a sample time period where the defendant would retrieve e-mails for one year and document the costs associated with the retrieval process. Then the court would be able to properly assess the appropriate level of discovery based on the costs and whether discoverable information was uncovered.

McPeek v. Ashcroft ("McPeek II"), 212 F.R.D. 33 (D.D.C. 2003). Following up on a previous ruling in the same case, the court held that after ordering the "sampling" of a large collection of backup tapes, the resulting data supported further discovery of only one of the tapes. The opinion includes a detailed description of the sampling methods used to reach the conclusion.

Medical Billing Consultants, Inc. v. Intelligent Medical Objects, Inc., No. 01 C 9148, 2003 WL 1809465 (N.D. Ill. Apr. 4, 2003) (mem.). In a copyright and trade secret appropriation case, the defendants moved to allow on-site inspection of the plaintiff's computers. The court held that absent any showing that the plaintiff's disclosures and responses to prior requests were inadequate or that more evidence was likely to be discovered, the request would be denied as unduly burdensome.

Nicholas v. Wyndham International, Inc., 373 F.3d 537 (4th Cir. 2004). In a personal injury suit brought by the parents of a minor child alleging that an employee of the defendant resort hotel had molested the child, the defendant sought discovery of computer information from the parents' non-party family business in another district under Fed. R. Civ. P. 45. The family business filed a motion for a protective order in its home district. After consultation with the judge presiding in the original litigation, the judge in the home district granted the protective order, finding that the requested discovery was cumulative, unduly burdensome, and harassing. The defendant appealed the district court's order. The Fourth Circuit found that the order denying discovery, unlike an order granting discovery, was not interlocutory, but final and ripe for appeal. That finding allowed the court to decide the issue of discovery. The appellate court applied the "abuse of discretion" standard and upheld the district court's findings and order.

SEC v. Beacon Hill Asset Management LLC, No. 02-CIV-8855, 2004 WL 1746790 (S.D.N.Y. Aug. 3, 2004). In an enforcement action by the Securities and Exchange Commission (SEC) against a hedge fund management company, the defendant listed a number of documents on a privilege log, which it produced to the SEC in a timely manner. Absent from the privilege log was a printout of customer contacts from the defendant's marketing management software. The printout appeared on a supplemental privilege log three weeks after the court-imposed deadline. The SEC moved to compel production of the printout, claiming that privilege was waived by the defendant's deliberate failure to list the printout on its privilege log. The defendant argued that it generated the printout only after it submitted the timely privilege log, and therefore the printout did not exist at that time. The court held that the defendant failed to list the database from which the printout was derived on its privilege log in a timely manner, and therefore the printout should be produced.

Stallings-Daniel v. Northern Trust Co., 52 Fed. R. Serv. 3d (West) 1406 (N.D. Ill. 2002). In an employment discrimination case, the plaintiff moved to allow her to use an expert to analyze the defendant's e-mail system. The plaintiff asked the court to reconsider a prior denial of a similar motion based on the "new" information that in another case the defendant may have tampered with documents. The court denied the plaintiff's motion because it was based on speculation as to the defendant's actions in an unrelated case.

Strasser v. Yalamanchi ("Strasser I"), 669 So. 2d 1142 (Fla. Dist. Ct. App. 1996). In a lawsuit involving the dissolution of a medical partnership, the plaintiff made a motion to access the computer system of the defendant. The court overruled the trial court and denied the plaintiff access. Some of the information in the system was privileged and "once confidential information is disclosed, it cannot be 'taken back.'" If the plaintiff could establish a strong likelihood that purged information would be relevant to the case and that the suggested means was the least intrusive method, then discovery might be appropriate. Cf. Strasser II, under "Data Preservation and Spoliation" at I.

Williams v. Massachusetts Mutual Life Insurance Co., 226 F.R.D. 144 (D. Mass. 2005). In an employment discrimination case, the plaintiff alleged that there was a discriminatory e-mail, but could not produce a copy of it. The defendants reported that they had no such e-mail and the plaintiff moved for appointment of a special master to conduct a forensic examination of the defendant's computer system. The defendant objected. The court rejected the motion noting that the plaintiff's belief of the existence of the e-mail was "at best [a] highly speculative conjecture." Without "some reliable information that the opposing party's representations are misleading or substantively inaccurate," the court was unwilling to grant the plaintiff access to the defendant's information system.

Wright v. AmSouth Bancorporation, 320 F.3d 1198 (11th Cir. 2003). In an age discrimination lawsuit, the Eleventh Circuit held that the trial court did not abuse its discretion when it denied the plaintiff's request for discovery of "[a] computer diskette or tape copy of all word processing files created, modified and/or accessed by, or on behalf" of five employees of the defendant over a two-and-one-half-year period. The request was not reasonably related to the plaintiff's age discrimination claims, and the court found that the request was overly broad and unduly burdensome.

III. Records Management

In re Cheyenne Software, Inc., Securities Litigation, No. CV-94-2771, 1997 WL 714891 (E.D.N.Y. Aug. 18, 1997) (mem.). In a securities litigation lawsuit, the court held that routine recycling of computer storage media must be halted during discovery when that is the most reasonable means of preserving available data. But the court refused to give an adverse jury instruction, because the plaintiff had not proved prejudice—instead the court ordered the defendant to pay $15,000 in fees and fines.

Heveafil Sendirian (Sdn.) Berhad (Bhd.) v. United States, Nos. 02-1085, 02-1086, 02-1087, 2003 WL 1466193 (Fed. Cir. Mar. 19, 2003) (order not to be cited as precedent). The Federal Circuit affirmed the judgment of the U.S. Court of International Trade in refusing to admit into evidence computerized business records that, in the trial court's view, were "at best, an unauthenticated duplicate of a database which may have been generated in the ordinary course of business." The Federal Circuit explained that the manufacturer "did not produce evidence explaining how the copy was made, such as an affidavit by an employee with pertinent knowledge verifying the accuracy of the database," and that key source documentation was not retained. The court stated, "[w]hile Commerce could have taken Heveafil's word for the authenticity of the diskette copy...we cannot conclude that Commerce abused its discretion in rejecting the diskette copy when the authenticity of that purported copy was not established."

Kozlowski v. Sears, Roebuck & Co., 73 F.R.D. 73 (D. Mass. 1976). Before the widespread use of computers, Sears, Roebuck recorded all customer complaints about products on index cards, which were organized by the name of the complainant and with no cross-indexing, making it almost impossible to search the vast collection for complaints about the same or similar products. When Sears was sued for selling children's pajamas made from highly flammable fabric, it argued that discovery of all complaints about flammable pajamas would be unduly burdensome and therefore should not be allowed. The court held that Sears was under an obligation to answer the discovery request, stating that "to allow a defendant whose business generates massive records to frustrate discovery by creating an inadequate filing system, and then claiming undue burden, would defeat the purposes of the discovery rules."

Landmark Legal Foundation v. EPA ("Landmark I"), 272 F. Supp. 2d 59 (D.D.C. 2003) (mem.). After news articles appeared nationally claiming that the Environmental Protection Agency (EPA) was trying to push through regulations before the Bush administration took office, the plaintiff filed a Freedom of Information Act (FOIA) request seeking records about the EPA's rule-making activities in the months before January 20, 2001. Dissatisfied with the response to the FOIA request, the plaintiff filed suit. In particular, the plaintiff claimed that the EPA violated FOIA by not maintaining agency e-mail in a central file in "readily reproducible" form. The court disagreed, holding that the EPA practice of printing out e-mail and filing it in various files by subject matter was a reasonable practice and did not violate FOIA. In addition, the court held that the EPA's search for responsive documents was reasonable and adequate, and that the plaintiff cannot require a particular search methodology in its FOIA request. Finally, the plaintiff complained that the EPA had destroyed documents subject to its FOIA request. The court held that although this was troubling, FOIA is not a records management statute, and the document destruction issue would be dealt with as a separate matter. Cf. Landmark II, under "Data Preservation and Spoliation" at I.

Public Citizen v. Carlin, 184 F.3d 900 (D.C. Cir. 1999). In a case disputing the validity of the records management schedule known as GRS 20, the National Archivist stated that federal agency e-mail could be migrated to archival media, and once migrated, original messages left in native format on desktop computers and network servers need not be preserved. The Archivist's migration plan preserved the content of the records and all necessary information from which the provenance of the records could be determined, although the archival media selected (in this case, paper) did not allow for easy searching and sorting. The district court held that GRS 20 violated the Records Disposal Act, 44 U.S.C. § 3303a(d) (see Public Citizen v. Carlin, 2 F. Supp. 2d 18 (D.D.C. 1998)). On appeal, the circuit court reversed the decision, noting that the plaintiff had confused form with substance and holding that the Archivist can reasonably "permit agencies to maintain their recordkeeping systems in the form most appropriate to the business of the agency."

Rambus, Inc. v. Infineon Technologies AG, 220 F.R.D. 264 (E.D. Va. 2004). In a complex patent infringement suit involving counterclaims of fraud, the defendant sought discovery of documents, including attorney—client communications, relating to the plaintiff's document retention program, on the theories that (1) the document retention program resulted in the intentional spoliation of relevant documents (as found by the court in a previous proceeding), and therefore the crime/fraud exception to the attorney—client privilege applied; and (2) by disclosing details of the document retention program in discovery, the plaintiff had waived any privilege. The document retention program featured a "Shred Day," on which employees of the plaintiff were rewarded with pizza and beer after destroying an estimated 2 million pages of documents. While there was no Fourth Circuit precedent for the court to rely on, the court held that "the crime/fraud exception extends to materials or communication created for planning, or in furtherance of, spoliation." The court found that the plaintiff's document retention program was developed at approximately the same time as plans to file this lawsuit. The plaintiff alleged that it instituted the program as a result of concerns over the cost of discovery. The court held that even if the plaintiff "did not institute its policy in bad faith, if it reasonably anticipated litigation when it did so, it is guilty of spoliation." The court ordered an in camera review of the documents on the plaintiff's privilege log to determine the extent to which both the crime/fraud exception and the subject-matter waiver applied.

Renda Marine, Inc. v. United States, 58 Fed. Cl. 57 (Fed. Cl. 2003). In a contract dispute filed by a marine dredging contractor against the U.S. Army Corps of Engineers, the plaintiff moved to compel production of backup tapes and for permission to access the contracting officer's computer hard drive. The policy of the corps was that after an e-mail was read, it was either deleted or moved to a personal folder immediately. The court found that this practice continued after the defendant had been put on notice that litigation might be pending, thereby breaching a duty to preserve documents. Thus, the court granted the plaintiff's motion to compel the defendant to produce the backup tapes at its own expense and to provide access to the contracting officer's computer hard drive.

IV. Form of Production

In re Bristol-Myers Squibb, 205 F.R.D. 437 (D.N.J. 2002). Early in the litigation of a securities fraud suit the parties had agreed to paper production and a per-page price for photocopying. However, the defendant did not disclose that the documents had been scanned, were being "blown back" to paper form at a cost below that of photocopying, and were available in electronic form for considerably less money. The court held the parties to the agreement to produce paper, but at the lower cost of the "blow backs," and ordered that the electronic versions also be produced, at the nominal cost of duplicating compact disks. The court rejected the defendant's argument that the plaintiff contribute to the cost of scanning the documents, as that action was taken unilaterally by the defendant, who, for its own purposes, didn't inform the plaintiff. Finally, the court lamented that the parties did not take the "meet and confer" obligations of Fed. R. Civ. P. 26(f) seriously in light of electronic discovery.

Hagemeyer North America, Inc. v. Gateway Data Sciences Corp., 222 F.R.D. 594 (E.D. Wis. 2004). In a dispute between two corporations, the plaintiff requested that the defendant search its backup tapes and identify responsive e-mails. The defendant objected, citing undue burden, because of the significant cost involved. The court, relying on the test in Zubulake v. UBS Warburg, 217 F.R.D. 309 (S.D.N.Y. 2003), ordered that information from a sample of backup tapes be taken to help determine "whether the burden or expense of satisfying the entire request is proportionate to the likely benefit."

In re Honeywell International, Inc., No. M8-85 WHP, 2003 WL 22722961 (S.D.N.Y. Nov. 18, 2003). In a putative securities class action, the plaintiffs served a subpoena on non-party PriceWaterhouseCoopers

(PWC), the defendant's auditor. PWC produced 63,500 pages of financial work papers in hard-copy form. The plaintiff moved to compel the production in electronic form, claiming that the data as produced were neither in business record order nor labeled to correspond to the categories of the request, as required by Fed. R. Civ. P. 34. PWC opposed the motion to compel because it had produced the information sought in paper form and recreating it electronically would cost $30,000. The court acknowledged that PWC had produced paper versions but stated it was "insufficient because they were not produced as kept in the usual course of business." The court required that PWC produce the data in electronic form and said that PWC could avoid the $30,000 expense by also producing the proprietary software to access the data. The court noted that the plaintiffs were not competitors and a confidentiality order was already in place, so PWC's trade-secret interests would be adequately protected.

In re Lorazepam & Clorazepate, 300 F. Supp. 2d 43 (D.D.C. 2004). In an anti-trust lawsuit, the plaintiff sought to compel the defendant to provide a searchable index of the "mountain" of electronic documents that had been provided. The defendant had previously given the plaintiff CD-ROMs with the material, but they proved unreadable and unsearchable. The court held that the plaintiff must have a company that specializes in computer forensics determine if the CD-ROMs were salvageable. McNally Tunneling Corp. v. City of Evanston, No. 00 C 6979, 2001 WL 1568879 (N.D. Ill. Dec. 10, 2001). In a lawsuit for breach of contract, the plaintiff made a motion to compel delivery of electronic documents, which it already had in hard copy. The court noted that case law was split on whether a party is entitled to discovery in electronic form as well as paper form, citing Williams v. Owens-Illinois, 665 F.2d 918 (9th Cir. 1982), which denied a request for computerized data to supplement paper production, and Anti-Monopoly, Inc. v. Hasbro, Inc., No. 94CIV.2120, 1995 WL 649934 (S.D.N.Y. Nov. 3, 1995), which held that a party is entitled to both hard-copy and computerized data. Since the motion was not supported by controlling case law, however, the court denied the defendant's motion because it "failed to demonstrate that it is entitled to both [a] hard copy and an electronic version[ ]."

Northern Crossarm Co. v. Chemical Specialties, Inc., No. 03-C-415-C, 2004 WL 635606 (W.D. Wis. Mar. 3, 2004). The plaintiff filed a motion to compel the production of 65,000 e-mail messages in electronic form after the defendant had produced the requested e-mails in paper form. The court held that the plaintiff was not entitled to its preferred form of production under Fed. R. Civ. P. 34. Absent a specific request for the production to be in electronic form, and absent any showing that the form chosen by the producing party constituted a "sharp tactic" or "gamesmanship," the court refused to grant the plaintiff's motion based only on "an unfortunate failure to communicate adequately."

Physicians Interactive v. Lathian Systems, Inc., No. CA 03-1193-A, 2003 WL 23018270 (E.D. Va. Dec. 5, 2003) (mem.). In a civil suit against alleged hackers for theft of customer lists and trade secrets, the plaintiff moved for expedited discovery to enter the sites where the defendants' computers were located and make "mirror" or bitstream images of the hard drives. The court stated the plaintiff must meet the four-part test from Blackwelder Furniture Co. v. Selig Manufacturing Co., 550 F.2d 189 (4th Cir. 1977), for a preliminary injunction which requires consideration of (1) the likelihood of irreparable harm to the plaintiff if the preliminary injunction is denied; (2) the likelihood of harm to the defendant if the requested relief is granted; (3) the likelihood that the plaintiff will succeed on the merits; and (4) the public interest, as well as the test for expedited discovery requiring "unusual circumstance...that would likely prejudice the party if they were required to wait the normal time." The court held that the plaintiff withstood the Blackwelder test and that "[e]lectronic evidence can easily be erased and manipulated," which met the requirement for expedited discovery. Therefore, the court granted the plaintiff's motion, with the condition that the imaging be done by a computer forensics expert and that discovery be limited to information related to the alleged attacks.

In re Plastics Additives, No. Civ. A. 03-2038, 2004 WL 2743591 (E.D. Pa. Nov. 29, 2004). In a complex antitrust class action, the plaintiffs made a motion to compel the defendants to "provide data in electronic format...and...provide technical assistance to the plaintiffs in understanding [the] data." The defendant objected to being compelled to provide technical assistance because the plaintiff did not carry the same burden. Agreeing with the defendant, the court found that "[b]oth parties must provide all transactional data in electronic format," however, the defendant was not required to provide technical assistance.

Super Film of America, Inc. v. UCB Films, Inc., 219 F.R.D. 649 (D. Kan. 2004). In a contract dispute over the sale of $115,000 worth of transparent film, the defendant sought discovery of e-mails, documents, databases, and spreadsheets that the plaintiff claimed were beyond its "knowledge or expertise" to retrieve and produce. The plaintiff offered to make computers available to the defendant so the defendant could retrieve the requested data. The defendant objected, and the court agreed that the offer was an unreasonable attempt to shift discovery costs to the requesting party. Noting that the plaintiff's claim that producing the documents would create an undue burden was conclusory and unsupported, the court granted the defendant's motion for discovery.

In re Verisign, Inc., No. C 02-02270, 2004 WL 2445243 (N.D. Cal. Mar. 10, 2004). In a class action securities suit, the defendants were ordered by the magistrate judge to produce all documents in electronic form. The order further stated that "[p]roduction of TIFF version alone is not sufficient," and that "[t]he electronic version must include metadata as well as be searchable." The defendants objected that the order required them to produce irrelevant material and to convert TIFF images already prepared for production into some other form. The district judge interpreted the order as essentially an order to produce in native format, but found that the order was neither "clearly erroneous [n]or contrary to law."

Zakre v. Norddeutsche Landesbank Girozentrale, No. 03 Civ. 0257, 2004 WL 764895 (S.D.N.Y. Apr. 9, 2004). The defendant produced over 200,000 e-mail messages on two CDs in a word-searchable electronic format. The plaintiff filed a motion to compel the additional production of "a meaningful and detailed document index." The court held that the defendant produced the e-mail messages "in as close a form as possible as they are kept in the usual course of business," and would not be required to produce an index or be "further obligated to organize and label them to correspond with Zakre's requests."

V. Use of Experts

Gates Rubber Co. v. Bando Chemical Industries, Ltd., 167 F.R.D. 90 (D. Colo. 1996). In a lawsuit over allegedly stolen trade secrets, one of the defendants deleted certain word processing files from his computer, claiming the files were unrelated to the litigation. The plaintiff obtained permission to utilize its own technician to recover the missing files. The technician installed a commercial data-recovery program, "Norton Unerase," on the defendant's computer, and in the process destroyed additional files estimated to be 7% to 8% of the remaining discoverable data. While acknowledging that the defendant's original intentional deletion of computer files warranted a sanction, the court noted the plaintiff's negligence in attempting to recover the files offset the potential sanction. The court stated that parties to judicial proceedings have "a duty to utilize the method which would yield the most complete and accurate results" to recover and preserve computer evidence. Despite the plaintiff's negligence, the court awarded the plaintiff 10% of the fees and costs related to bringing the sanctions motion, an unusual reprimand stemming from the unique difficulty of isolating the cost of one discovery motion among many.

Northwest Airlines v. Local 2000, No. Civ. A.00-08 (D. Minn. Jan. 11, 2000), discussed in Michael J. McCarthy, Data Raid: In Airline's Suit, PC Becomes Legal Pawn, Raising Privacy Issues, Wall Street J., May 24, 2000, at A1. In an unreported case, an airline sued a flight attendants' union, alleging that certain union activists attempted an illegal "sick out" to coincide with the millennium holiday. The airline sought discovery of the home computers of two of the most vocal union leaders, claiming that these individuals used their personal e-mail accounts to organize the job action. The magistrate judge granted the airline's discovery request, ordering inspections of the two home computers under protocols similar to the one adopted in Playboy Enterprises, Inc. v. Welles. However, the representations made by the airline and its computer experts regarding the amount of time and level of intrusiveness the inspection would involve turned out to be wildly inaccurate, and the neutrality of the experts came into question, leading to accusations in the public press that the requested discovery was an unwarranted invasion of privacy and amounted to harassment of the defendants. After more than 30 days of inspection, no significant relevant evidence was found and the case was dismissed.

Playboy Enterprises, Inc. v. Welles, 60 F. Supp. 2d 1050 (S.D. Cal. 1999). In a lawsuit for trademark infringement and dilution, the plaintiff sought discovery for the defendant's hard drive, which may have contained deleted e-mails. The defendant objected, citing concerns that some of the e-mails were privileged. To protect privilege, confidentiality, and the integrity of the evidence, the court appointed a qualified neutral expert to conduct discovery of the defendant's computer hard drive and approved a detailed protocol for the expert to follow.

Rowe Entertainment, Inc. v. William Morris Agency, Inc., 51 Fed. R. Serv. 3d (West) 1106, aff'd, 53 Fed. R. Serv. 3d (West) 296 (S.D.N.Y. 2002). In allowing the requesting party direct access to the respondent's computer files, the court adopted a protocol in which the requesting party's expert recovered files and the requesting party's attorney reviewed them for relevance before the responding party reviewed them for privilege. See also Rowe, under "Costs and Cost Allocation" at VI.

Simon Property Group, L.P. v. mySimon Inc., 194 F.R.D. 639 (S.D. Ind. 2000). In a trademark infringement lawsuit, the plaintiff sought to compel discovery of the defendant's hard drive to access deleted documents. The court adapted a similar approach as that used in Playboy Enterprises v. Welles, 60 F. Supp. 2d 1050 (S.D. Cal. 1999). The plaintiff was to choose an expert to create a "mirror image" of the hard drive and the expert was to furnish it to the defendant's counsel to identify and redact any documents that were privileged. The plaintiff would then have access to all material that was not privileged.

Tempo Electric Heater Corp. v. Temperature Engineering Co., No. 02 C 3572, 2004 WL 1254134 (N.D. Ill. June 3, 2004). In a suit concerning theft of trade secrets, the defendant moved for summary judgment, stating that the plaintiff had failed to produce key evidence to support its claim. In particular, the plaintiff failed to show by direct evidence that any unauthorized files existed on the defendant's computers. The circumstantial evidence offered by the plaintiff was that the defendant did not return several "access keys" and proprietary programs at the end of the parties' working relationship. The direct evidence offered in rebuttal was that the defendant hired an independent service bureau to inspect all of its computers for remnants of the plaintiff's proprietary software, and the service bureau reported that none were found. The court held that the plaintiff ultimately has the burden of proof, and that mere circumstantial evidence and failure to conduct its own investigation of the defendant's computers did not meet that burden.

YCA, LLC v. Berry, No. 03 C 3116, 2004 WL 1093385 (N.D. Ill. May 7, 2004). In a lawsuit for breach of an employee non-solicitation, non-disclosure, and non-recruitment agreement, the defendant Berry moved to strike the testimony of the plaintiff YCA's computer forensics expert on the grounds that YCA had failed to identify the expert and the nature of the evidence the expert would offer in a timely manner. The expert had recovered a "plethora" of documents apparently deleted by Berry from his company-issued computer. The court denied the motion on the grounds that Berry had deliberately misled YCA during discovery by denying that he had used his company-issued computer to further his plans to establish a competing business. YCA could not be faulted for relying on Berry's representations and making a rational cost-benefit decision to not hire an expert. YCA's analysis changed at the close of discovery when Berry admitted that his previous statements were false.

VI. Costs and Cost Allocation

In re Air Crash Disaster at Detroit Metropolitan Airport, 130 F.R.D. 634 (E.D. Mich. 1989). In a lawsuit stemming from the crash of a passenger jet, the defendant made a motion to compel the plaintiff to produce a nine-track tape with simulation runs on it. The plaintiff opposed the motion because it stated that the Federal Rules of Civil Procedure do not require it to create new documents it does not already have. Relying on National Union Electric Corp. v. Matsushita Electric Co. Ltd., 494 F. Supp. 1257 (E.D. Pa. 1980), the court granted the defendant's motion. However, since the plaintiff did not already have the tapes, the court allocated the cost of generating them to the defendant.

In re Brand Name Prescription Drugs Antitrust Litig., Nos. 94 C 897, MDL 997, 1995 WL 360526 (N.D. Ill. June 15, 1995) (mem.). In an antitrust lawsuit, the plaintiff made a motion to compel the defendant to retrieve deleted e-mails at the defendant's expense. The defendant contended the request for discovery was overly broad and the expense of retrieval, $50,000 to $75,000, made the request overly burdensome. The court held that the defendant must bear the cost of retrieval since the plaintiff had no control over the type of record-keeping the defendant maintained. However, the plaintiff was required to narrow the scope of discovery to limit costs and to pay $.21 for each page of the e-mails that were to be copied.

Computer Associates International, Inc. v. Quest Software, Inc., 56 Fed. R. Serv. 3d (West) 401 (N.D. Ill. 2003). The plaintiff in a software copyright and trade secret infringement case requested that the defendant image the computer hard drives of six key employees. After the imaging, the defendant spent between $28,000 and $40,000 to remove privileged e-mails from the backups and create a privilege log. The defendant then filed a motion to require the plaintiff to pay these preparation costs. The court reviewed the eight factors articulated in Rowe Entertainment, Inc. v. William Morris Agency, Inc., 205 F.R.D. 421 (S.D.N.Y. 2002), and determined that none of them favored cost shifting, analogizing these preparation costs to costs for attorney review.

Federal Trade Commission v. U.S. Grant Resources, LLC, No. Civ. A.04-596, 2004 WL 1396315 (E.D. La. June 18, 2004). The defendant is this civil fraud action was also defending a related criminal fraud action brought by the State of Louisiana. The defendant in this case served a subpoena under Fed. R. Civ. P. 45 for hard-copy records the state seized from it in the criminal action. The state's attorney filed a motion to quash the subpoena on the basis that it was overbroad and duplicative, and that the defendant should pay the costs of copying the documents. The federal court denied the motion, stating that although the defendant already had computer files representing the alleged fraudulent transactions, it was entitled to hard copies of its own documents held by the state, and that under the three-part test established by In re Exxon Valdez, 142 F.R.D. 380 (D.D.C. 1992), the cost of photocopying the documents was not an undue burden that entitled the state to reimbursement, even though it was not a party to this action.

Laurin v. Pokoik, No. 02 Civ. 1938, 2004 U.S. Dist. LEXIS 24010 (S.D.N.Y. Nov. 30, 2004). In a hostile work environment case, the defendant alleged that the plaintiff made a particular entry in the defendant's computer system shortly before she was terminated. The plaintiff requested any document that would prove the date the entry was actually made. The court directed the plaintiff to file a motion to compel inspection of the defendant's computer system if and when she was willing to retain a forensic computer expert at her own expense.

Medtronic Sofamor Danek, Inc. v. Michelson, 56 Fed. R. Serv. 3d (West) 1159 (W.D. Tenn. 2003). In an intellectual property case involving spinal fusion medical technology, the defendant sought discovery of information from 996 computer backup tapes and 300 megabytes of data on the desktop computers of the plaintiff's employees. The plaintiff objected that the proposed discovery would be unduly costly and burdensome. The court agreed and applied the eight factors articulated in Rowe Entertainment, Inc. v. William Morris Agency, Inc., 205 F.R.D. 421 (S.D.N.Y. 2002) (see below), to determine that the defendant should shoulder most of the costs of the proposed discovery. The court then ordered a detailed protocol for the parties to follow in conducting discovery of the backup tapes and hard drives. Finally, the court granted the defendant's request that a special master be appointed under Fed. R. Civ. P. 53, with the costs to be borne equally by the parties.

Multitechnology Services, L.P. v. Verizon Southwest, No. 4:02-CV-702-Y, 2004 WL 1553480 (N.D. Tex. July 12, 2004). In a commercial lawsuit involving allegations of unfair trade practices, the plaintiff propounded interrogatories seeking information from the defendant's customer databases. The defendant sought a protective order shifting the cost of the database searches, but the plaintiff objected, stating that cost shifting would not be appropriate under the factors announced in Zubulake v. UBS Warburg, 217 F.R.D. 309 (S.D.N.Y. 2003), because the requested data were "accessible." The court held that Zubulake was neither controlling nor exactly applicable to the situation. However, applying the Zubulake cost-shifting factors, the court found that an even sharing of the cost would accommodate the plaintiff's need for the information while balancing the defendant's desire to control the costs. In addition, the court classified the expenditures as "court costs," rendering them recoverable by the prevailing party.

Murphy Oil USA, Inc. v. Fluor Daniel, Inc., 52 Fed. R. Serv. 3d (West) 168 (E.D. La. 2002). In a lawsuit for breach of contract, the plaintiff made a motion to compel the defendant to reproduce e-mails from its backup tapes. Following Rowe Entertainment, Inc. v. William Morris Agency, Inc., 205 F.R.D. 421 (S.D.N.Y. 2002), the court offered the defendant two options for proceeding with discovery of e-mail from the backup tapes. Under option one, the plaintiff would pay the cost of recovering the e-mails and would assess whether any of the documents were relevant, then the defendant could review those documents to determine whether any were privileged. Under the second option, the defendant could review, at its own cost, all relevant documents recovered by the expert and produce only the non-privileged documents to the plaintiff.

OpenTV v. Liberate Technologies, 219 F.R.D. 474 (N.D. Cal. Nov. 18, 2003) (order re discovery). In an intellectual property infringement suit, the magistrate judge ruled that a portion of the costs of producing relevant computer source code should be shifted from the responding party to the requesting party. The plaintiff had requested production of some 100 additional versions of source code for software products being developed by the defendant. The defendant objected, stating that locating and duplicating the requested source code would be unduly burdensome and would yield only marginally relevant results. Instead, the defendant offered to make its complete source code database available at its facilities, along with a complete index to the database and a software engineer to provide technical assistance. The plaintiff rejected the offer, arguing that it essentially shifted production costs to the plaintiff, the requesting party. The court agreed that the offer effectively shifted costs, yet because extracting the source code would take the defendant 125 to 150 hours, the court found that the requested electronic data were inaccessible for purposes of discovery and that cost-shifting would be appropriate. Applying the Zubulake factors (see Zubulake I in this section), the court determined that the costs for extraction should be split evenly, although the cost of duplication should be borne solely by the defendant.

Oppenheimer Fund, Inc. v. Sanders, 437 U.S. 340 (1978). In a class action before the Supreme Court, the issue was whether the defendant would have to pay the cost of extracting information to certify the class. The Court held that the request fell under Fed. R. Civ. P. 23(d), governing class actions, not Fed. R. Civ. P. 26, governing general discovery, because the issue was notifying a class, and not "to define or clarify issues of the case." Also, either party would require the services of a third-party to extract the information, negating any potential cost saving were the defendant to do it. Therefore, the court held it was inappropriate to shift the burden of costs to the defendant.

Rowe Entertainment, Inc. v. William Morris Agency, Inc., 205 F.R.D. 421 (S.D.N.Y. 2002). In an action against talent agencies alleging racial discrimination in bookings, the plaintiffs requested e-mail from the defendants' backup media. The four defendants objected, citing the high costs estimated by electronic discovery consultants to restore the backup media to accessible form and the legal costs associated with screening the e-mails for relevance and privilege. Balancing eight factors derived from the case law, the court required the plaintiffs to pay for the recovery and production of the defendants' extensive e-mail backups, except for the cost of screening for relevance and privilege. The eight "Rowe factors" are

1. the specificity of the discovery request;
2. the likelihood of discovering material data;
3. the availability of those data from other sources;
4. the purposes for which the responding party maintains those data;
5. the relative benefits to the parties of obtaining those data;
6. the total costs associated with production;
7. the relative ability and incentive for each party to control its own costs; and
8. the resources available to each party.

Toshiba America Electronic Components, Inc. v. Superior Court of Santa Clara County, 21 Cal. Rptr. 3d 532 (Cal. Ct. App. 2004). A California state court judge found that California's Code of Civil Procedure, section 2031(g)(1), was fundamentally different from Fed. R. Civ. P. 26(b)(2), in that it clearly placed the responsibility for the reasonable expense of translation of computer data, if necessary, on the requesting party. Although this litigation was in state court, neither party actually cited the California rule, basing their arguments for and against cost shifting on federal practice. The court found these arguments by both sides misplaced, stating that the parties should have relied on California's statute.

Wiginton v. CB Richard Ellis Inc. ("Wiginton II"), N. 02-C-6832, 2004 U.S. Dist. LEXIS 15722 (N.D. Ill. Aug. 9, 2004). In a class action lawsuit alleging sexual harassment and a hostile work environment, the plaintiffs requested a search through the defendant's e-mail backup tapes for pornographic images and sexually suggestive messages. By agreement, the plaintiffs' computer discovery expert was provided with 94 selected backup tapes and with a set of search terms to use. The expert identified between 142 and 567 arguably responsive documents at a cost of $249,000. The plaintiffs filed a motion for costs. Considering the cost-shifting factors announced in Rowe Entertainment, Inc. v. William Morris Agency, Inc., 205 F.R.D. 421 (S.D.N.Y. 2002), and Zubulake v. UBS Warburg, 217 F.R.D. 309 (S.D.N.Y. 2003), the court opted to modify the Zubulake factors to emphasize the proportionality test of Fed. R. Civ. P. 26(b)(2)(iii). The factors the court considered were

1. the likelihood of discovering critical information;
2. the availability of such information from other sources;
3. the amount in controversy as compared to the total cost of production;
4. the parties' resources as compared to the total cost of production;
5. the relative ability of each party to control costs and its incentive to do so;

6. the importance of the issues at stake in the litigation;
7. the importance of the requested discovery in resolving the issues at stake in the litigation; and
8. the relative benefits to the parties of obtaining the information.

Finding that while most of the factors weighed in favor of cost shifting, the court stated the plaintiff had not entirely overcome the presumption that the responding party bears its own costs. Therefore the court ordered that the plaintiffs should bear 75% of the costs and the defendant only 25%.

Xpedior Creditor Trust v. Credit Suisse First Boston (USA), Inc., 58 Fed. R. Serv. 3d (West) 855 (S.D.N.Y. 2003). A corporation brought a putative class action against an investment banking house, alleging breach of contract in an Initial Public Offering (IPO), and sought discovery of electronic data from two decommissioned computer systems. The defendant moved for a protective order that would shift to the plaintiff the costs of restoring the computer systems to access the data. Applying the seven-part test enunciated in Zubulake v. UBS Warburg LLC (Zubulake I), 217 F.R.D. 309 (S.D.N.Y. 2003), the judge found that the plaintiff's request was narrowly tailored, the information was not available from any other source, and the cost of the proposed restoration ($400,000), while high, was not extraordinary in light of the total monetary stake. She also noted that the plaintiff was a bankrupt corporation with no assets and the defendant was an international firm with assets of over $5 billion. The final factors—ability to minimize costs, public interest in the issues at stake, and the usefulness of the information to both parties—were neutral. Therefore, although the information requested was inaccessible without incurring costs, there was no justification to shift those costs to the requesting party.

Zenith Electronics Corp. v. WH-TV Broadcasting Corp., 2004 WL 1631676 (N.D. Ill. July 19, 2004). In a breach of contract action, the court entered judgment against the defendant in favor of two third-party defendants. The third-party defendants then filed a bill of costs for $357,618.82, naming both Zenith and WH-TV Broadcasting as jointly liable. Zenith challenged the bill of costs, which included several items related to electronic discovery. The court reviewed the items in light of 28 U.S.C. § 1920. It found that the considerable cost ($109,627.46) of printing documents originally in electronic format, including consulting time for the conversion of documents from electronic to print formats, was incurred for the convenience of the parties and was not recoverable under the statute, nor was the cost ($182,595.47) of hiring an independent computer consultant to review the electronic documents for privilege and relevance under a court-ordered protocol.

Zubulake v. UBS Warburg LLC ("Zubulake I"), 217 F.R.D. 309 (S.D.N.Y. 2003). In a sex discrimination suit against a financial services company, the plaintiff requested e-mail beyond the approximately 100 pages produced by the defendants. She presented substantial evidence that more responsive e-mail existed, most likely on backup tapes and optical storage media created and maintained to meet SEC records-retention requirements. The defendants objected to producing e-mail from these sources, which they estimated would cost $175,000 exclusive of attorney review time. The judge held that the plaintiff's request was clearly relevant to her claims, but both parties raised the question of who would pay for the discovery and urged the court to apply the Rowe factors. The court held that for data kept in an accessible format, the usual rules of discovery apply. The responding party should pay the costs of producing responsive data. A court should consider cost shifting only when electronic data are relatively inaccessible, such as on backup tapes. Furthermore, requiring the responding party to restore and produce responsive documents from a small sample of the requested backup tapes is a sensible approach in most cases. Finally, in conducting the cost-shifting analysis, the court rejected the Rowe factors and substituted a seven-factor test. The "Zubulake factors" are, in order of importance or weight:

1. the extent to which the request is tailored to discover relevant data;
2. the availability of those data from other sources;
3. the total cost of production, relative to the amount in controversy;
4. the total cost of production, relative to the resources available to each party;
5. the relative ability and incentive for each party to control its own costs;
6. the importance of the issues at stake in the litigation; and
7. the relative benefits to the parties in obtaining those data.

Zubulake v. UBS Warburg LLC ("Zubulake III"), 216 F.R.D. 280 (S.D.N.Y. 2003). Following the May 13, 2003, Opinion and Order above, the defendants restored and reviewed five backup tapes selected by the plaintiff at a cost slightly over $19,000. Six hundred e-mail messages were deemed to be responsive to the plaintiff's discovery request. The defendants estimated that the cost for production of the entire 77-tape collection would be $165,954.67 for restoration and $107,694.72 for review. Analyzing each of the seven factors announced by the court in the previous decision, the court determined that the balance tipped slightly against cost shifting, and that requiring the defendants to bear 75% of the costs would be fair. However, the court determined that none of the costs for attorney review of the data, once they had been made accessible, should be borne by the requesting party.

VII. Privacy and Privilege

Collaboration Properties, Inc. v. Polycom, Inc., 224 F.R.D. 473 (N.D. Cal. 2004). In a lawsuit over patent infringement, a dispute arose over privilege for 58 e-mails between non-attorneys of the defendant that were forwarded to attorneys. The plaintiff argued that the defendant should provide redacted copies of the 58 e-mails, because the defendant had not demonstrated that all portions of the 58 e-mails were privileged. The defendant complied, but, according to the plaintiff, the redactions were still overbroad. In particular, the defendant redacted information showing the author and recipient of each withheld e-mail. The court ordered the defendant's counsel to show to the plaintiff's counsel nonredacted copies of the e-mails, with the defendant reserving its right to assert any applicable privilege, in order to discuss more meaningfully the scope of any privilege and correlative redactions. Over the defendant's objections, the court concluded that the limited disclosure in the context of a mandated meeting of counsel did not waive the attorney—client privilege.

In re Currency Conversion Fee, No. MDL 1409, M 21-95, 2003 WL 22389169 (S.D.N.Y. Oct. 21, 2003). Under the "functional equivalent" exception to the corporate attorney—client privilege, the privilege is maintained even though the communications are disclosed to a third party, if that third party is the functional equivalent of a corporate employee. The court held that the exception did not apply to otherwise privileged documents processed by an outsourced computer data-processing firm.

Fraser v. Nationwide Mutual Insurance Co., 352 F.3d 107 (3d Cir. 2003). In a wrongful discharge suit, the Third Circuit upheld the district court's ruling that an employer's search for e-mails of an employee found on the workplace computer network did not violate the Electronic Communications Privacy Act (ECPA), 18 U.S.C. §§ 2510, 2701. Title I of the ECPA prohibits "interceptions," which are universally defined as searches of messages during transmission, not searches of messages that have reached their destination and are being stored. Title II of the ECPA prohibits "seizure" of stored e-mails, but exempts actions taken by the "person or entity providing the wire or electronic communications service," in this case the employer.

Haynes v. Kline, 298 F. Supp. 2d 1154 (D. Kan. 2003). In a suit by a former employee of the Kansas State attorney general, the plaintiff moved for a preliminary injunction prohibiting the attorney general's office from further accessing his private files on his former work computer. The court granted the injunction, holding that the employee demonstrated a Fourth Amendment right in the privacy of his personal computer files. The court found that although the employer stated, as part of the employee orientation, that there was "no expectation of privacy in using this [computer] system," the orientation went on to distinguish between "public" and "private" files and to warn that access to any other employee's files without permission was forbidden. Passwords were issued to each employee to prevent unauthorized access, and prior to this litigation there had been no evidence that any other employee's personal computer files had been monitored or viewed by supervisors. The defendant offered no evidence to justify its search of the employee's personal computer files. The court held that given the totality of the circumstances, the plaintiff's expectation of privacy was both subjectively and objectively reasonable.

Holland v. GMAC Mortgage Corp., No. 03-2666-CM, 2004 WL 1534179 (D. Kan. June 30, 2004). The parties in this civil suit stipulated to a broad protective order, which they offered to the court. The order provided that categories of documents, including "computer records or other confidential electronic information," be designated as "confidential," and that any confidential material to be filed with the court would be filed under seal. The court refused to endorse the order, stating that "[t]he mere fact that a document is a computer record or an electronic document does not warrant protection from disclosure," and that "the fact that the parties may agree to a protective order which provides for the filing of confidential materials under seal does not dispense with the requirement that the parties establish a harm sufficient to overcome the public's right of access to judicial records."

Jicarilla Apache Nation v. United States, 60 Fed. Cl. 413 (Fed. Cl. 2004). In one of the many Indian land trust fund mismanagement cases, the Court of Federal Claims found that good cause existed to issue a protective order to facilitate discovery while meeting the requirements of a number of federal confidentiality laws. However, the court excluded "attorney—client privilege, the deliberative process privilege, and the attorney work product doctrine" as applicable laws. (The complete text of the order and a list of the applicable laws are published with this decision.)

Navigant Consulting, Inc. v. Wilkinson, 220 F.R.D. 467 (N.D. Tex. 2004). In a suit by a corporation against a group of former employees for trade secret theft, the defendants moved to compel the production of e-mails and other documents related to the corporation's internal investigation of the defendants and other employees. The corporation objected, claiming attorney—client privilege and work product protection. Among the documents withheld was a detailed forensic analysis of one employee's laptop computer, including a printout of data contained therein. Applying Texas law, the court held that the attorney—client privilege applies only to communications "made for the purposes of facilitating the rendition of professional legal services" and does not apply when the attorney is "functioning in some other capacity—such as an accountant, investigator, or business advisor." The mere fact that the corporation was contemplating litigation did not turn the attorneys' business assistance and advice into privileged attorney—client communications.

Portis v. City of Chicago, No. 02 C 3139, 2004 WL 1535854 (N.D. Ill. July 7, 2004). In a class action suit brought by citizens who claimed unlawful detention by city police for nonviolent ordinance violations that carry no jail time, attorneys for the plaintiff class obtained approximately 20,000 relevant arrest records from the city. They proceeded to create a computerized database from the arrest records at a cost of approximately $90,000. The city then filed a motion to compel the plaintiffs to produce the database, stating that although the database is attorney work product, it is not "opinion" work product, and that the city has a "substantial need" for the database, which it cannot recreate itself from the available information without "undue hardship." The court found that the database was a hybrid of "fact" and "opinion" work product, but that disclosure to the city would not reveal the plaintiffs' legal strategy or counsels' mental impressions. The court went on to find that the database, as distinct from the individual arrest records, was an essential piece of evidence. The crux of the lawsuit was the claim that there was a pattern of unlawful detention, and such a pattern could only be established through computer analysis using the database. The court concluded that ordering the plaintiff to share the database would advance the interests of the litigation as a whole and would not violate the attorney work product doctrine, but that the parties must split the database development costs.

United States v. Rigas, 281 F. Supp. 2d 733 (S.D.N.Y. 2003). In a criminal case involving executives of the Adelphia Communication Corporation, the government issued grand jury subpoenas to Adelphia, pursuant to which Adelphia created twenty-six bitstream images of employee computer hard drives. The government accidentally provided privileged information along with the material required for discovery. Upon realizing the mistake, the government petitioned to have the file returned, but the defendants responded that the government had waived its privilege. Declining to adopt a bright line rule that inadvertently volunteering privileged material always or never constituted a waiver, the court adopted a four-part test to gauge the fairness of waiving privilege. The test balances

1. the reasonableness of the precautions taken to prevent inadvertent disclosure of privileged documents;
2. the volume of the discovery versus the extent of the specific discovery at issue;
3. the length of time taken by the producing party to rectify the disclosure; and
4. the overarching issue of fairness.

Applying the test to this case, the court held that the government had taken reasonable precautions, the documents relinquished were only a small portion of the total discovery, the government promptly notified the court of the mistake, and finally the court found it would not prejudice the defendants counsel to not have the material. The court held that defendants were required to return the documents to the government.

United States v. Stewart, 287 F. Supp. 2d 461 (S.D.N.Y. 2003). A year before her indictment on charges related to securities fraud, but after the investigation had been made public, Martha Stewart prepared a detailed e-mail relating her side of the facts and sent it to her attorney. The next day she accessed the e-mail and forwarded it to her daughter, without alteration. Later, attorneys for Martha Stewart Living Omnimedia (MSLO) produced documents and computer files in response to a grand jury subpoena. Both e-mails appeared on MSLO's privilege log; however, only the e-mail to the attorney was removed from the actual production. An assistant U.S. attorney later found the copy sent to the daughter. Stewart objected to MSLO's production of the e-mail on the basis that it was privileged. The court held that the e-mail to the attorney would have been privileged as attorney—client communication, but that Stewart waived the privilege when she forwarded the e-mail to her daughter. However, the court found that the work product protections offered by Fed. R. Civ. P. 26(b)(3) and Fed. R. Crim. P. 16(b) are broader than the attorney—client communication privilege, and that sharing factual work product with a family member did not waive those protections.

United States Fidelity & Guaranty Co. v. Braspetro Oil Services Co., 53 Fed. R. Serv. 3d (West) 60 (S.D.N.Y 2002). In a surety action, the defendants provided their testifying experts with more than 50 CD-ROM disks containing 1.1 million documents, including many attorney—client communications and work product documents. The plaintiffs claimed that by providing the experts with unfettered access to the entire litigation support database, the defendants had waived any privileges and were required to produce the database under Fed.

R. Civ. P. 26(a)(2) as material "considered" by the experts. The court acknowledged that while the scope of what is "considered" by an expert is unclear in the case law, the burden is on the party resisting discovery to clearly identify for the court the material that the expert did not "consider" out of the mass provided. Finding that the defendant provided no such guidance, the court held that the entire litigation support database was discoverable, as was the index and OCR-created text files the experts used in searching the database.

New York State Bar Association, Committee on Professional Ethics, Opinion 749 (December 14, 2001). Topic: Use of computer software to surreptitiously examine and trace e-mail and other electronic documents (found

at http://www.nysba.org/Content/NavigationMenu/Attorney_ Resources/Ethics_

Opinions/Committee_on_Professional_Ethics_Opinion_749.htm). The receipt by an attorney of an electronic file does not constitute permission to open and read the metadata or imbedded data that file might contain. Opening and viewing such data is presumptively unauthorized and unethical. Similarly, placing a tracer "bug" in an e-mail to track the distribution and modification of the message after it has left the attorney's computer system is unethical. For a short analysis of this ethics opinion and useful links to background technical information, see David Hricik, The Transmission and Receipt of Invisible Confidential Information, E-Ethics, vol. 2, no. 3, October 2003 (found at http://www.hricik.com/eethics/ 2.3.html).

VIII.   Rule 37 Sanctions

See also "I. Data Preservation and Spoliation."

Aero Products International, Inc. v. Intex Recreation Corp., No. 02 C 2590, 2004 WL 417193 (N.D. Ill. Jan. 30, 2004). In a patent infringement suit involving the manufacture and sale of air mattresses, the defendant was found to have been routinely deleting all its e-mail every thirty days during the first year of the litigation. The court entered an order requiring the defendant to recover as much destroyed electronic data as possible and authorizing the plaintiff to petition the court for appointment of a computer forensics expert at the defendant's expense. The defendant engaged its own expert, who submitted a report and forty-five pages of recovered data. The plaintiff stated that the production was inadequate, but never petitioned the court for appointment of an expert or filed any other motion to compel further production. Instead, the plaintiff filed a motion under Fed. R. Civ. P. 37 for sanctions amounting to a default judgment against the defendant. The court denied the sanctions as inappropriate and unwarranted, given the plaintiff's failure to pursue the discovery opportunities offered to it.

Invision Media Communications, Inc. v. Federal Insurance Co., No. 02 Civ. 5461, 2004 WL 396037 (S.D.N.Y. Mar. 2, 2004). In an insurance suit stemming from business disruption caused by the 9/11 attacks, the plaintiff and the defendant filed cross-motions to compel discovery and for sanctions. Two of the many incidents alleged involved electronic discovery. In the first incident, the plaintiff's general counsel testified that as the company's offices were closed and employees laid off, she directed that hard drives of those employees' computers be "wiped." The defendant requested sanctions for spoliation, which were denied by the court in the absence of any showing that the wiped hard drives would have rendered relevant evidence. In the second incident, the defendant requested e-mails from a three-month period around September 2001. The plaintiff initially responded that there were no responsive e-mails, as the policy had been to delete all e-mails after two weeks. However, the e-mails were eventually found and produced. The court found that a "reasonable inquiry by the plaintiff's counsel prior to responding to [the defendant's] document request...would have alerted counsel that the plaintiff possessed electronic mail that fell within the scope of [the defendant's] document request." The plaintiff was directed to pay costs and reasonable attorneys' fees resulting from the additional discovery required.

Kucala Enterprises, Ltd. v. Auto Wax Co., 56 Fed. R. Serv. 3d (West) 487 (N.D. Ill. 2003). In a patent infringement case, the defendant repeatedly requested documents from the plaintiff, including business records and correspondence from the plaintiff's computer system. After three motions to compel production, the defendant was allowed access to the plaintiff's computer to conduct an inspection. The computer forensics expert conducting the inspection discovered that the plaintiff had used a commercially available disk-wiping software, "Evidence Eliminator," to "clean" approximately 3,000 files three days before the inspection, and another 12,000 on the night before the inspection between the hours of midnight and 4:00 a.m. The magistrate judge found that, based on the totality of the circumstances, the spoliation was intentional and recommended to the trial judge that the plaintiff's case be dismissed with prejudice, and that the plaintiff pay the defendant's attorneys' fees and costs from the time the Evidence Eliminator was first used. On de novo review, the district court judge rejected the recommendation to dismiss the plaintiff's case with prejudice, favoring adjudication of the claims and counterclaims, but upheld the recommendation that the plaintiff bear attorneys' fees and costs. Kucala Enterprises, Ltd. v. Auto Wax Co., No. 02 C 1403, 2003 WL

22433095 (N.D. Ill. Oct. 27, 2003) (rulings on objections dated October 27, 2003).

Procter & Gamble Co. v. Haugen, 2003 WL 22080734 (D. Utah Aug. 19, 2003) (order). Procter & Gamble (P&G) sued several independent distributors of rival Amway products, claiming unfair trade practices for allegedly distributing e-mail associating P&G with Satanism. P&G immediately informed the defendants of their duty to preserve computer evidence crucial to the case, but neglected to impose a similar duty upon itself, resulting in the destruction of e-mail records of five key P&G employees. Without citing Fed. R. Civ. P. 37, the court granted the defendant's motion to dismiss the case on three grounds, each of which the court stated were sufficient alone to grant dismissal. The three grounds were (1) the plaintiff failed to preserve evidence it knew was "critical" to the case, (2) the plaintiff's actions rendered an effective defense "basically impossible," and (3) the plaintiff destroyed the very evidence it would need to support its proposed expert testimony on damages, rendering the testimony inadmissible on Daubert grounds. In a previous decision, the trial court sanctioned the plaintiff $10,000—$20,000 for each of the five key employees whose files had been destroyed. Procter & Gamble Co. v. Haugen, 179 F.R.D. 622 (D. Utah 1998), rev'd on other grounds, 222 F.3d 1262 (10th Cir. 2000).

Sheppard v. River Valley Fitness One, L.P., 203 F.R.D. 56 (D.N.H. 2001). The plaintiff made a motion for sanctions against the defendants' counsel for abuses of discovery. Numerous times the plaintiff requested electronic documents, but was only given information from floppy discs in the defendants' counsel's office. The court attributed the defendant attorney's failure to produce requested computer records to lack of diligence as opposed to intentional obstruction of discovery, hence he was fined $500 and Aubin, a third party, was precluded from testifying at trial.

Stevenson v. Union Pacific Railroad Co., 354 F.3d 739 (8th Cir. 2004). In a negligence action arising out of a railroad crossing collision, the trial court granted the plaintiff partial summary judgment and imposed an adverse-inference instruction on the defendant as a sanction for the destruction of recorded voice communications between the train crew and dispatchers and destruction of track maintenance records both before and after commencement of litigation. On appeal, the circuit court looked at the circumstances of each allegation of spoliation and applied the test of Lewy v. Remington Arms, 836 F.2d 1104 (8th Cir. 1988), to determine the extent of the duty of preservation. It held that the trial court did not abuse its discretion in imposing the adverse-inference instruction sanction for destruction of the tape recordings, as the tape recordings were clearly relevant to reasonably anticipated litigation, there were no alternative records, and there was evidence that such recordings had been preserved in other litigation. Likewise, the destruction of track maintenance records after litigation commenced warranted the sanction. However, the routine destruction of track maintenance records pursuant to a records management policy prior to litigation did not give rise to a presumption of bad faith to justify the adverse-inference instruction. And on remand, the trial court was instructed to allow the defendant to present evidence challenging the rebuttable presumption that an adverse-inference instruction creates.

Theofel v. Farey-Jones, 341 F.3d 978 (9th Cir. 2003). In a commercial lawsuit, the defendant issued a subpoena to the plaintiff's Internet service provider (ISP) requesting "all copies of e-mail sent or received by anyone" employed by the plaintiff, with no limitations of time or scope. The ISP, which was not represented by counsel, complied, producing many privileged and irrelevant messages. The plaintiff moved to have the subpoena quashed and for sanctions for discovery abuse, which the magistrate judge granted. Individual employees of the plaintiff also filed civil suits against the defendant under the Stored Communications Act, Wiretap Act, and Computer Fraud and Abuse Act, which the district court dismissed. The appellate court reversed the dismissal of the claims under the Stored Communications Act and Computer Fraud and Abuse Act, stating that although the subpoena was purported to be a valid request under Fed. R. Civ. P. 45, it "transparently and egregiously" violated the standards of Rule 45 and the "defendants acted in bad faith and with gross negligence in drafting and deploying it." In so ruling, the appellate court negated any argument that the ISP knowingly consented to the request. By remanding the statutory claims to the district court, the appellate court left open the possibility of civil penalties against the defendant.

Tulip Computers International B.V. v. Dell Computer Corp., 52 Fed. R. Serv. 3d (West) 1420 (D. Del. 2002). In a patent infringement case, the defendant Dell failed several times to answer discovery requests, provide any reasonable explanations for its failures, or provide any witnesses who could answer questions about its records management systems, paper or computerized. The parties resolved the dispute regarding paper documents themselves, agreeing on Tulip's request for access to a document warehouse. For the computer records, the court ordered that Tulip could search a hard drive with e-mails from Dell executives, other than Michael Dell, using agreed upon search terms. Then Dell would be permitted to look through the e-mails derived from the queries to filter the privileged documents.

Zubulake v. UBS Warburg LLC ("Zubulake IV"), 220 F.R.D. 212

(S.D.N.Y. 2003) (opinion and order dated Oct. 22, 2003). (For factual background, see Zubulake I and Zubulake III under "Costs and Cost Allocation" above at VI.) After restoring backup tapes to locate missing e-mails, the defendant found that certain relevant tapes were missing. The plaintiff moved for sanctions, including a spoliation-inference instruction. The court found that (1) a duty to preserve the missing tapes existed; (2) the defendant was negligent and possibly reckless in failing to preserve the tapes; but (3) the plaintiff failed to demonstrate a reasonable likelihood that the missing tapes contained evidence that would have been relevant to the lawsuit. Had the plaintiff shown either that the defendant had acted with malicious intent or that the missing tapes actually held evidence that would have been damaging, a spoliation-inference instruction would have been appropriate. In the absence of either of those elements, the appropriate sanction was limited to awarding the costs of additional depositions taken pursuant to the discovery. Cf. Zubulake V, under "Data Preservation and Spoliation" at I, in which the adverse-inference jury instruction was granted after further discovery revealed intentional deletion of e-mail.

Appendix B
Glossary

The following terms are included to assist the reader in understanding this book and computer forensics. This glossary was copied from the National Institute of Justice's special report titled "Forensic Examination of Electonic Evidence: A Guide for Law Enforcement". This is a free publication that can be found on the NIJ's website, www.ojp.udsoj.gov/nij, NCJ 199408. This is an excellent guide that is worth reading if you desire to learn more about computer forensics (and it is free).

Acquisition: A process by which digital evidence is duplicated, copied, or imaged.

Analysis: To look at the results of an examination for its significance and probative value to the case.

BIOS: Basic Input Output System. The set of routines stored in read-only memory that enables a computer to start the operating system and to communicate with the various devices in the system such as disk drives, keyboard, monitor, printer, and communication ports.

CD-RW: Compact disk-rewritable. A disk to which data can be written and erased.

CMOS: Complementary metal oxide semiconductor. A type of chip used to store BIOS configuration information.

Compressed file: A file that has been reduced in size through a compression algorithm to save disk space. The act of compressing a file will make it unreadable to most programs until the file is uncompressed. Most common compression utilities are PKZIP with an extension of .zip.

Copy: An accurate reproduction of information contained on an original physical item, independent of the electronic storage device (e.g., logical file copy). Maintains contents, but attributes may change during the reproduction.

Deleted files: If a subject knows there are incriminating files on the computer, he or she may delete them in an effort to eliminate the evidence. Many computer users think that this actually eliminates the information. However, depending on how the files are deleted, in many instances a forensic examiner is able to recover all or part of the original data.

Digital evidence: Information stored or transmitted in binary form that may be relied on in court.

Duplicate: An accurate digital reproduction of all data contained on a digital storage device (e.g., hard drive, CD-ROM, flash memory, floppy disk, Zip, Jaz). Maintains contents and attributes (e.g., bit stream, bit copy, and sector dump).

Electromagnetic interference: An electromagnetic disturbance that interrupts, obstructs, or otherwise degrades or limits the effective performance of electronics/electrical equipment.

Encryption: Any procedure used in cryptography to convert plain text into cipher text in order to prevent anyone but the intended recipient from reading that data.

Examination: Technical review that makes the evidence visible and suitable for analysis; tests performed on the evidence to determine the presence or absence of specific data.

File name anomaly: Header/extension mismatch; file name inconsistent with the content of the file.

File slack: Space between the logical end of the file and the end of the last allocation unit for that file.

File structure: How an application program stores the contents of a file.

File system: The way the operating system keeps track of the files on the drive.

Forensically clean: Digital media that are completely wiped of nonessential and residual data, scanned for viruses, and verified before use.

Hashing: The process of using a mathematical algorithm against data to produce a numeric value that is representative of that data.

Host protected area: An area that can be defined on IDE drives that meets the technical specifications as defined by ATA4 and later. If a Max Address has been set that is less than a Native Max Address, then a host protected area is present.

IDE: Integrated drive electronics. A type of data communications interface generally associated with storage devices.

Image: An accurate digital representation of all data contained on a digital storage device (e.g., hard drive, CD-ROM, flash memory, floppy disk, Zip, Jaz). Maintains contents and attributes, but may include metadata such as CRCs, hash value, and audit information.

ISP: Internet service provider. An organization that provides access to the Internet. Small Internet service providers provide service via modem and an integrated services digital network (ISDN), while the larger ones also offer private line hookups (e.g., T1, fractional T1).

MAC address: Media access control address. A unique identifying number built (or "burned") into a network interface card by the manufacturer.

MO: Magneto-optical. A drive used to back up files on a personal computer using magnetic and optical technologies.

Network: A group of computers connected to one another to share information and resources.

Original evidence: Physical items and the data objects that are associated with those items at the time of seizure.

Password protected: Many software programs include the ability to protect a file using a password. One type of password protection is sometimes called "access denial." If this feature is used, the data will be present on the disk in the normal manner, but the software program will not open or display the file without the user entering the password. In many cases, forensic examiners are able to bypass this feature.

Preservation Order: A document ordering a person or company to preserve
potential evidence. The authority for preservation letters to ISPs is in 18 USC 2703(f).

Proprietary software: Software that is owned by an individual or company and that requires the purchase of a license.

Removable media: Items (e.g., floppy disks, CDs, DVDs, cartridges, tape) that store data and can be easily removed.

SCSI: Small Computer System Interface. A type of data communications
interface.

Steganography: The art and science of communicating in a way that hides the existence of the communication. It is used to hide a file inside another. For example, a child pornography image can be hidden inside another graphic image file, audio file, or other file format.

System administrator: The individual who has legitimate supervisory rights over a computer system. The administrator maintains the highest access to the system. Also can be known as sysop, sysadmin, and system operator.

Unallocated space: Allocation units not assigned to active files within a file system.

Write protection: Hardware or software methods of preventing data from being written to a disk or other medium.

Appendix C
Questions to Ask a Forensic Specialist

These questions are designed to help someone interview and select a computer forensic specialist to assist them in a legal case or investigation. You may have additional questions that we did not think of, but these will hopefully get you off to a good start. After these questions we have some tips or guidance to help you separate the wheat from the chaff as you interview people. Just because they have a nice certification or two does not mean the individual is a qualified examiner. Likewise, very few examiners will have the best answer to every question, but if they do you may want to do a little more due diligence because this is rare.

1. How long have you been doing computer forensics?
2. How many computer forensic cases have you done?
3. How many hard drives have you imaged?
4. What kinds of storage media have you imaged and/or analyzed?
5. What software/hardware have you used in your work?
6. Are you certified in computer forensics?
7. Which certifications? (verify these)
8. Have you ever presented at a conference on computer forensics? (usually verifiable, sometimes on line)
9. What professional groups are you involved in?
10. Do you have any past clients I can call for a reference?
11. Has the evidence on which you have worked ever been admitted into court?
12. How many times have you attempted to qualify as an expert witness?

13. How many times have you qualify as an expert witness in computer forensics?

14. What were the cases you gave court testimony in? (then verify these)

Tips on Answers you can expect

1. Be careful on this one, have they done 1 case 5 years ago and thus claim they have been doing computer forensics for 5 years? A full time computer forensic specialist will do 30 plus cases a year.

2. Anything below 30 cases is generally a beginner or novice. They may be able to do the work, but there is no substitute for experience. In many computer forensic labs an examiner's first 10 cases or 3 to 6 months are done under direct supervision of an experienced examiner.

3. This will help determine if they did one case 5 years ago or do 30+ cases a year.

4. A lot of computer forensic work involves IDE hard drives, which are common in personal computers (workstations and laptops). If you need someone to image and analyze something more, like servers or larger mid-range/mainframe computers, then look for evidence they the person has imaged RAID servers, optical drives, backup tapes, or other configurations that may be found at the client's site.

5. A computer forensic specialist will normally use several tools to get the job done. There may be several imaging tools they use and if they do not mention it, ask how they ensure the original storage media is protected to ensure there are no writes to it. If the person claims that this one tool does it all, keep looking this is not the person you want. Many times even Encase and SMART do not do everything an examiner will need in the course of an examination—and these are two of the most versatile tools on the market in my opinion.

6. Certifications are good, but will only show a minimum level of ability, they are NOT a substitute for actual experience and do not make the person an expert. Think about the CPA certification. This shows that the person has a minimum level of competency in accounting. It does not make the person an expert in Tax or Non-profit accounting, though many experts in this area have the CPA certification.

7. Make sure the certification has something to it. Some time the most valuable part of a certification is the frame it came in. Computer forensics is a relatively new profession;

there are some good certifications and some that are very questionable.

8.   This is similar to the Guild test some courts use to use to determine if the person knew their stuff. Many conferences in computer forensics are organized by people in the field. So if the computer forensic specialist has spoken as conferences it is an indication that their peers think they know something. Also, it takes a lot more research and preparation to present a class than to sit through it.

9.   Professional group memberships are generally open to everyone, but are a great place to network with other in the profession and to get continuing education. I have found the friends made in these groups to be a very valuable resource when I have questions. If the person is not a member of any professional groups and there are some in the area I would wonder why?

10. Nothing beats a good reference. If they are available, make sure you call them.

11. In many cases all you need is to get the evidence admitted into court. What is their track record? I have been told that in civil legal cases over 80% never go to court. So if the examiner does not do criminal work (which many do not) it many not be surprising to find a computer forensic specialist that has never been to court even after several years of full time work.

12. 12, 13, & 14. If the person has attempted to qualify (successful or not) as an expert you should be able to verify this with a service from someone like Lexis-Nexis or Findlaw.

Appendix D
Websites

This is not a list of every website worth visiting regarding computer forensics, just a few we thought you might find interesting. There are litterly thousands of websites, some good & some bad, that you can find information on computer forensics and electronic discovery on. If they were all listed it would be a book by itself.

Digital Detective

This company provides training and tools for computer forensics. The tools are reasonably priced and some are free. For more information go to their website: http://www.digital-detective.co.uk/.

Encase

Guidance Software's suite of EnCase® solutions provide an enterprise investigative infrastructure that enables corporations, government and law enforcement agencies to conduct effective digital investigations, respond promptly to eDiscovery requests and other large-scale data collection needs, and take decisive action in response to external attacks. Guidance also offers training and has the EnCE certification. For more information see the company's website, www.encase.com.

AccessData

AccessData's suite, Ultimate Toolkit ™, includes its forensics software, password recovery software, registry viewer software, drive wiping software, and its distributed network attack software (to recover passwords faster). The company also offers training and the ACE certification. For more information, please see the company's website—http://www.accessdata.com/.

ASR Data

SMART is a software utility that has been designed and optimized to support data forensic practitioners and Information Security personnel in pursuit of their respective duties and goals. The SMART software and methodology have been developed with the intention of integrating technical, legal and end-user requirements into a complete package that enables the user to perform their job most effectively and efficiently. For information regarding training or about SMART, please visit the company's website—http://www.asrdata.com/.

Paraben

Paraben's line of forensic software is a must have for any investigator. From acquisition, to final report, from hard drives to cell phones, Paraben has a product for you. The modular nature of our forensic suite allows you to purchase one component or all of them to make your toolbox complete. Paraben also offers training. More information is available at the company's website, http://www.paraben-forensics.com/.

ProDiscover

The ProDiscover® family of security products combines high quality, performance, and ease of use at affordable prices. Technology Pathways provides products and services for a variety of uses including computer forensics, systems audits, and digital discovery. ProDiscover is a product of Technology Pathways. Technology Pathways also offers training. For more information please see their website: http://www.techpathways.com/.

DataLifter

DataLifter is a suite of products built on years of investigative experience. They have been specifically designed to assist with Computer Forensics, Information Auditing, Information Security and Data Recovery. DataLifter is a product of StepaNet Communications, Inc. The company also offers training. For more information please see the company's website—http://www.datalifter.com/.

Symantec

Symantec's Norton SystemWorks™ 2005 Premier contains the file recover utilities, disk editor and imaging software that have been used by computer forensic specialist for years. Though Symantec does not develop these tools for computer forensics, they are still nice tools.

More information is available at the company's website—http://www.symantec.com/.

Maresware

All Maresware is command line driven, and designed for reliable, extremely rapid processing of very large data files. The software is simple to use, yet quite versatile, with capabilities well beyond those documented. Most programs in the packages are also available individually. Site licenses and volume discounts are available for both individual programs and for the packages. For information about the software or training, please visit the company's website—http://www.dmares.com/ or http://www.norcrossgroup.com/.

HTCIA

The High Technology Crime Investigation Association (HTCIA) is designed to encourage, promote, aid and affect the voluntary interchange of data, information, experience, ideas and knowledge about methods, processes, and techniques relating to investigations and security in advanced technologies among its membership. More information is available at the organization's website—http://www.htcia.org/.

IISFA

The International Information Systems Forensics Association (IISFA) is a nonprofit organization whose mission is to promote the discipline of information forensics in the form of evangelism, education, and certification. For more information about the organization, please see their website—http://www.iisfa.org/.

ISCFE

The International Society of Computer Forensic Examiners is a private Florida corporation affiliated with Key Computer Service, Inc. Although the ISFCE is a for-profit corporation, our goal is not to gain profits, but to provide a quality certification at a minimum cost. We are dedicated to providing a universally recognized, unblemished certification that is available to all who can qualify, for a reasonable cost. For more information on the organization or the CCE certification (Certified Computer Examiner) please go to their website—http://www.isfce.com/.

Cyber Crime Institute

The Cybercrime Institute is a division of Continuing Education at KSU in existence to fill a void in training for those interested in information security and computer forensics. The Cybercrime Institute was created in response to increasing demands for forensic and security expertise in business, law enforcement, and government sectors. With rapid technological advancements, it only makes sense that the bad guys are using sophisticated equipment and knowledge to commit crime. Their website is http://www.kennesaw.edu/coned/sci/index.htm.

Southeast CyberCrime Summit

This joint venture between the Atlanta HTCIA and the Southeast Cybercrime Institute at Kennesaw State University brings together more than 60 of the nation's top security experts, and over 20 exhibitors, to address critical issues in the areas of information security and computer forensics. Designed for individuals working in the areas of information security, law enforcement, and computer forensics. Attendees also gained valuable hands-on training using software tools from Guidance Software, AccessData, Deloitte & Touche, and other. For more information go to—http://www.cybercrimesummit.com/.

Techno Security & Techno Forensics

Techno has become known as a world class training and networking event now having had attendees register from 40 different countries. We're not trying to be the biggest conference, just the best. This conference generally has seven concurrent training tracks. These will consist of seven extensive Techno Security tracks. For more information on the conferences offered by The TrainingCo, LLC please see their website -
http://www.technosecurity.com/.

Intelligent Computer Solutions

Formed in 1990 is the industry leader in hard drive duplicators. In the past year they have developed a forensic hand-held hard drive duplicator geared specifically toward the Law Enforcement and Security professionals. For more information, visit their website at http://www. ics-iq.com/.

Logicube

Logicube is the recognized world leader in hard drive and media duplication, back-up, and computer forensics systems. Logicube's hard drive cloning and duplication systems are used throughout the world in thousands of IT departments, as well as by the world's leading law enforcement agencies. Whether you are looking for software duplication, drive imaging and diagnostic, back-up, file management, or computer forensic and data recovery solutions, Logicube has the ideal system for you. For more information see their website, http://www.logicube. com/.

Forensic Computers

Forensic-Computers.com is the producer of "The Ultimate Computer Forensic Hardware". Their forensic towers and portables are setting the new industry standard for overall quality and speed. Some of the largest corporations and government agencies in the world have chosen their equipment to run their forensics laboratories. Their website is http:// www.forensic-computers.com/.

ICFP

The Institute of Computer Forensic Professional's mission is to create best practices of digital forensics through standardization, guidelines, and procedures for computer forensic specialists. More information is available at their website, http://www.forensic-institute.org/.

Computer Forensics Tool Testing

There is a critical need in the law enforcement community to ensure the reliability of computer forensic tools. A capability is required to ensure that forensic software tools consistently produce accurate and objective test results. The goal of the Computer Forensic Tool Testing (CFTT) project at the National Institute of Standards and Technology (NIST) is to establish a methodology for testing computer forensic software tools by development of general tool specifications, test procedures, test criteria, test sets, and test hardware. The results provide the information necessary for toolmakers to improve tools, for users to make informed choices about acquiring and using computer forensics tools, and for interested parties to understand the tools capabilities. Our approach for testing computer forensic tools is based on well-recognized international methodologies for conformance testing and quality testing. The website is http://www.cftt.nist.gov/.

ForensicExams.org

This is a computer forensic portal for examiners/investigators to share information and investigative techniques. A website with lots of information on computer forensics and a listing of computer forensic specialist. The website is http://www.forensicexams.org/.

FIOS

Fios provides electronic discovery services to corporate counsel and their law firms, enabling them to reduce costs, ensure defensibility in court and increase the likelihood of success by fully leveraging the growing universe of electronic evidence that is a part of every litigated matter. Their website is http://www.fiosinc.com/.

Kroll Ontrack

Kroll Ontrack provides large-scale electronic and paper-based discovery and computer forensics services and software to help attorneys, investigators, corporations, and legal professionals quickly, efficiently and cost-effectively recover, review, manage, and produce information and documents. Formerly known as ONTRACK Data International, Inc. Their website is http://www.krollontrack.com/.

Appendix E
Model Case Management Orders

These 3 are included only as examples of what others have done and were found on Kenneth J. Wither's website. We do not make an endorsement of any particular form or order. Websites where samples of forms may also be found at:

- Federal Judicial Center's website—http://www.fjc.gov/public/home.nsf/pages/196.
- Kroll Ontrack's website—http://www.krollontrack.com/legalresources/sample.asp
- Ken Wither's website—http://www.kenwithers.com/rulemaking/index.html

IN THE UNITED STATES DISTRICT COURT
EASTERN DISTRICT OF ARKANSAS
WESTERN DIVISION

In re: :   MDL Docket No. 4:03CV1507-WRW
                                          :
PREMPRO PRODUCTS LIABILITY   :   ALL CASES .
LITIGATION   :
                                          :

ORDER CONCERNING ELECTRONIC DISCOVERY HEARING

Purpose and Areas of Discussion

My responsibilities as the discovery Judge in this case are to insure that all significantly relevant and discoverable materials are preserved and produced, to expedite the discovery process, to minimize costs, and to achieve a reasonable balance between the legitimate discovery needs of the parties and the corresponding burden on the producing party. Because of the nature of the litigation, it is probable that the most significant discovery problems will arise in connection with Plaintiffs' discovery of Defendant's materials.

To carry out these responsibilities, a hearing on electronic discovery has been scheduled for December 16, 2003. The parties and I can make every attempt to tie down issues now, in an effort to head off problems and to facilitate discovery.

To do this it is necessary to obtain information evaluate the proposed Practice and Procedure Order No. #3, and make sure that I can discharge my duty to monitor the discovery process.

Defendant acknowledges the existence of a significant amount of discoverable electronic data. As the parties know, preservation, discovery, and production of electronic materials presents special problems.

I am interested in learning about the following:

1.   Defendant's electronic document depository. A presentation and demonstration will be welcome.

2.   Defendant's corporate structure and operations, including which departments or divisions would be involved in research and development, government approval, marketing, and monitoring the involved product.

3.   The identities of the key individuals within each of the above areas of responsibility that would have been involved with the product.

4.   The time frame during which relevant electronic or other discoverable information may have been created.

5.   Basic information about the process of obtaining government approval for the product in question, including citations to regulations covering retention of research and other materials involved in the approval process.

6.   Basic information about necessary record-keeping and reporting to the government during the time the product is marketed.

7.   Defendant's computer systems, including servers, networks, e-mail systems, voice mail systems, data bases, desktop or laptop computers, PDAs, and backup or archival tapes or other similar storage media.

8.   Changes made in Defendant's systems during the relevant period and any information as to the existence of any relevant and discoverable electronic data which is not located on currently used electronic devices (legacy data).

9.   Whether relevant and discoverable electronic data may exist in third party storage or processing entities, such as internet storage or servicing facilities.

10. Any steps taken to insure preservation of relevant and discoverable materials—in addition to in-house counsel's memorandum to employees dated July 17, 2002, directing the preservation of hard copy and electronic documents. Whether any individuals have been given the responsibility of monitoring the process, and, if so, their names and positions.

11. Whether the parties anticipate special problems with discovery by Defendant of the various Plaintiffs' medical and other relevant and discoverable information.

No later than Wednesday, December 10, 2003, Defendant must submit information about its basic corporate structure, as listed in items 2 and 3 above,[1] and information about the government approval and monitoring process as mentioned in paragraph 5 above.

Defendant must also have present for the hearing the individual or individuals most knowledgeable about its computer system. Any additional information bearing on the above categories which the parties could submit prior to the hearing would be welcome.

---

[1] The Court needs somewhat more detailed information than that listing "management, medical affairs, regulatory affairs and labeling, and marketing," which appeared in Wyeth's Statement Regarding Document Preservation, Collection and Production filed June 2, 2003. Perhaps the organizational charts listed in the proposed order, if not too extensive, would be helpful.

Steering Committee Concerns

Proposed Practice and Procedure Order No. 3 was presented before the appointment of the Steering Committee. That was one of the reasons that the Order has not been entered. I believe it is in the interest of the Parties for the Steering Committee to have an opportunity to participate in this critical step of the litigation. The Steering Committee should review the proposed Order and express any concerns they might have. If such concerns exist, **the committee must specifically state those concerns in a motion or other appropriate pleading, which must be filed no later than Monday, December 8, 2003, with copies to opposing counsel.**

Preservation of Data

One concern I have with the proposed document depository is that the documents are being produced in Tagged Image File Format (.tif). Thus, although the documents would be in electronic form, it appears the production is the functional equivalent of a "hard copy" production and no "metadata" such as document history, earlier or deleted versions, electronic marginal comments, etc., would be available. Of further concern is Defendant's statement that after a document is scanned and the ".tif" image created, Wyeth is "returning the original documents needed for ongoing business to the files."[2] As to electronic documents, this may result in destruction or alteration of relevant data. Therefore, all parties and their counsel are reminded of their duty to preserve evidence that may be relevant to this action. The duty extends to documents, data, and tangible things in the possession, custody, and control of the parties to

---

[2] See Wyeth's Statement Regarding Document Preservation, Collection and Production filed June 2, 2003, pages 5-6.

4

this action, and any employees, agents, contractors, carriers, bailees, or other non-parties who possess materials reasonably anticipated to be subject to discovery in this action. Counsel is under an obligation to exercise reasonable efforts to identify and notify such non-parties, including employees of corporate or institutional parties.

"Documents, data, and tangible things" is to be interpreted broadly to include writings; records; files; correspondence; reports; memoranda; calendars; diaries; minutes; electronic messages; voicemail; E-mail; telephone message records or logs; computer and network activity logs; hard drives; backup data; removable computer storage media such as tapes, disks, and cards; printouts; document image files; Web pages; databases; spreadsheets; software; books; ledgers; journals; orders; invoices; bills; vouchers; checks; statements; worksheets; summaries; compilations; computations; charts; diagrams; graphic presentations; drawings; films; charts; digital or chemical process photographs; video, phonographic, tape, or digital recordings or transcripts thereof; drafts; jottings; and notes. Information that serves to identify, locate, or link such material, such as file inventories, file folders, indices, and metadata, is also included in this definition.

"Preservation" is to be interpreted broadly to accomplish the goal of maintaining the integrity of all documents, data, and tangible things reasonably anticipated to be subject to discovery under Fed. R. Civ. P. 26, 45, and 56(e) in this action. Preservation includes taking reasonable steps to prevent the partial or full destruction, alteration, testing, deletion, shredding, incineration, wiping, relocation, migration, theft, or mutation of such material, as well as negligent or intentional handling that would make material incomplete or inaccessible.

If Defendant's business practices involve the routine destruction, recycling, relocation, or mutation of such materials, Defendant must, to the extent practicable for the pendency of this order, either (1) halt such business processes; (2) sequester or remove such material from the business process; or (3) arrange for the preservation of complete and accurate duplicates or copies of such material, suitable for later discovery if requested.

Before or after the hearing, Defendant may apply to the court for further instructions regarding the duty to preserve specific categories of documents, data, or tangible things. Defendant may seek permission to resume routine business processes relating to the storage or destruction of specific categories of documents, data, or tangible things, upon a showing of undue cost, burden, or overbreadth.

IT IS SO ORDERED this 17th day of NOVEMBER 2003.

UNITED STATES DISTRICT JUDGE
WM. R. WILSON, JR.

6

Figure Appendix E.1—<u>Order Concerning Electronic Discovery</u>, from Prempro Products Liability MDL, 03-CV-1507 (E.D. Ark., November 17, 2003).

Model Order Regarding Preservation

The primary purpose of this model order is to have the parties to meet and confer to develop their own preservation plan. If the court determines that such a conference is unnecessary or undesirable, Section
3 may be modified to serve as stand-alone preservation order.

1. Order to Meet and Confer
    To further the just, speedy, and economical management of discovery, the parties are ORDERED to meet and confer as soon as practicable, no later than 30 days after the date of this Order, to develop a plan for the preservation of documents, data, and tangible things reasonably anticipated to be subject to discovery in this action. The parties may conduct this conference as part of the Rule 26(f) conference if it is scheduled to take place within 30 days of the date of this Order. The resulting preservation plan may be submitted to this Court as a Order under Rule 16(e).

2. Subjects for Consideration The parties should attempt to reach agreement on all issues regarding the preservation of documents, data, and tangible things. These issues include, but are not necessarily limited to:
    A. The extent of the preservation obligation, identifying the types of material to be preserved, the subject matter, time frame, the authors and addressees, and key words to be used in identifying responsive materials.
    b. the form and method of providing notice of the duty to

preserve to persons identified as custodians of documents, data, and tangible things.

   c. the identification of persons responsible for carrying out preservation obligations on behalf of each party.

   d. mechanisms for monitoring, certifying, or auditing custodian compliance with preservation obligations;

   e. whether preservation will require suspending or modifying any routine business processes or procedures, with special attention to document management programs and the recycling of computer data storage media;

   f. the methods to preserve any volatile but potentially discoverable material, such as voicemail, active data in databases, or electronic messages;

   g. the anticipated costs of preservation and ways to reduce or share these costs;

   h. an mechanism to review and modify the preservation obligation as discovery proceeds, eliminating or adding particular categories of documents, data, and tangible things.

3. Duty to Preserve.

   a. until the parties reach agreement on a preservation plan, all parties and their counsel are reminded of their duty to preserve evidence that may be relevant to this action. the duty extends to documents, data, and tangible things in the possession, custody and control of the parties to this action, and any employees, agents, contractors, carriers, bailees, or other non-parties who possess materials reasonably anticipated to be subject to discovery in this action. counsel is under an obligation to exercise reasonable efforts to identify and notify such non-parties, including employees of corporate or institutional parties.

   b. "documents, data, and tangible things" is to be interpreted broadly, to include writings; records; files; correspondence; reports; memoranda; calendars; diaries; minutes; electronic messages; voicemail; email; telephone message records or logs, computer and network activity logs; hard drives; backup data; removable computer storage media such as tapes, disks, and cards; printouts; document image files; web pages; databases; spreadsheets; software; books; ledgers; journals; orders; invoices; bills; vouchers; checks; statements; worksheets; summaries; compilations; computations; charts; diagrams; graphic presentations;

drawings; films; charts; digital or chemical process photographs; video, phonographic, tape, or digital recordings or transcripts thereof; drafts, jottings, and notes. information that serves to identify, locate, or link such material, such as file inventories, file folders, indices, and metadata, is also included in this definition.

c. "preservation" is to be interpreted broadly to accomplish the goal of maintaining the integrity of all documents, data, and tangible things reasonably anticipated to be subject to discovery under fed. r. civ. p. 26, 45, and 56(e) in this action. preservation includes taking reasonable steps to prevent the partial or full destruction, alteration, testing, deletion, shredding, incineration, wiping, relocation, migration, theft, or mutation of such material, as well as negligent or intentional handling that would make material incomplete or inaccessible.

d. if the business practices of any party involve the routine destruction, recycling, relocation, or mutation of such materials, the party must, to the extent practicable for the pendency of this initial order, either:
   (i) halt such business processes,
   (ii) sequester or remove such material from the business process, or
   (iii) arrange for the preservation of complete and accurate duplicates or copies of such material, suitable for later discovery if requested.

e. before the conference to develop a preservation plan, a party may apply to the court for further instructions regarding the duty to preserve specific categories of documents, data, or tangible things. a party may seek permission to resume routine business processes relating to the storage or destruction of specific categories of documents, data, or tangible things, upon a showing of undue cost, burden, or overbreadth.

4. Procedure in the Event No Agreement Is Reached If after conferring to develop a preservation plan, counsel do not reach agreement on the subjects listed under Section 2 of this Order or on other material aspects of preservation, the parties are to submit to the court within three days of the conference a statement of the unresolved issues together with each party's proposal for their resolution of the issues. The court will consider the statements with any outstanding applications under Section 3.E. of this order in framing an

order regarding the preservation of documents, data, and tangible things.

Entered this _____ day of _____, 20__.

_____
District Court Judge

Model Order Regarding Preservation, prototype of Form 40.25 now found in the Manual for Complex Litigation (4th Edition).

CHRISTOPHER A. SEEGER*+
STEPHEN A. WEISS*
DAVID R. BUCHANAN*+

MICHAEL L. ROSENBERG*+&
DIOGENES P. KEKATOS*+

ADMITTED IN
*NY +NJ °CT
&MA ^CA @PA #IL
*COUNSEL

SEEGER WEISS LLP
ATTORNEYS AT LAW
ONE WILLIAM STREET
NEW YORK, NEW YORK 10004-2502
(212) 584-0700
FAX (212) 584-0799

AMY F. ALBERT*+~
PATRICIA D. CODEY+
MICHAEL S. PARKAS*+
LORI A. HEFFELFINGER*+
SETH A. KATZ*
DAVID N. KRUGLER*+
LAURENCE V. NASSIF*+
JAMES A. O'BRIEN III*@
STUART P. SLOTNICK*+
LAWRENCE P. TROMBINO*+
ELIZABETH A. WALL*+

December 19, 2002

BY HAND
Hon. Shira A. Scheindlin
United States District Court Judge
United States District Court for the
  Southern District of New York
500 Pearl Street
New York, New York 10007

Re: *In re Initial Public Offering Securities Litigation*
       21 MC 92 (SAS)
       (Electronic Data Preservation Protocol)

Dear Judge Sheindlin:

I write as Plaintiffs' liaison counsel on electronic preservation issues in connection with Plaintiffs' and the Underwriter Defendants' discussions concerning an appropriate protocol for the preservation of electronic data that may be subject to discovery in these actions.

I am pleased to report that Plaintiffs and the majority of Underwriter Defendants have resolved all points of dispute concerning the proposed electronic data preservation protocol, which was previously presented to the Court, and the associated preservation questionnaire, which is proposed by the parties at the Court's suggestion. The parties' agreed-upon proposal is reflected in proposed Case Management Order Relating to Preservation of Electronic Data, which is submitted herewith.

As Your Honor will note, while plaintiffs consent to the proposed CMO, certain smaller Underwriter Defendants ("smaller" in terms of either institutional size or number of actions in which they are defendants) object to certain provisions of the protocol. These objecting Underwriter Defendants have designated two liaisons to communicate with plaintiffs in an effort to address their concerns. Plaintiffs have spoken with the objecting Underwriter Defendants' liaison counsel and will continue to do so over the next 30 days. Plaintiffs will return to the Court at that point with a preservation proposal

UNITED STATES DISTRICT COURT
SOUTHERN DISTRICT OF NEW YORK

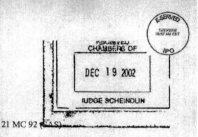

In re
**INITIAL PUBLIC OFFERING
SECURITIES LITIGATION**

This Document Relates to All Cases

21 MC 92 (SAS)

**PROPOSED CASE
MANAGEMENT ORDER
RELATING TO
PRESERVATION OF
ELECTRONIC DATA**

SHIRA A. SCHEINDLIN, U.S.D.J.:

Annexed hereto as Exhibit 1 is a Protocol for the Preservation of

Electronic Data ("Protocol") that has been submitted by the parties listed in Schedules A

and B thereto. IT IS HEREBY ORDERED that the parties identified in Schedules A and

B to the Protocol abide by the provisions thereof.

Shira A. Scheindlin, U.S.D.J.

Dated: December 19, 2002
           New York, New York

Plaintiffs' and Underwriter Defendants'
Joint Proposed Electronic Data Preservation Protocol

1.   As used herein, the term "potentially discoverable electronic information" refers to Underwriter Defendants' and Institutional Named Plaintiffs' electronic "documents" that contain or potentially contain information relating to facts at issue in the litigation, where the term "documents" is used as it is defined in Fed. R. Civ. P. 34(a).[1]

2.   During the pendency of these actions, the Underwriter Defendants and the Institutional Named Plaintiffs shall securely maintain, to the extent that they currently exist and may contain potentially discoverable electronic information: (i) e-mail back-up tapes, and (ii) network back-up tapes (together, the "Back-Up Tapes") created in the ordinary course of business during the period from August 1997 through August 2002 as set forth in the following sentence. The Underwriter Defendants and the Institutional Named Plaintiffs shall be obligated to retain only one day's Back-Up Tapes among all Back-Up Tapes created in the ordinary course during a given month, provided that such day's Back-Up Tapes represent a complete back-up of the data contained on the subject servers on that day (as opposed to merely an incremental back-up of the subject servers). If only incremental back-up tapes have been retained for a given month, then all such incremental tapes shall be retained. All Back-Up Tapes other than those specifically required to be preserved pursuant to this paragraph and paragraph 3 below may be recycled, overwritten, or erased, as the case may be, pursuant to each Underwriter Defendant's and Institutional Named Plaintiff's otherwise applicable retention schedule.

3.   All electronic information or data archived or backed up during the period from August 1997 through August 2002 as part of a special back-up (a back-up made other than in the ordinary course of business by an Underwriter Defendant or Institutional Named Plaintiff), whether due to system upgrade, transition planning, system migration, disaster recovery planning, Y2K testing, or any other reason, that potentially contains potentially discoverable electronic information shall be securely retained, to the extent that they currently exist, for the remainder of the litigation.

4.   All current or legacy software and hardware necessary to access, manipulate, print, etc., potentially discoverable electronic information that either is "live" or has been archived or backed up shall be securely retained, to the extent that they currently exist, for the remainder of the litigation.

---

[1]   The Underwriter Defendants consenting to this protocol are set forth in Schedule A, annexed hereto. The agreed-upon Institutional Named Plaintiffs subject to this protocol are set forth in Schedule B, annexed hereto.

5.   The Underwriter Defendants and the Institutional Named Plaintiffs shall circulate retention notices designed to ensure the preservation of potentially discoverable electronic and other information to those employees potentially possessing such information. Thereafter, the Underwriter Defendants and the Institutional Named Plaintiffs shall quarterly re-notify their employees of their continuing obligation to preserve such information.

6.   The Underwriter Defendants and the Institutional Named Plaintiffs shall take the following measures to secure and retain, to the extent that it exists, the potentially discoverable electronic information that is on the desktop and laptop hard drives of their respective employees. Either: (i) hard drives containing potentially discoverable electronic data shall be retained with all potentially discoverable electronic data contained therein retained intact; or, (ii) employees shall be instructed to copy all potentially discoverable electronic information to a secure, backed-up network storage device or back-up medium for the remainder of the litigation, making all reasonable efforts to retain all meta-data (file creation dates, modification dates, etc.) associated with the potentially discoverable electronic information at issue. The periodic retention notifications disseminated pursuant to paragraph 5 above shall advise employees potentially possessing potentially discoverable electronic information of their obligation to store discoverable electronic information on a secure, backed-up network storage device or back-up medium to ensure its preservation and instruct such employees in the manner of doing so in accordance with this paragraph.

7.   Plaintiffs within 15 days of receiving the list of business units referred to below shall identify by name, title, or departmental category employees of each Underwriter Defendant for which the respective Underwriter Defendant shall be responsible for maintaining the hard drive, or a mirror image copy (i.e., a bit by bit copy) of such hard drive, during the pendency of this litigation. Defendants shall within 15 days of receiving the list of business units referred to below identify by name, title, or departmental category of employees of Institutional Named Plaintiffs for which the respective Plaintiff shall be responsible for maintaining the hard drive, or a mirror image copy (i.e., a bit by bit copy) of such hard drive, during the pendency of this litigation. In no event shall the number of computers subject to the provisions of this paragraph be greater than 40 for each Underwriter Defendant and 5 for each Institutional Named Plaintiff. The hard drives or image copies of such hard drives preserved pursuant to this paragraph shall be labeled to identify the employee who primarily used the computer associated with that hard drive. In order to facilitate the identification of the appropriate employees, the parties will provide to each other identification by business unit and positions the employees they reasonably believe could have potentially discoverable electronic information. The parties will meet and confer in good faith and exchange additional information as may be necessary to facilitate the identification, and limit the number, of employees for whom the provisions of this paragraph shall be applicable.

8.   To the extent that any Underwriter Defendant or Institutional Named Plaintiff has implemented a system for the purpose of preserving external emails (emails sent to or received by a given Underwriter Defendant's or Institutional Named Plaintiff's employees) in an easily accessible form, other than an email server or the Back-up Tapes

identified in paragraph 2 or 3 above, all emails that were created during the period from August 1997 through August 2002, that contain potentially discoverable electronic information, and that are stored on any such system as of the date hereof, shall be preserved during the pendency of this litigation.

9.   Within 45 days, each Underwriter Defendant and each Institutional Named Plaintiff will provide written answers to the best of its ability to the questions concerning information system and electronic document retention practices set forth in attached Schedule C. Should any Underwriter Defendant or Institutional Named Plaintiff believe that it cannot in good faith answer any of the questions as posed, the relevant parties will confer to resolve any disputes and, if necessary, seek Court intervention.

10.   By agreeing to preserve potentially discoverable electronic information in accordance with the terms hereof, none of the Underwriter Defendants and none of the Institutional Named Plaintiffs are waiving any objection to the ultimate discoverability of such information at such point when discovery is authorized in these actions.

11.   Nothing herein shall be deemed to affect the Underwriter Defendants' and Institutional Named Plaintiffs' obligations to preserve hardcopy documents pursuant to paragraph V of the Court's August 8, 2001 Order. If counsel to an Underwriter Defendant or an Institutional Named Plaintiff learns that potentially discoverable hardcopy documents pertaining to a given public offering were destroyed by such party subsequent to being named as a party in, and receiving a copy of, a complaint pertaining to that public offering, counsel for such party shall notify opposing counsel in writing of such destruction within two weeks of learning so.

12.   Nothing herein shall preclude any party from raising with counsel or the Court the limitation or modification of the foregoing in response to particular facts relevant to that party.

13.   Nothing herein relieves any other party of its obligations under the Federal Rules of Civil Procedure, the Private Securities Litigation Reform Act, or any other applicable law.

3

SCHEDULE A

Underwriter Defendants Consenting to
Plaintiffs' and Underwriter Defendants'
Joint Proposed Electronic Data Preservation Protocol

1. Banc of America Securities, LLC (f/k/a NationsBanc Montgomery Securities)

2. The Bear Stearns Companies Inc. and Bear, Stearns & Co. Inc.

3. CIBC World Markets Corp. (f/k/a CIBC Oppenheimer Corp.)

4. Credit Suisse First Boston Corp.

5. Dain Rauscher Wessels (acquired by Royal Bank of Canada in September 2000 and renamed RBC Dain Rauscher, Inc.)

6. Deutsche Bank Securities Inc. (f/k/a Deutsche Bank Alex. Brown and BT Alex. Brown)

7. Epoch Partners (acquired by The Goldman Sachs Group, Inc. in June 2001)

8. E*Offering Corporation (merged into Wit SoundView Corporation, a susidiary of Wit SoundView Group, Inc., in October 2000; subsequently known as SoundView Technology Corporation)

9. Everen Securities Holdings, Inc. (a subsidiary of Everen Captial Corporation, acquired by First Union Corporation in April 1999)

10. The Goldman Sachs Group, Inc. and Goldman, Sachs & Co.

11. J.C. Bradford & Co. (acquired by Paine Webber Group, Inc. in April 2000)

12. J.P. Morgan Securities Inc. (Hambrecht & Quist, LLC, Chase Securities, Inc., and J.P. Morgan Securities merged into a single entity)

13. Lazard Freres & Co., LLC

14. Lehman Brothers Holdings, Inc. and Lehman Brothers, Inc.

15. Merrill Lynch & Co., Inc., Merrill Lynch, Pierce, Fenner & Smith Incorporated and Merrill Lynch International

16. Morgan Stanley Dean Witter & Co., Morgan Stanley & Co. and Morgan Stanley Online

17. Needham & Company, Inc.

18. Paine Webber Group, Inc. (acquired by UBS Warburg, LLC in November 2000 to form UBS Paine Webber, Inc.)

19. Prudential Securities Incorporated (individually and as successor in interest to Volpe Brown Whelan & Co., LLC)

1

20. Raymond James & Associates

21. Robert Fleming Inc. (acquired by Chase H&Q in August 1999)

22. Robertson Stephens, Inc. (f/k/a BancBoston Robertson Stephens, Inc. and FleetBoston Robertson Stephens, Inc.)

23. Salomon Smith Barney, Inc.

24. SG Cowen Securities Corp.

25. SoundView Technology Group, Inc. (a wholly owned subsidiary of Wit Capital Group, Inc. as of January 2000; subsequently known as Wit SoundView Corporation and SoundView Technology Corporation)

26. SunTrust Robinson Humphrey Capital Markets a division of SunTrust Capital Markets, Inc.

27. Thomas Weisel Partners, LLC

28. Tucker Anthony Inc. (acquired by the parent of RBC Dain Rauscher Inc. in November 2001 and merged into RBC Dain Rauscher Inc. in March 2002)

29. UBS Paine Webber, Inc. (formed by November 2000 acquisition of Paine Webber Group, Inc. by USB Warburg, LLC)

30. UBS Warburg, LLC (formed by June 1998 merger of SBC Warburg and Union Bank of Switzerland)

31. U.S. Bancorp Piper Jaffray, Inc.

32. Wit Capital Group, Inc. (subsequently known as Wit SoundView Group Inc., and SoundView Technology Group, Inc.)

33. Wit SoundView Group Inc. (formerly known as Wit Capital Group, Inc.)

SCHEDULE B

Institutional Plaintiffs

Issuer	Docket Number	Plaintiff
Avanex	01 Civ. 6890	International Brotherhood of Electrical Workers
eBenX, Inc.	01 Civ. 9411	Rennel Trading Corp.
eGain Comm., Corp.	01 Civ. 9414	Rennel Trading Corp.
Eloquent, Inc.	01 Civ. 6775	Pond Equities
GRIC Communications, Inc.	01 Civ. 6771	Colbert Birnet, LP
InforMax, Inc.	01 Civ. 10834	Coastline Corporation, Inc.
Internet Capital Group, Inc.	01 Civ. 3975	AFA Management Partners, LP
Metasolv Software, Inc.	01 Civ. 9651	Colbert Birnet, L.P.
Numerical Technologies	01 Civ. 9513	Pond Equities
On Semiconductor Corp.	01 Civ. 6114	Fuller & Thaler Asset Management
Palm, Inc.	01 Civ. 5613	Plumbers and Pipefitters National Pension Fund
Perot Systems Corp.	01 Civ. 6820	Robinson Radiology Ltd. Profit Sharing Plan and Trust
Radio One, Inc.	01 Civ. 10160	Colbert Birnet, L.P.
Wireless Facilities, Inc.	01 Civ. 4779	Fuller & Thaler Asset Management

SCHEDULE C

Plaintiffs' and Underwriter Defendants'
Proposed Document Retention Questionnaire

Network Servers

The below questions concern the current and former database and file servers on your network that now store or previously stored discoverable electronic data (hereinafter referred to as "network servers").

1. Do you have at least one complete (i.e., non-incremental) backup of each of your network servers for each month since August 1, 1997 to the present?

   1.1. If not, for which months do you not have at least one complete backup?

   1.2. For those months, if any, for which you do not have a complete backup, do you have incremental backups or other backups from which a full backup can be created of all data as of a given date in each such month?

   1.3. If so, please describe the nature of such incremental or other backups and identify the months for which you have them.

2. Can specific files contained on network backups be selectively restored?

3. As a matter of firm policy, do you overwrite, reformat, erase, or otherwise destroy the content of the backups of your network servers on a periodic basis?

   3.1. If so, what is the rotation period?

   3.2. If the rotation period has changed since August 1, 1997, describe the changes.

Email Servers

The below questions concern the current or former servers on your network ("email servers") that now or previously stored discoverable electronic internal or external peer-to-peer messages, including email, Bloomberg email, other third party email sources, and instant messages (collectively, "email").

4. Identify the systems (client and server-side applications) used for email and the time period for the use of each such system.

5. Are end-user emails that appear in any of the following folders stored on (i) the end-user's harddrive, (ii) an email server, or (iii) a server of a third party application service provider:

- "In Box"?

- "Sent Mail"?

- "Delete" or "trash" folder?

- End user stored mail folders?

6. If any of your emails systems have changed since August 1, 1997, identify the legacy system, the new system, and the date of the last backup made with the legacy system.

7. Do you have at least one complete (i.e., non-incremental) back up of each of your email servers for each month since August 1, 1997 to the present?

  7.1. If not, for which months do you not have at least one complete backup?

  7.2. For those months, if any, for which you do not have a complete backup, do you have incremental or other backups from which a full backup can be created of all data as of a given date in each such month?

  7.3. If so, please describe the nature of such incremental or other backups and identify the months for which you have them.

8. Does each complete email backup contain all messages sent or received since creation of the immediately prior complete email backup?

  8.1. Do your email backups contain the messages that are in each employee's "in box" as of the time such backup is made?

  8.2. Do your email backups contain the messages that are in each employee's "sent mail" folder as of the time such backup is made?

  8.3. Do your email backups contain the messages that are in each employee's "delete" or "trash" folder as of the time such backup is made?

  8.4. Do your email backups contain the messages that are in each employee's stored mail folders as of the time such backup is made?

9. Can specific email boxes contained on email backups be restored selectively?

10. As a matter of firm policy, do you overwrite, reformat, erase, or otherwise destroy the content of the backups of your email servers on a periodic basis?

  10.1. If so, what is the rotation period?

  10.2. If the rotation period has changed since August 1, 1997, describe the changes.

2

11.   Do you have a computer system that maintains electronic copies of all emails sent or received by certain of your employees?

   11.1. If so, describe the system(s) and the date(s) of first use.

   11.2. If so, does such system(s) contain copies of all emails captured from the date of first use until the present?

   11.3. If so, does such system(s) capture a copy of all emails sent or received by employees in investment banking, equity research functions, or senior management?

Hard Drives

The below questions concern the current and former local or non-network drives contained in current or former employees' laptop and desktop computers or workstations.

12.   As a matter of firm policy, are employees' desktop and laptop hard drives backed up in any way?

   12.1. If so, under what circumstances?

   12.2. If so, how long are such backups retained?

13.   As a matter of firm policy, are employees permitted to save files, emails or other data (excluding system and application generated temporary files) to their desktop or laptop hard drives?

14.   Since August 1, 1997, has it been technically possible for firm employees to save files, emails, or other data (excluding system and application generated temporary files) to their desktop or laptop hard drives?

15.   Do you implement technical impediments to minimize the opportunity for employees to save files, emails or other data (excluding system and application generated temporary files) to their desktop or laptop hard drives?

16.   As a matter of firm policy, are employees' desktop and laptop hard drives erased, "wiped," "scrubbed" or reformatted before such hard drives are, for whatever reason, abandoned, transferred or decommissioned?

   16.1. If so, are, as a matter of firm policy, files, emails or other data stored on such hard drives copied to the respective employee's replacement drive, if any?

   16.2. If so, are, as a matter of firm policy, such files, emails or other data copied on a "bit-by-bit" basis?

3

Non-Firm Computers

17.   Does firm policy permit, prohibit or otherwise address employee use of computers not owned or controlled by the firm to create, receive, store or send work-related documents or communications?

    17.1.   If so, what is that policy?

18.   Is there any technical impediment to employees using computers not owned or controlled by the firm to create, receive, store or send work-related documents or communications?

4

Figure Appendix E.3—<u>Electronic Data Preservation Order</u> <u>Document Retention Questionnaire</u>, from Initial Public Offering Securities Litigation, 21 MC 92 (S.D. N.Y., December 19, 2002).

Appendix F
Answers to Cases

Whistle Blower Case

Answers:

1. Was the computer forensics specialist brought onto the team at the best time?

No—the computer forensic specialist should have been brought onto the team at the beginning. The specialist could have help the team plan how computer forensics should be utilized and help preserve any potential evidence.

2. What are the consequences of the IS auditor's 'poking round'?

When the IS auditor poked around the computers any evidence that was recovered from these computers was spoiled. This altered the contents of the computer's hard drives and if nothing else the time stamps of the files accessed. Once this is done there is no way to tell what was and what was not done. The defense can claim that the IS auditor planted the information on the computers because they wanted to be the hero of the audit, they wanted a promotion, or because they were mad at someone. What ever their story is, you can not disprove it in court. So the information found on the computers may be enough to fire them or to bluff with, but it will not hold up in court.

3. Did the computer forensic specialist bring any value to the investigation?

Yes value was added, but not as much as it could have been. The specialist can inform the investigation team about the spoilage of the evidence so they know not to present it in court. If this had been presented in court and then thrown out because the work of the IS auditor had spoiled it, think about how it could effect the rest of the case. It could have tainted anything else the investigation team found. The items found by the specialist helped lead the investigation team to individuals that could help prove what was going on and testify about it.

4.   Can anything else be done?

The email server backup tapes! These were removed from the rotation, locked up, and forgotten about. These are unspoiled by the IS auditor's poking around! These tapes can be given to the computer forensics person, imaged, validated, analyzed, and if anything is found presented in court. A review of the corporate policies and procedures may lead to another unspoiled source of potential evidence.

Last Minute Examination

Answers:

1. How could the use of a computer forensics specialist been more effective?

On day one, the hard drives and backup tapes of the computers in question should have been obtained and imaged by a computer forensic specialist. Even if they are not reviewed this is cheap insurance in case you do need them. This action would also prevent the situation of the people being investigated acquiring new computers and the old ones being discarded. Remember, if anything inappropriate had taken place involving a computer, it would have been done prior to this investigation on the old computers. If they had kept a second set of books for the accounts being manipulated, they would be on the old computer. Why would anyone copy these files over to a new computer after an investigation has been started? The fraudulent scheme had been discovered and corrected; these were of no value and could be a huge liability if they are discovered.

2. Did the investigating attorney leave himself open to any potential problems?

The attorney leading the investigation may have left himself open to lawsuits. He knew the external auditors wanted the forensic review done before they would sign off on the audit report. He knew or should have known that the people under investigation used computer in their day-to-day work, email, Excel files, Word documents, personal databases, etc. He should have also realized that these tools, especially email, are used in their daily communication and if collusion had taken place there was a high probability of email communication on the subject. Does his scooping out of potential electronic evidence leave to door open for a legal malpractice suite? Even if it does not, how would you justify scoping out of the potential electronic evidence to a judge in court.

3.   Are there any issues that could prevent the printed email that the auditors found from being admitted as evidence?

The sender and the person receiving the email are no longer employed by the company and had no known access to the company's resources, including the email system. There is no way to tie this email to a specific person. There is no way to tell who or why the email was sent. Was it really sent from one person to another or was there just one person involved in the email, was it real or a hoax.

4.   How could the investigation process concerning the Excel file, Original—Bonus Ins.xls been improved? What issues could keep this out of court?

This item has several flaws. First it was not properly imaged; there have been several cases that address the issue of copying vs. forensic image. The fact that the file was copied using Windows creates problems if you want to get something admitted into court. Next, the files were not validated with a hash as soon as they were copied. This might provide the integrity to the items so that it can be admitted into court, just maybe. Then the attorney modified the file. After this you can forget about getting the item in to court as evidence. The potential evidence has been spoiled beyond repair.

If the forensic specialist had been brought in to just image the hard drives in the beginning, this Excel file would be ready for court. If a forensic specialist had imaged the hard drive before the attorney copied everything over and validated the images the acts of the attorney would not matter. After the attorney made all of his changes the forensic specialist could then carve the Excel out from the image he made. The forensic specialist could then validate the number in the attorney's Excel file. In this case it would have been a cheap insurance policy for the investigating attorney.

5.   Could the two computers found by the CIO be of any value to the case?

Maybe, they could be of value to the case, but these images have their own problems. There are no issues with them being imaged with Ghost; this is a tool that has been validated by many people for use in computer forensics. The problems arise because there are not chain-of-custody forms, they were not validated with a hash number, and then there was the way the auditor acted. Why did the auditors take the images, especially before they could be validated? Also, why did the executives get new computers and no one knows about it? These computers have lots of issues and there is a god chance they are useless, though a skilled attorney and forensic specialist might get some use out of them.

End Notes

---

[1] ASR Data website from www.archive.org.

[2] The Sedona Principles – Best Practices, Recommendations, & Principles for Addressing Electronic Document Production, July 2005 version – Page 3.

[3] http://www.mul-t-lockusa.com/craft.asp

[4] Desmond Rowland and James Bailey, The Law Enforcement Handbook, page 152.

422933

Made in the USA